PRAISE FOR *THE NEW SCIENCE OF RADICAL INNOVATION*

"If you are serious about innovation in your organization, this book is a must read. Sunnie Giles sets a new standard for understanding innovation and provides profound insights on how innovation happens and what you can do to harness that potential."

—JONATHAN ROSENBERG, COAUTHOR OF *NEW YORK TIMES* AND *WALL STREET JOURNAL* BESTSELLER *HOW GOOGLE WORKS* AND FORMER SVP OF PRODUCTS AT GOOGLE

"Complexity is scary. So is radical innovation. But Sunnie Giles is here to tame those twin beasts. Surveying the topic from neuroscience to artificial intelligence, she extracts profound insights and an actionable set of skills she calls Quantum Leadership. Using these skills, any leader can push his/her organization to new heights of innovation and advantage."

—DANIEL PINK, #1 *NEW YORK TIMES* BESTSELLING AUTHOR OF *DRIVE* AND *TO SELL IS HUMAN*

"This book provides a clear theoretical framework to understand the seemingly idiosyncratic business practices of successful Silicon Valley high tech companies and actual practices companies must master to win in this new world. *The New Science of Radical Innovation* should be a bible for every leader aspiring for innovation."

—MARSHALL GOLDSMITH, WORLD'S #1 LEADERSHIP THINKER, RENOWNED BUSINESS EDUCATOR AND COACH, AND AUTHOR OF 35 BOOKS

"Paranoid about disruptive innovators? Read this book and you can learn how to become one. Well researched and practical, this book is a must-read for any leader who wants to win in today's unpredictable, complex world by producing radical innovation consistently. Whether you are a C-level executive seeking to build an innovative organization or a first line manager seeking to build an innovative team, this book will give you the insights, strategies, and behaviors to redefine the rules of the game."

—SEAN COVEY, *WALL STREET JOURNAL*
#1 BESTSELLING COAUTHOR OF *THE 4 DISCIPLINES OF EXECUTION*

The

NEW SCIENCE

of RADICAL

INNOVATION

The

NEW SCIENCE
of RADICAL
INNOVATION

The Six Competencies Leaders
Need to Win in a Complex World

SUNNIE GILES

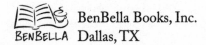 BenBella Books, Inc.
Dallas, TX

BenBella Books, Inc.
10440 N. Central Expressway, Suite 800
Dallas, TX 75231
www.benbellabooks.com
Send feedback to feedback@benbellabooks.com
Printed in the United States of America
10 9 8 7 6 5 4 3 2 1

Library of Congress Cataloging-in-Publication Data
Names: Giles, Sunnie, 1965- author.
Title: The new science of radical innovation : the six competencies leaders
   need to win in a complex world / Sunnie Giles.
Description: Dallas, TX : BenBella Books, [2018] | Includes bibliographical
   references and index.
Identifiers: LCCN 2017052702 (print) | LCCN 2017054660 (ebook) | ISBN
   9781946885234 (electronic) | ISBN 9781946885029 (trade cloth : alk. paper)
Subjects: LCSH: Leadership. | Information technology—Management.
Classification: LCC HD57.7 (ebook) | LCC HD57.7 .G5195 2018 (print) | DDC
   658.4/063—dc23
LC record available at https://lccn.loc.gov/2017052702

Editing by Vy Tran
Copyediting by Miki Alexandra Caputo
Proofreading by Kim Broderick and Cape Cod Compositors, Inc.
Indexing by Jigsaw Indexing Services
Author photo by Michael Schoenfeld
Cover design by Oceana Garceau
Jacket design by Sarah Avinger
Text design and composition by Aaron Edmiston
Printed by Lake Book Manufacturing

Distributed to the trade by Two Rivers Distribution, an Ingram brand
www.tworiversdistribution.com

May you see the signature of eternity that weaves through all the wonders of the world and find deeper meaning.

For Courtney.

CONTENTS

INTRODUCTION

*To arrive at the truth, once in your life you have to commit yourself
to undoing all the opinions that you have formerly taken for
granted, and reconstruct anew all the systems of your knowledge.*
—RENÉ DESCARTES, *REMARQUES SUR
LES SEPTIÈMES OBJECTIONS*

With brows knitted and head cocked slightly, he rubbed his forehead back and forth, furiously weighing his options, a black stone held between his fingers. Just a couple of days ago, the second-highest reigning world champion told the press he would win in a landslide victory, but now it seemed that his opponent was much stronger than he thought. At stake was not just a $1 million prize but the primacy of human intelligence. His opponent never had to take a break during the five-hour match and never got tired, hungry, or swayed by emotion.

"Oh, wow!" the crowd exclaimed in disbelief, as he grimly placed a captured white stone on the board to signal his resignation.

More than two hundred million people around the world watched this historic match, which was streamed live from South Korea in March 2016. The five-game matchup between Korean Lee Sedol, the legendary champion of the ancient Chinese board game Go (or *baduk* in Korean),

Wikimedia Commons

and AlphaGo, an artificial intelligence (AI) developed by Google's DeepMind, was over.[1] Lee lost the five-game series one to four to AlphaGo.

Go is a 2,500-year-old Chinese board game played by forty million people daily. Players take turns placing black or white stones on a board, trying to maximize territory. Go has long been viewed as the most challenging of classic games for artificial intelligence because of its enormous search space and the difficulty of evaluating board positions and moves.[2] The average number of possible moves for a given turn in Go is 250 (in chess, it's 35). The number of possible board configurations is 10^{170}, far more than the 10^{80} atoms in the universe. A typical Go game lasts 150 moves, often taking more than five hours—no wonder my mom threw out my dad's Go stones, totally exasperated! Intuition—the ability to judge the game from the overall picture of the board—is essential to win. It's a result of lifelong learning and experience in the game. For centuries, Go masters have been hailed not only for their ability to correctly analyze complex sequences of moves to maximize territory in local areas of the board but also for their far-reaching finesse in positioning stones early in the game to maximize influence before any territory has been staked. These factors make brute-force search, which is how IBM's Deep Blue won a chess match against Garry Kasparov in 1997, impractical. You might have to wait until the next big bang to see the end of the game! The cows might never come home . . . the horizontally challenged lady might never sing . . . You get the point.

As I watched the match unfold, I became intensely curious about how AlphaGo beat Lee Sedol. How did AI achieve this seemingly impossible feat ten years faster than industry sages anticipated? I ended up discovering several principles behind AlphaGo's victory and was fascinated to find that these are the exact same principles that Google and many other Silicon Valley tech companies use for managing people to spawn radical innovation and redefine the rules of the game. These principles have not just helped these companies tweak things here and there to make *incre-mental* improvements but have catapulted their organizations far ahead of their competition and radically changed how the game is played in their industry. These principles work because they're based on laws of nature that govern all living organisms, including people and organizations. These same principles govern how complexity is created in the business environment. Complexity, as used in this book, is the holistic, unpredictable result of many self-organizing, interdependent agents learning by profuse trial-and-error experiments, following simple rules. To better understand how complexity is created and how it works, let's first take a closer look at the examples of AlphaGo and Google.

Complexity is the unpredictable result of many self-organizing, interdependent agents learning by profuse trial-and-error experiments, following simple rules.

PRINCIPLES OF COMPANIES (AND AI) THAT WIN

Self-organizing agents

AlphaGo and Google both use self-organizing agents. In AI, agents are nodes where computation happens, similar to individual neurons in our brains. They take input from sensors and direct their activities toward certain goals. In AlphaGo, the agents learn on their own, instead of relying on pre-programmed instructions from Go grandmasters to decide the next move.

Google's stance on this principle is seen in how it manages people: "Hire the best people and get out of their way."[3] Google allows people to self-organize. At Google, managers are encouraged to delegate as much as possible, to the point where they start feeling slightly uncomfortable.[4] Self-organization is also evident in Google's 20 percent–time policy, where employees spend 20 percent of their time working on what *they* think will most benefit Google. This freedom empowers them to be more innovative.

Some wildly successful projects have come from this policy, such as the multibillion-dollar AdSense business.[5]

Using simple rules

To provide some cohesive direction and coordination among the many self-organizing agents pursuing different things, both AlphaGo and Google use simple rules. AlphaGo uses two sets of simple rules to consider each move. One group of rules, called policy networks, evaluates board positions and reduces the *breadth* of the search, and another set of rules, called value networks, predicts the probability of winning in a given position and reduces the *depth* of the search. It has to simplify the search space because a brute-force evaluation of every possible move is not practical.

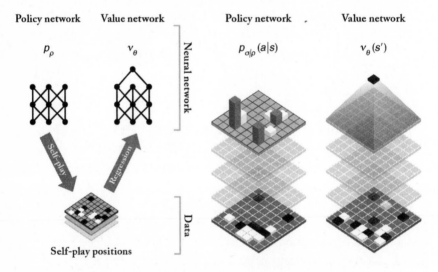

Figure 0.1 *Neural network training pipeline and architecture in AlphaGo by Google DeepMind, published in* Nature[6]

Using these rules increases the speed of computation by reducing the input AlphaGo needs to process. Human brains do the same thing; we use mental models to process the same input more quickly next time.

Google, too, uses simple rules as loose guidelines for a diverse population of self-organizing employees. Without these simple rules, thousands of employees doing different things would result in chaos, with no consistency in direction. Google's simple rule to decide priorities? Focus on the user and all else will follow. When to add a layer under a manager? Have a minimum of seven employees.[7] What about office space? Keep it open to maximize interaction. Ethics? "Don't be evil." How to allocate corporate funds? Spend 70 percent on existing products, 20 percent on emerging products, and 10 percent on moon-shot projects.

These simple rules not only provide cohesive parameters by which employees can self-organize but also speed up decision-making, another essential criterion for innovation. In today's complex business environment, where things are changing constantly, speed of execution is a lot more important than perfect execution.

> In today's complex business environment, where things are changing constantly, speed of execution is a lot more important than perfect execution.

Lots of trial and error

In the process of implementing self-organization and at the same time deciding which simple rules work best, both AlphaGo and Google employees learn from repeated experiments of trial and error. AlphaGo played against *itself* 30 million times, using reinforced learning. These trial-and-error results are used either to amplify or attenuate the input, which slowly improves the algorithm. AlphaGo *had* to lose many times to slowly improve its win rate because failures are a necessary input to improvement.

In an interview with me, Jonathan Rosenberg, SVP of Products at Google and one of the coauthors of *How Google Works*, expounded on how this aspect of AlphaGo is analogous to Google's own culture:

> *One of the things I observed in listening to the expert commentary on AlphaGo was that AlphaGo's algorithm threw out moves that violated the basic principles that most Go masters held to be self-evident for many, many years and tried them. One of the things that we embrace at Google culturally is people often flip things on their head and throw out very crazy suggestions and then run with them and see where they go.*

Success comes from learning, and learning requires failures, which means success *requires* failures for both AI and organizations. Tolerating failures and learning from each iteration of trial and error is essential in today's complex business environment.

Diversity of input

To maximize the potential of many self-organizing agents and produce right answers, both AlphaGo and Google ensure diversity of input. Diversity of input improves AlphaGo's performance. Developers trained AlphaGo with 160,000 games played by decent amateurs, which is how it learned to predict what the next move would be. Research has shown that the collective wisdom of many ordinary people is more accurate than one expert's opinion.[8]

Rosenberg and former executive chairman of Google Eric Schmidt agree:

> *Homogeneity in an organization breeds failure. A multiplicity of viewpoints, aka diversity, is your best defense against myopia. People from different backgrounds see the world differently. These differences of perspective generate insights that can't be taught. When you bring these together in a work environment, they integrate to create a broader perspective that is priceless.[9]*

From this vantage point, *diversity is not a compliance issue—it is a strategic issue.*

General intelligence versus narrow intelligence

To increase the diversity of input and minimize chances of errors, both AlphaGo and Google use general intelligence, as opposed to narrow intelligence. Unlike a narrow AI, which is used for very specific purposes, AlphaGo is an artificial general intelligence (AGI)—a single system that can operate on a wide range of tasks. The problem with narrow AI, such as those used in smart homes, is that it breaks when faced with unexpected situations outside of handcrafted, preprogrammed solutions. Imagine asking your smart home system, "I forgot to brush my teeth this morning—what is the impact on my future?" As Johnny 5 would say, "Malfunction! Need more input!" General-purpose algorithms like AlphaGo's are much more resilient and adaptive.

Rosenberg and Schmidt explain how they see the quandary of the generalist versus the specialist:

> *Favoring specialization over intelligence is wrong, especially in high tech. The world is changing so fast across every industry and endeavor. Hiring a specialist in such a dynamic environment can backfire. A specialist brings an inherent bias to solving problems that spawns from the very expertise that is his putative advantage and may be threatened by a new type of solution that requires a new expertise. A generalist doesn't have a bias and is free to survey a wide range of solutions and gravitate to the best one.*[10]

Specialists' inherent bias results in mental frames through which they view the world, limiting their ability to respond to new, never-seen-before challenges. A generalist doesn't have this bias and hence can respond better to new challenges.

During my interview with him, Rosenberg explained the importance of using the generalist approach:

> *The generalist approach builds a new platform on which incremental innovation can build, much like Google's AdWords, the transistor, the steam engine, and electricity. These things were developed for initial point solutions but evolved into much bigger things, like a framework for lots of other innovations to build on.*

A generalist approach is not a perfect solution for all things but produces enough solutions to most problems that it gets adopted as a standard framework. Partly because of its culture of using the generalist approach over specialists, Google has been ranked among Boston Consulting Group's top three most innovative companies ten years in a row.[11]

These principles, which helped AlphaGo beat Lee Sedol, are the same principles that help Google create a culture that can serve as a primordial soup to spawn radical innovation. Google and other companies that follow these principles—which I call Quantum Companies—are creating and harnessing complexity. When an organization achieves a higher level of complexity, it increases the organization's options and ability to respond to external challenges and produce radical innovation. It can also dramatically improve the capacity for innovation *all* companies need to successfully compete.

That is what this book is about: demystifying radical innovation—what it is, how it comes about, and what companies, and leaders within them, need to do to consistently produce it. That is a challenge because of the unpredictable nature of business environments, but this book will teach you how to harness complexity and jump-start radical innovation. It will reveal how to use complexity to your advantage instead of becoming paralyzed by or irrelevant because of it. It will teach you the concepts and tools necessary to adopt and exploit positive complexity, stimulating radical innovation with your products and services. It will reveal the secret DNA that many Quantum Companies have in common—what makes them so successful. It will also teach you how to transform traditional companies into Quantum Companies by implementing the tools and concepts in this book. Every company and every leader can benefit from applying the leadership principles in this book. Even if you are a line manager and the rest of the company has not bought the concepts in this book, you can start experimenting with these tools and concepts within your own sphere of control. Before you know it, you will be making radical changes and the rest of the company will be curious to learn about what you're doing. Then you can increase your circle of influence by sharing with them how to use the tools in this book.

This book is not about how to make *incremental* improvements. There are myriads of books out there to help you achieve that goal. This book is about *radical* innovation, the kind that causes everyone to play by the rules that *you* define, changes the fundamental dynamics of an industry, catapults your company a generation ahead of the competition, and sets a new framework—a new platform for others to build on, with 10x improvements, as Peter Thiel calls it.[12]

These are the principles that I wish I had known when I was managing my teams. In many aspects, I failed as a leader because I didn't know the role of a leader and, even worse, how to become a good one. If I had known these tools and concepts, I would have been a much more effective leader. It is my sincere hope that this book will help leaders in all walks of life to transform their organizations and lives and make the world a better place for all of us.

Chapter 1

A NEW PARADIGM
OF LEADERSHIP

O n Friday, June 24, 2016, more than $2 trillion of wealth was wiped out in equity markets around the world in the highest one-day sell-off in history.[1] This dramatic decline was a result of the British public voting for Brexit, despite the plea of thirty-six prominent CEOs from the FTSE 100 (Financial Times Stock Exchange 100 Index) to vote against the referendum that would decide if Britain should stay with or leave the European Union. In a letter to the editor of the *Times*, these executives had voiced deep concern about losing unrestricted access to the vast EU market of five hundred million consumers and the resulting job losses and decreased profits. Never could they—or the voting public, or perhaps anyone in the world—have imagined that such an outcome all started with a fruit vendor who set himself on fire in Tunisia six years earlier.

December 17, 2010, began as a typical day for Mohamed Bouazizi, a young fruit vendor in Tunisia. He headed to the market to sell produce in the streets to support his family. The night before, he had purchased his produce on credit. Now he pushed his cart to market, hopeful of good profit . . . until the police arrived. Because he had no permit, they attempted to extort the equivalent of seven dollars from him, which was more than he could hope to make in a single day.

"What do you want me to do?! Steal?! Die?! How do I make a living?!" he exclaimed with a desperate cry, punching the air with his fist.[2]

In despair, with no other way to protest, he doused himself with gasoline in the midst of traffic. He stood in front of the municipality building, his clothes dripping in gasoline and his cheeks flushed with rage. Then he struck a match, igniting himself—and the frustration of all Arab youth.

People around him took pictures and videos of this incident, and the news rapidly went viral on social media. His plight resonated with a massive number of people, inciting huge demonstrations and riots. At Mohamed's funeral, marchers chanted, "Farewell, Mohamed, we will avenge you. We weep for you today; we will make those who caused your death weep." Twenty-eight days after Mohamed's self-immolation, Tunisian president Zine El Abidine Ben Ali fled to Saudi Arabia, stepping down after twenty-three years in power. So began the Arab Spring.

When the Syrian people rose up against Bashar al-Assad, instead of stepping down, like many of his counterparts in other Arab countries, he led his country into civil war, producing millions of refugees. Seeking safety and opportunity, these refugees poured into Europe and Britain, stretching the limits of social support systems and challenging the practicality of the Schengen Agreement that had made it possible for people to move freely within the EU boundaries. The growing public discontent about these refugees pouring in from Europe, compounded by other complicated factors such as financial disparity among the nations in the European Union and resulting burdens on bigger, healthier countries such as the United Kingdom, led to the Brexit referendum to leave the European Union.

This chain of events shows just how complex the world is today. If fewer people had cell phones, as was the case just a decade ago, they wouldn't have been able to capture Bouazizi's self-immolation. If fewer people were connected on social media, the news wouldn't have gone viral. If fewer people had access to TV, radio, and internet, they wouldn't have been inspired to rise up against their own regimes. If fewer refugees had access to transportation to take them from Turkey, Italy, or Greece, they wouldn't have been as able to flee to England or Germany, the more affluent countries of the European Union. The increased interdependence among the many variables involved resulted in Brexit—something that couldn't possibly have been predicted from the initial event of one fruit vendor's self-immolation. It is similar to a game of Go: one can't guess how the event will turn out from the initial moves, because the outcome is so interdependent on moves throughout the game.

Unpredictability is itself a hallmark characteristic of complexity, and this is the complex environment businesses operate in today. You might have even heard it referred to as a VUCA environment, a concept that originated in the early nineties from students at the US Army War College to describe the volatility, uncertainty, complexity, and ambiguity of the world after the Cold War.[3] Since then, these elements have also taken on a business context as characteristics of various challenges that demand different types of responses from leaders.

When unpredictable events happen outside the organizational boundaries, they can be negative or positive, but both present greater volatility, uncertainty, complexity, and ambiguity, which makes it a lot more difficult for leaders to make decisions now. An example of positive complexity is your product going viral and becoming an internet sensation. The Tunisian fruit vendor is an example of negative complexity for business and political leaders.

Negative complexity can, in fact, be harnessed to create positive complexity because the underlying principles that govern both are the same.

In this sense, negative complexity and VUCA are used synonymously throughout this book. But negative complexity isn't necessarily bad news or as doom and gloom as it sounds—negative complexity can, in fact, be harnessed to create positive complexity because the underlying principles that govern both are the same. But before we learn how to harness the negative or dive into what positive complexity entails, it's helpful to understand the factors that create complexity in the first place. Let's look at another example of the VUCA environment we live in today:

A two-year-old boy's body, efflorescent with hemorrhagic blisters, lay limp in his mother's arms. Just a few days ago, after eating the bushmeat of fruit bats from the market, he showed flu-like symptoms. Two days later, blood-filled blisters had grown as big as plums on deadened patches of his skin. Now, bouts of seizures were punctuated with vomiting and bleeding from his eyes and ears. His mother's hysteric wailings ricocheted through the palm-leaf roofs of the village as she rocked her fading boy in the dark, forgetting her own feverish body.

A couple of days later, on December 6, 2013, this boy died in Guéckédou Prefecture, Guinea, in West Africa. He was patient zero of the Ebola outbreak of 2014, one of the deadliest epidemics to ever hit the human race, with a case fatality rate of up to 90 percent. A week later, it killed his mother, sister, and grandmother. Two mourners at the funeral spread the virus to their village. By the time health officials started noticing the spreading disease in March 2014, it had killed dozens. The number of prevalent cases reported in Guinea, Liberia, and Sierra Leone hit a turning point in August 2014; it had taken eight months to amass about 1,600 cases by the end of July 2014. In August, the prevalent cases almost doubled to 3,100 from the previous month; in September, to 7,000; and in October, 13,500. By May 2015, Ebola cases totaled 27,000.[4]

This was not the first Ebola outbreak—there had been three dozen occurrences before 2014, which were quickly contained. The worst previous outbreak had not affected more than 450 people.[5]

What made the Ebola outbreak of 2014 spin so out of control? The 2014 outbreak was different in four important aspects:

1. *New variables* were introduced to the equation—that is, new roads and political instability. The epicenter of the disease was the village of Guéckédou, Guinea, bordering Sierra Leone and Liberia at the intersection of the three countries. Up to this point, all previous outbreaks occurred in remote villages, not at a population hub. Additionally, all three countries had recently emerged from long periods of conflict and political instability, which pushed the limits of the health-care system that was already treating many injured patients.

2. *The level of interdependence* among the variables was higher than in previous cases. This interdependence among the related variables—that is, political instability and weakened hospitals, labs, and health-care personnel—was much more pronounced than before because the outbreak happened in a more developed,

central location with a lot more moving parts, each playing specialized roles and more deeply interconnected with other parts, than in remote villages. For example, hospitals, labs, and health-care workers often played overlapping roles in remote villages, where, if one part of the health system broke down, other parts could easily fill in.

Political conflicts in the area also meant health-care personnel were neither sufficiently staffed nor trained for infection prevention and control. It resulted in inadequate isolation wards, which enabled contagions to go unchecked. Further, insufficient laboratory capacity delayed detection of the disease. The increased interdependence among all these variables contributed to the failure of the entire health-care system when the inflow of patients exceeded the health-care system's ability to contain it.

3. *The speed of interaction* among the variables was faster than in previous cases. The prefecture of Guéckédou had newly installed roads all around it. The accelerated transportation at the junction of three countries enabled the disease to travel much faster than in other cases before.

4. *The density of interaction* among the variables was higher. The population of all three countries, and indeed the sixteen countries in Western Africa, has been increasing at a 45° slope since the mid-1990s and early 2000s, averaging between 2 and 4 percent annually, which has created higher density of interactions among the people.[6]

As a result of the 2014 Ebola outbreak, the World Bank estimated that somewhere between $2.2 billion and $7.4 billion in GDP was lost in 2014 and another $25.2 billion in 2015 in Guinea, Liberia, and Sierra Leone.[7] Because of reduced access to health-care services, an estimated additional 10,600 lives were lost to HIV, tuberculosis, and malaria during the epidemic in these three most affected countries. More than 17,300 children have been orphaned because of Ebola; each student had lost approximately 1,848 hours of education owing to school closures, ranging from around thirty-three weeks in Guinea to thirty-nine weeks in Sierra Leone. Routine immunizations decreased by 30 percent when funding and logistics previously dedicated to vaccination campaigns were redirected to fight the epidemic or were postponed to avoid public gatherings.[8] Major events were canceled (for example, Morocco requested a postponement of the 2015 Africa Cup of Nations, which it was scheduled to host, and was subsequently disqualified by organizers due to Ebola).

To help fight the epidemic, the United States committed three thousand troops to West Africa. The TSA rolled out enhanced screening at major US airports, affecting some thirty-six thousand passengers. Connecticut had declared a public health emergency, which allowed for the isolation of anyone deemed at risk of passing on the virus.

If you are a leader of an organization from the other side of the world, the ripple effect of something that you have no control over can be devastating. It requires a totally new framework to manage this level of unpredictable complexity.

The same phenomenon of complexity prevails in businesses, but our tools and skills have not kept pace. *Effective leadership must change with the times to reflect the changes happening in the environment.* The Industrial Revolution is the single most influential force that catapulted the world from the feudal society to the twentieth century. Now we are in the midst of, and some even say post, another megatrend of the same magnitude that is reshaping the world: the *Digital Revolution.* Effective leadership must be redefined to reflect this reality.

CHANGES IN THE BASIS OF COMPETITION

I mentioned that unintended negative complexity tends to occur when unforeseeable events happen *outside* an organization's boundaries. However, when an unpredictable result of many self-organizing, independent agents happens *inside* the organizational boundaries, that is, *intended*, it usually creates positive complexity because it feeds innovation. In essence, a leader's job in this VUCA age is to respond constructively to negative complexity outside the organizational boundaries and increase positive complexity inside.

In essence, a leader's job in this VUCA age is to respond constructively to negative complexity outside the organizational boundaries and increase positive complexity inside.

A whole different set of leadership skills is required to achieve these goals. The good news is that both necessitate the same skills, but the bad news is that many businesses and their leaders don't know about, and hence are not developing, these skills. They are still using tools, models, frameworks, structures, and management practices designed for the much simpler economy of the Industrial Revolution.

The basis of competition—how value is created and how you win—has changed massively over time. I define *winning* as creating more value faster than competition. In the simple economy of the Middle Ages, the basis of competition was access to capital: a feudal lord put workers on land to create economic value with little competition. Leadership meant giving orders in a one-to-one relationship, although bound by the expectation of providing paternalistic patronage in exchange for the workers' obligations. Primary responses to perturbations in the environment were force and coercion (to use Adam Smith's terms) with the primary management goal of preserving or increasing capital.

The Industrial Revolution changed all that. The basis of competition became maximizing efficiency through a division of labor, specialization, and standardization, which produced the economies of scale from the experience curve (as one gains more experience, the efficiency improves). To achieve this goal, organizations concentrated power among a few smart leaders at the top, who developed strategy, allocated resources, and disseminated orders in a one-to-many relationship. In this model, information, power, and responsibility all resided at the top. Information is formed at the edge of the organizational boundaries, the point of interaction with customers, which was then sent up through the ranks to the top. This hierarchical model was designed to increase efficiency by reducing variances or inconsistent outcomes. Primary responses to perturbations in the environment were contingency planning with the primary management goal of eliminating variances. Corporations wanted to measure, control, and minimize variance, which gave rise to corporate initiatives such as Six Sigma, total quality management, and enterprise resource planning. In this mechanistic, predictable environment, effective leadership was defined by individual skills, such as charisma, vision, and technical expertise.

The Digital Revolution of the twenty-first century has changed the rules of competition in a massive way yet again, requiring flexibility and adaptability. In a post–Digital Revolution era, trying to predict, control, and eliminate variances is a losing game. For one, efforts to reduce variance inevitably meet the law of diminishing marginal returns: the cost of reducing variance eventually exceeds the benefit. In addition, the goal of controlling and minimizing variance is deceptive, because we don't know what to measure in a complex environment that changes fast, and we can't control what we can't measure. The minute we figure it out, what we need to measure has changed. Primary responses to perturbations in the environment now call for adaptability, speed, decentralization, and pattern recognition, with the primary management goal of accelerating learning and harnessing complexity. Contingency planning can't possibly cover all the exponential number of combinations and permutations from thousands of new variables.

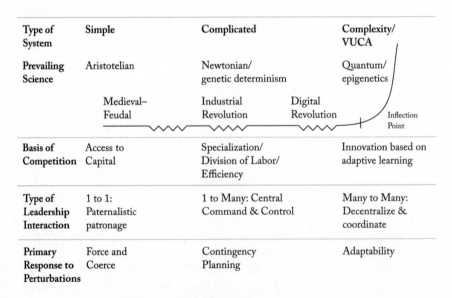

Type of System	Simple	Complicated		Complexity/ VUCA
Prevailing Science	Aristotelian	Newtonian/ genetic determinism		Quantum/ epigenetics
	Medieval–Feudal	Industrial Revolution	Digital Revolution	Inflection Point
Basis of Competition	Access to Capital	Specialization/ Division of Labor/ Efficiency		Innovation based on adaptive learning
Type of Leadership Interaction	1 to 1: Paternalistic patronage	1 to Many: Central Command & Control		Many to Many: Decentralize & coordinate
Primary Response to Perturbations	Force and Coerce	Contingency Planning		Adaptability

Figure 1.1 *Changes in the rules of engagement*

The speed with which this fast-changing dynamic environment is producing new information has exceeded the speed at which traditional bureaucratic hierarchy can send information up and down through its chain of command. As a result, decoupling of information, power, and responsibility has taken place. Information resides with frontline employees but power and responsibility reside with top managers. Hence, employees cannot take action in a timely fashion, which creates inefficiency and ineffective decision-making, a deadly situation in this fast-changing complex world.

RESPONDING TO THE COMPLEXITY OF TODAY'S BUSINESS ENVIRONMENT

In the past, our model of success in business started with a strong charismatic leader with superior intelligence who could see through the end of the game, pick the best solution, and hand out orders to employees, who then executed them with specialized division of labor in functional silos. This is similar to how an AI with a brute-force approach could win a chess game that is not as complex as Go. It can simulate all possible scenarios from each move and make a move based on the highest probability of winning.

The increasing complexity of today's business world makes that model obsolete. Just as AI had to be upgraded from the brute-force approach to a speedier and more flexible approach to win a complex game like Go, so leaders must up their game to successfully navigate today's complex business environment. Even the best AI can't direct current moves based on the expert knowledge that sees through the end of a game of Go from each move. The game has become too complex.

Four factors have dramatically increased the level of complexity today:

- the increased number of new variables introduced
- the increased speed of interaction among those variables
- the increased density of population and resulting higher density of interactions
- the increased degree of interdependence among all variables involved

A combination of these four mutually reinforcing conditions can quickly push a phenomenon over the tipping point from predictable to uncontrollable, demanding new approaches and reactions from incumbents (current market leaders) or else we must face the consequences: a Silicon Valley start-up from a garage can render an existing player's business model irrelevant overnight.

First, the number of new variables introduced in the leader's decision-making space is increasing in the form of new technologies and innovations every day. Consider these research findings on how much a human brain can process: the maximum number of chunks of information humans can process simultaneously is seven (plus or minus two).[9] Focused attention can only hold up to four concepts at a time.[10] The number of interdependent variables, and the resulting permutations of outcomes a leader must consider to make good decisions, has long exceeded seven, let alone four. Similarly, AlphaGo couldn't have won if it followed the brute-force search method that worked for narrow AI to beat humans in other less complex games with less variables to consider.

Second, the speed with which new variables enter the system is accelerating exponentially. It took ninety-nine years for the telephone, invented in 1876, to reach 90 percent of US households but only twenty years for the cell phone, first sold in 1984, to achieve the same 90 percent penetration level—and the internet spread even faster.[11]

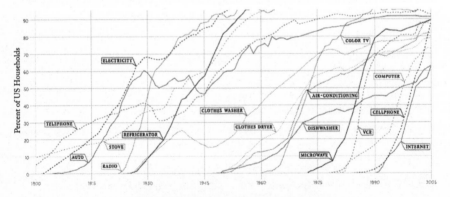

Figure 1.2 Consumption spreads faster today
Nicholas Felton, New York Times

Third, as the economic standards rose, which has lengthened life expectancy, the world population has increased exponentially. The resulting increased density creates more frequent interactions among the members of and entities in the economies, which result in a higher level of complexity.

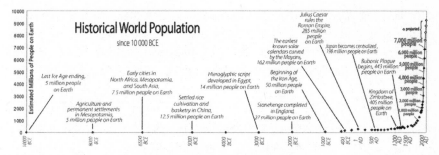

Figure 1.3 *Historic world population*
UNEP-GRID and US Census Bureau, 2011

Fourth, as the number, speed, and density of variables multiply, the degree of interdependence among the variables is also intensifying, producing a butterfly effect: a flap of a butterfly's wing in Beijing can set off a cascade of atmospheric events that, weeks later, spurs the formation of a tornado in Texas. When variables involved are interdependent, a small change in one state causes large effects at a later stage, because of the sensitive dependence on initial conditions. The increasing level of interdependence and the resulting unpredictability in the world today makes doing business very challenging for leaders.

HARNESSING COMPLEXITY

The more complex post–Digital Revolution business environment makes the mechanistic efficiency model ineffective. The very premise of Six Sigma—that we can predict, control, and reduce variability—is at odds with the principle of unpredictability and complexity in today's business world. *Variability is the essence of the game, not a noise to be eliminated.* Leaders should not be afraid of complexity but rather *increase* complexity to use it to their advantage.

Leaders should not be afraid of complexity but rather *increase* complexity to use it to their advantage.

Turning complexity on its head, organizations can use the very principles that pose significant challenges to their advantage by increasing the speed, interdependence, density of interaction, and variety of input in the organization to improve one's chances of survival and radical innovation. As we've seen at Google, self-organization, flexibility, diversity of thoughts, simple rules, and profuse experiments do just that. Therefore, new leadership competencies required in this more complex environment include tolerance for ambiguity and diversity, agility, flexibility, transparency, adaptability, resilience, and connection with others. For example:

- To increase the volume of new variables, organizations need to increase variability of input by creating diversity of thought.
- To increase the speed of interaction, teams in organizations must share information with complete transparency, remove any friction in the communication process, and constantly make iterative improvement using simple rules. Increase self-organization of frontline employees who have more information. Push power and responsibility down to where information resides so that information, power, and responsibility can all reside at the same place.
- To increase density of interactions, increase frequency of interactions. House employees in cubicles with low walls in confined spaces. Design a path to the cafeteria and snacks so that employees from departments that would never interact in a normal course of business would have to run into each other.
- To increase interdependence among employees, a networked team structure should be in place to improve connection among team members, creating a many-to-many relationship, replacing the obsolete traditional silos in hierarchical order of one-to-many relationships. Create an environment where people feel a sense of belonging and connection.

This is how AlphaGo beat Lee Sedol and how Google became one of the most innovative companies in the world—and it's how any organization can transform itself to succeed in this new digital era and create positive complexity. We'll cover more on how to harness complexity in the next chapter.

(By the way, in case you lose sleep over the possibility of a DeepMind-turned Skynet obliterating the human race, Google is developing a kill switch—and it's not sniffer dogs. Rest assured, the android terminators won't take over our world.)

HOW RADICAL INNOVATION HAPPENS

Radical innovation germinates for a long time, surfacing at the critical inflection point when momentum has become large enough (as some would call self-organized criticality). Radical innovation happens when many self-organizing employees experiment profusely and learn—to see how to adapt to the environment best and adjust their behavior iteratively using simple rules. The iterative adaptation based on the results of this experimentation builds the momentum, often well below the radar screen. The employees take cues from the environment in an open-feedback system. Radical innovation is a result of these employees coevolving with the environment in an open system where information for feedback and adaptation flows without friction. Radical innovation is created by an adequate level of random perturbations from the environment and the complex system's adaptations to them. It often results from accidental, spontaneous recombination of existing ideas and tools.

In the process of this constant adaptation to signals from the environment, employees use simple rules to speed up the reaction time, rather than executing with perfect accuracy, because spontaneous second order change happens as a result of growth of variances or errors from imperfect execution. As such, speed to generate meaningful variances from iterations of trials is far more important for radical innovation than perfection.

Radical innovation cannot be planned or choreographed; it can only be fostered and nurtured. Putting someone in charge of an "innovation" department, allocating some budget, and tasking that person with managing the innovation pipeline can only yield incremental innovation, such as packaging innovation or line extension. To maximize chances of radical innovation, the kind that produces 10x improvements, individuals with differentiated, unique expertise, skill sets, and perspectives must be forged in solid connection as a coherent team.

Radical innovation involves a cultural shift and the accompanying changes in HR and leadership practices. Once manifested, radical innovation sustains for a relatively long period, until the next radical innovation redefines industry dynamics. To summarize, I define *radical innovation as a holistic, serendipitous result of many self-organizing, interdependent employees learning from profuse experiments using simple rules often to produce a minimum of 10x improvements, dramatically changing the existing industry dynamics and providing a new platform for other innovations to build on.* Radical innovation is a specific manifestation of complexity. Each of these concepts will be unpacked in the remaining chapters.

THE ROLE OF NEUROSCIENCE IN LEADERSHIP

Our business environment is no longer deterministic, and neither are our brains. Both can adapt to a new environment. In our desire to create positive complexity, understanding how our brains work can help us greatly. The principle of *neuroplasticity*—our brains' ability to change and adapt in response to experience—is now accepted by all neuroscientists. Neuronal plasticity can occur at the genetic level. Epigenetics is a relatively new field of biology that relates to how DNA or genes expression can be modified in cells. In neuroscience, this relates to how the environment influences gene expression and may even affect the genes we inherit from our parents and how our DNA will be activated and transmitted to the next generation. The prefix *epi-* means "above" or "in addition to" and genetics is about the information encoded in DNA. Epigenetics reveals that the changes in our genetic materials can come from our life experiences. Epigenetics is redefining molecular biology, neuroscience, epidemiology, and many other related fields of study. It turns out that epigenetics holds vast promise for leaders (and followers) everywhere.

Our brains' responses to stimuli were originally thought to be predictable and predetermined. Recent neuroscience studies substantiate that neuronal connections and brain structures—once thought to be inherited and unchangeable—change substantially over time as emotions and experiences *change our brains' firing patterns*. Depending on which neuronal circuits get stimulated, certain neuronal connections may become stronger and more efficient, while others are pruned. This function is facilitated through the feedback loop with the environment where the neuronal activities closer to the desired outcome strengthen the neuronal connection and those farther away from the desired outcome weaken it. As the plasticity of the brain creates different neural connections, new emotions, behaviors, and even types of learning become available.

Why epigenetics matters to business leaders

How does this relate to the skills required to win in the complexity that we covered in the previous section? Our past experiences program and shape our neuronal connections, which can make it difficult for leaders to practice the skills necessary to harness complexity, such as embracing diversity of thought, practicing transparency in communication, and allowing others to self-organize.

Have you ever worked for a boss who was inflexible, hoarded information, micromanaged, and was not open to your ideas? If you have, you know how miserable your life can get. If you *are* one, well, heaven help you . . . no, that's all the more reason you need to keep reading this book, so you can learn how to change! These bosses do not only make our lives miserable and sap the last drop of life energy out of us; they are also unable to navigate through complexity, and thus compromise the organization's ability to produce radical innovation. Chances are, they perceive that acting in this ineffective way is their best option—which highlights the need for self-management.

Understanding and harnessing the epigenetic nature of our brains can help us modify the past programs that subconsciously affect how we tend to behave. For example, becoming aware of how one's body tightens when other people voice contrary opinions helps leaders identify a tendency to downplay others' ideas. This awareness assists leaders to change how they interpret incoming signals and trace the source of the tension, which is often a result of past experiences. Then they can make a thoughtful decision to consciously change how they interpret the incoming signal and change how they respond. *Emotions follow meaning*. We can consciously choose what meaning we assign to incoming signals instead of jumping to the first meaning our lower brain fires automatically.

Understanding and harnessing the epigenetic nature of our brains can help us modify the past programs that subconsciously affect how we tend to behave.

MY RESEARCH

The oldest of three children, I was born in the bucolic farm town of Suwon in Korea. One spring day during my sophomore year in high school, I sat down with my parents to decide whether I would be taking the liberal arts or math and science track. The conventional wisdom in rural Korea three decades ago was that girls didn't go to college but instead got married and took care of the household. So my parents gave me a blank stare and said, "Why are you trying to go to college? If we send you to college, you won't even spend money on a bus ride for us because you will get married and will become a stranger to us. But we'll get an airplane ride out of your brothers." I knew they were half joking, but that day I decided I would go to college with or without their help. I came to Brigham Young University with only seventy dollars in my pocket and began working a job where I got up at four in the morning to scrub toilets on campus. With God's grace and scholarships, I graduated with honors and no student loans.

When I got my first job after college, I bought an airplane ticket and flew out my mom—she did get an airplane ride out of me after all. When she saw how I was living, she said, "You are a dragon born in a stream. I thought you were a salamander. Dragons belong in the ocean not in the humble stream where you were born."

This book is about how *you* go from a salamander to a dragon that opens up an entire new ocean—radical innovation.

My PhD program at Brigham Young University opened the door for my interest in systemic psychology, systems theory, and neuroscience, which led me to complex adaptive systems theory, which led me to quantum mechanics. I was fascinated to find how these principles also explained the phenomena in people, business, organizations, and so many of life's puzzles. As my curiosity grew and my investigative efforts became more intense, I began to see how my diverse background—practicing corporate accounting with my CPA, strategy consulting for Accenture where I learned about and solved the challenges many Fortune 500 companies faced, and various experiences in marketing and systemic psychology—gave me precisely the skill sets that help me see the thin thread that connects all these diverse disciplines. Ironically, my lack of aptitude in math helped me translate the quantum mechanics principles into a language that laypeople can understand—I had to understand the core principles of those concepts and then apply them in everyday situations that others can relate to.

Given the ever-growing complexity of the business environment, and armed with the knowledge of the epigenetic nature of our brains, I set out to learn the following:

- What are effective leadership competencies for organizations in a complex environment?
- How do "good" and "bad" leadership competencies affect the bottom line?
- How much money are people willing to forgo to work for a "good" boss and how much more do they require to tolerate working for a "bad" boss?
- Which leadership competencies best predict good performance evaluation and employee-turnover intention?
- Which leadership competencies are most necessary for radical innovation?

As an organizational scientist, leadership trainer and consultant, and professional certified executive coach, I have worked with many executives around the globe and long wrestled with these questions. In search of answers, I conducted two rounds of global leadership research.

I wanted to learn what leaders see as the most important leadership competencies, based on their evaluation of their own bosses, given the complex nature of the business environment. The first-round research findings were published by *Harvard Business Review*.[12] The article generated a huge response from readers all around the globe because it confirmed the universal belief that *HBR* readers intuitively hold about what makes leadership effective and what makes life difficult for followers.

Through sophisticated statistical modeling, the second round of research data revealed the following:

1. There are two distinct groups of leaders: those who excel at leadership competencies vital to win in complexity by stimulating radical innovation—whom I dub Quantum Leaders (40 percent of all leaders)—and those who don't, whom I call Mechanistic Leaders (60 percent).
2. The difference in the turnover intent of followers who work for these two groups is 37 percent, which translates to a $448 million hit to operating expenses for each Fortune 500 company.
3. People are willing to forgo up to 39 percent of their compensation to work for a Quantum Leader.

What is amazing about these findings is that the leadership competencies identified by global leaders—safety, connection, and learning—are *exactly* the same needs, in that order, that our brains have been optimized to fulfill by evolution.

Our brains demand safety, connection, and learning, in that order

The human brain has evolved over millions of years, which has ultimately led to us becoming the dominant species, on top of the food chain. The most primitive part evolutionarily of our brains is the brain stem, which is in charge of keeping us *safe* by recognizing even subliminal signals of threat within milliseconds. If the incoming signal is deemed safe, then it proceeds to the limbic system, which is in charge of providing emotional saliency to what we experience, through which we experience *connection*. Once we feel connected, the signal can be processed in the next, most evolved part of our brains, the cortex, which is in charge of *learning* and adapting based on feedback. These three layers of our brains are hierarchical,[13] meaning the safety needs of the brain stem trump the connection needs of the limbic system, which in turn trump the learning and innovation needs of the cortex brain. The responses of leaders all around the world confirm neuroscience! We cannot learn and create radical innovation before we feel safe and attached. A deeper review on this topic will be covered in chapter 3.

Leadership competencies to harness complexity

At the INSEAD business school in France and at Xerox in Palo Alto, researchers discovered that in a number of industries, long periods of incremental improvement tend to be interrupted by short periods of radical innovation: sudden shifts that determine a new pattern of technology diffusion, rather than a series of small improvements over time, which are dubbed punctuated equilibria.[14] This type of radical innovation requires many failures in iterative experiments by interdependent, self-organizing employees, which gives rise to an unpredictable, holistic emergent pattern in which the whole is greater than the sum of its parts—another definition of complexity.

My research identifies six competencies required to win in a complex world by creating more value faster than competition. Let's look at the hierarchical building blocks leaders must achieve to lead an organization through complexity, in ascending order:

- Self-management
- Providing safety
- Creating differentiation
- Strengthening connection
- Facilitating learning and adapting
- Stimulating radical innovation

Each of these competencies will be covered in more detail in respective chapters.

TOWARD A NEW PARADIGM OF LEADERSHIP

This book is a culmination of my primary research with hundreds of leaders throughout the world, secondary research from hundreds of social scientists, and insights and observations from the countless hours I've spent coaching, consulting, and delivering training workshops to many executives and teams. In this book, I will use research-based evidence, as well as case examples observed in my clients, to show you how to harness and thrive in complexity and consistently produce radical innovation.

I will reveal what these effective leadership proficiencies are and how they can permanently change an organization and the individuals in it. In the process, I will also provide quantified bottom-line impact for each leadership competency group, so you can prioritize what you need to work on the most.

You can take a complimentary leadership assessment to see where you rank vis-à-vis other global leaders on these leadership competencies and see how you compare to other global leaders by going to my website: www. sunniegiles.com. Reviewing the results will make the content of this book more relevant to you.

I will offer additional insights from my research, including the following:

* The discrepancy between what people identify as important leadership attributes versus what actually drives people's decisions
* Which leadership qualities have the greatest impact on individual performance evaluation
* Which leadership attributes and competencies make the greatest difference in preventing turnover
* Which leadership attributes and competencies make the greatest difference between Quantum Leaders and Mechanistic Leaders
* How Quantum Leaders facilitate radical innovation

I will also address the dilemma of the current corporate learning model: people are taught, but they are not learning. According to the *Wall Street Journal*, US firms spent about $156 billion on employee learning in 2011, but some 90 percent of new skills are lost within a year! That is because current learning models are not harnessing the nature of our brains and the nature of humans and organizations as living *systems*, so they produce only temporary learning effects. I will show you how to harness the nature of our brains and people as living systems, discover your subconscious programs that make practicing the Quantum Leadership skills difficult, and how to permanently change them.

Let's start with a deeper understanding of complex systems, which will also reveal common patterns—shared among all living organisms as diverse as people, organizations, coral reefs, and termite colonies—and establish the concepts we will use throughout this book.

Chapter 2

COMPLEX ADAPTIVE SYSTEMS: HOW ALL LIVING THINGS WORK

THE BIRTH OF THE BUTTERFLY EFFECT

"Ah, not again!" Professor Edward Lorenz sighed with frustration as his computer froze. It was the winter of 1962, and Lorenz, a mild-mannered mathematician turned meteorologist researcher at MIT was trying to run a model to simulate formation of air convection, using input variables such as air velocity, temperature, density, and pressure. In 1962 it was notoriously difficult to predict weather, but then again, it still is today (and you will soon learn why it's so difficult). He was trying to find ways to predict weather patterns of convection, a relatively easier task than predicting turbulence such as hurricanes. But the computer he was using was shared with many others at the university, and he was forced to take a break when the computer froze. He was prepared for this interruption and had written down the numbers he used for the input. When the computer came back online, he reentered his data and then went for a coffee.

When he came back after his coffee break, he was baffled by the simulation results. It was nothing like his first run.

"Why is it so different? It should just be a repeat of the first run. I don't understand," he muttered to himself.

It shouldn't have been different, since all the numbers he used for input were the same. But were they? Checking the numbers over and over, he finally solved the mystery. He had truncated one of the numbers from 0.506127 to 0.506. This tiny variation in the initial condition, 0.000127, transformed the whole pattern of more than two months of simulated weather data into something unrecognizable from the first run.

Lorenz's curiosity kicked in. What was going on with the data? He reviewed the results of three thousand simulations. The simulations showed steady predictable results, apart from the initial erratic pattern, through the 1,650th iteration. But then something strange happened. Lorenz saw that at this point, a critical state was reached from each preceding iteration, after which seemingly unpredictable, erratic simulation results were observed.[1] Take a look at the figure below from his paper:

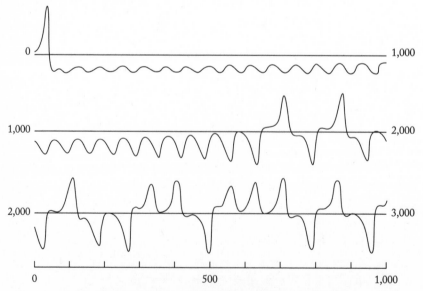

Figure 2.1 *Numeric solution of the convection equations. Graph of Y as a function of time for the 1,000 iterations (upper curve), second 1,000 iterations (middle curve), and third 1,000 iterations (lower curve).*

Edward Lorenz, Deterministic Nonperiodic Flow

Figure 2.1 on the previous page shows a numerical solution of the convection equations as time goes by. Notice how relatively predictable the pattern is portrayed until it hits 1,650, after which the pattern becomes unpredictable. Figure 2.2 below shows the same information with two-dimensional projections. The numeral 14 indicates positions at the 1,400th iteration; 15 at the 1,500th iteration; and 16 at the 1,600th iteration. Notice how 14, 15, and 16 are in the same quadrant and relatively predictable, but 17, 18, and 19 are all in different quadrants.

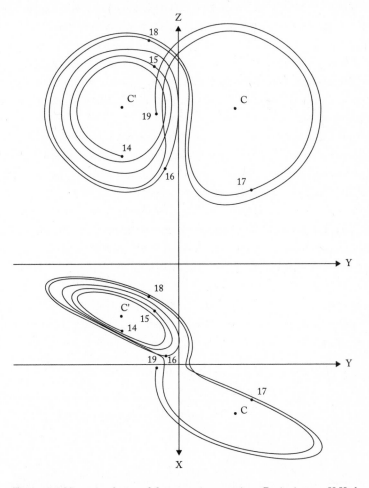

Figure 2.2 *Numeric solution of the convection equations. Projections on X-Y plane and the Y-Z plane in phase space of the segment of the trajectory extending from the 1,400th to 1,900th iterations. Numbers 14, 15, etc. denote positions at the 1,400th, 1,500th, etc. iterations. States of steady convections are denoted by C and C'.*

Edward Lorenz, Deterministic Nonperiodic Flow

His discovery and following insights rocked the world, introducing the concept of chaos theory in a 1963 paper titled "Deterministic Nonperiodic Flow," published in the *Journal of Atmospheric Sciences*. This is one of the most cited papers in history (about nineteen thousand times at the time of publication of this book). The key concept here is how a small change of initial parameters could produce dramatically different outcomes, transforming regular, predictable patterns into seemingly random chaos. It also showed how the momentum for large change is invisible in the beginning while it is building under the surface, but after the critical state, it manifests itself into a disproportionately large divergence, unrecognizable from the initial pattern. This divergence happens because the variables (air temperature, wind speed, and density, in Lorenz's simulation) are interdependent, and each iteration of small adaptations to changes over time escalates into compounding errors in future behaviors as they influence and are influenced by each other.

Chaos theory is a field of mathematics that studies how small differences in initial conditions, such as those from rounding errors in Lorenz's simulation, yield vastly different outcomes, rendering long-term predictions impossible. Lorenz describes chaos as a condition in which "the present determines the future, but the approximate present does not approximately determine the future," which happens because of the "sensitive dependence on initial conditions"—otherwise dubbed as the butterfly effect.[2]

In 1972 Lorenz gave a speech called "Predictability: Does the Flap of a Butterfly's Wings in Brazil Set Off a Tornado in Texas?" The result of Lorenz's simulation—with two circles resembling the wings of the butterfly as shown in Figure 2.2—was nicknamed the butterfly effect, a phrase we have since used in common parlance to denote how small causes can have large effects, even cropping up in the popular movie *Jurassic Park*.

In Steven Spielberg's blockbuster movie, there is a foreboding scene where Dr. Ian Malcolm (Jeff Goldblum), explains—from the backseat of a moving Jeep—to Dr. Ellie Sattler (Laura Dern), why humans will fail to control the growth of dinosaurs:

MALCOLM: See, the tyrannosaur doesn't obey set patterns or
    park schedules—the essence of chaos.
ELLIE: I'm still not clear on chaos.

MALCOLM: Oh, oh—it simply deals with unpredictability in complex systems. The shorthand is the butterfly effect. A butterfly can flap its wings in Peking and in Central Park you get rain instead of sunshine.

Here Malcolm is trying to make a connection between the chaos theory and the tyrannosaurs at Jurassic Park, although in reality Ellie should already be familiar with it, being a paleobotanist. No respectable paleobotanist would be unfamiliar with the concepts of chaos and complex adaptive systems now, but this movie was made in 1993 when the concept of chaos was still very new. Ellie, with a sheepish smile, gestures with her hand to show this information has gone right over her head. Malcolm dips his hand into the glass of water and then conducts a makeshift experiment on her hand to explain his point.

MALCOLM: Put your hand flat, like a hieroglyphic. Now, let's say a drop of water falls on your hand. Which way is the drop going to roll off? Which finger, or over the thumb, or over the other side?

ELLIE: Thumb.

Malcolm places a drop of water on the back of Ellie's hand, and it quickly rolls off toward her thumb. Malcolm then does the same thing again, showing that the next water drop rolls off a different direction. He is trying to explain that aperiodicity is one of signature characteristics of chaos.

MALCOLM: It changed. Why? Because tiny variations—the orientation of the hairs on your hand, the amount of blood distending in your vessels, imperfections in the skin . . . Microscopic, microscopic—and never repeat, and vastly affect the outcome. That's what?

ELLIE: Unpredictability.

Though this makeshift experiment may not make the grade for publication in a peer-reviewed journal, it does bring the unpredictable nature of chaos a little more down to earth.

COMPLEX ADAPTIVE
SYSTEMS THEORY

Chaos theory opened the doors for complex adaptive systems theory, which explains how all living organisms work. When it comes to complex adaptive systems—including all living systems, such as ecosystems, people, families, organizations, trees, insects, animals, coral reefs, and neurons—a slight variation in input produces an unpredictable outcome. Often this outcome exhibits a holistic pattern where the whole is greater than the sum of its parts, unrecognizable from its parts. This is how nature selects the fittest, and it's repeated in all complex systems.

Darwin's Paradox revisited

In 1859 Charles Darwin's thoughts on natural selection were published in *The Origin of Species* and turned the world of biology upside down. But there is a question that Darwin couldn't explain: How do coral reefs that cover only 0.1 percent of the surface of the ocean support over 25 percent of all marine species? How do the corals, battered by waves, form a thriving ecosystem when only a few yards away the vast desert of the lifeless Pacific Ocean extends for thousands of miles? Similarly, why is the earth the only planet inhabited by life (as far as we know) among the billions of planets in the universe?

This is the famous Darwin's Paradox. Solving this paradox involved studying the properties of the coral reef in the context of its environment. Understanding the principles that solve this paradox can be applied to the leadership competencies necessary to facilitate radical innovation.

Corals are colonies of small animals embedded in calcium carbonate shells living in shallow waters. The heads of the coral are made up of animals called polyps, which don't photosynthesize but have a symbiotic relationship with the microscopic algae that live inside them. Corals use tentacles to capture plankton for nutrients. Plankton's waste is used by the symbiotic algae as nutrients. The algae photosynthesize, producing sugar, which the corals in turn use as nutrients. As the corals proliferate, they attract many fish, which graze on algae, keeping them in check from overpopulating and smothering the corals. Cleaner shrimp keep these fish healthy by eating parasites off them. Snails graze on algae and sometimes become food for sea stars. Sea squirts, tunicates, and mollusks filter and clean the water by sieving and eating phytoplankton.

Reefs grow as corals and algae deposit calcium carbonate at the base, functioning as barriers against huge waves and protecting the ecosystem of many marine species. At the same time, a habitat without waves is not an optimal solution, since the waves stir up the bottom of shallow water to make nutrients more accessible to corals. An adequate number of waves is necessary for a thriving colony. Adaptation to the environment through complex collaboration and biodiversity is key to a thriving coral reef.

Over many millennia, coral reefs found a radically innovative way to coevolve with—taking input from and adapting to—the environment and create an ecosystem that benefits not only themselves but many other forms of marine life. Coral reefs and all the other life forms in the colony are (1) self-organizing agents, (2) interdependent on each other and on the environment to adapt to signals from the environment, (3) learning from an open-feedback system and (4) simple rules (5) to conduct many, many trial-and-error experiments, (6) coevolving with the environment over millions of years. The holistic result of this constant adaptation is efficiency inside the coral reef and the vibrant, sustainable ecosystem with extensive biodiversity, creating an emergent whole greater than the sum of its parts.

Sounds familiar? Yes, these are the concepts we have used to define complexity and the principles behind AlphaGo and Quantum Companies' management practices. These principles behind nature's emergent phenomena also govern how radical innovation happens in business. Following these principles increases your chances of success as a system (e.g., family, organization, or society). These principles work for people and organizations because they are based on laws of nature.

Another example of how many self-organizing individual agents create an emergent whole greater than the sum of their parts can be found in the East African savanna, which features harsh daily and seasonal temperature fluctuations. Here we discover extraordinarily sophisticated structures that use the convection principle to provide advanced functions, such as ventilation and temperature control, throughout the year. They contain storage chambers for food and ventilation systems to expel waste gases and bring in fresh oxygen. They draw water from sources two hundred feet below ground.

These are not descriptions of an ancient African civilization but of termite colonies! The constant eighty-six degrees Fahrenheit is optimal for growing fungi inside the mound, which they use as food. The water they draw from deep underground helps keep the queen's chamber at almost 100 percent humidity, optimal for egg laying. There is something synergistic that emerges when individual termites do their job, even though they are unaware of how their individual efforts contribute to the intricate whole. No termite can exist without the colony, and the colony cannot be sustained without individual members. The result is a marvelously vibrant, densely populated colony that is better than any one of them can produce alone, and unrecognizable from the sum of their individual efforts.

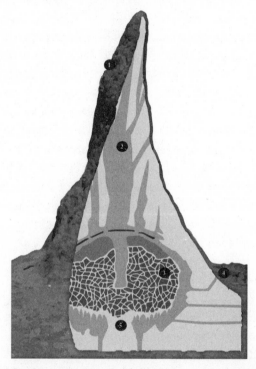

Figure 2.3 Inside a termite mound: (1) a porous mound constructed with soil, termite saliva, and dung, which enables ventilation; (2) a chimney, a ventilation system; (3) living space and a fungal garden for food; (4) openings for entering and exiting; (5) a cellar six feet below ground, a cooling system for the whole colony.

Emergence

But what is this holistic synergy? How do simple termites and corals achieve these extraordinary feats?

The answer lies in (1) the self-organizing agent adapting to changes in the environment and each other, (2) following simple rules and (3) profuse iteration of experiments to find the best way to adapt, and (4) the positive-feedback loop that builds momentum in the process while they (5) conduct profuse experiments to see what works best, pooling resources together and (6) coevolving with others in the ecosystem. In the language of complexity theory, this holistic synergy is called *emergence*. Self-organizing agents following simple rules can give rise to an extraordinarily complex structure. A flock of self-organizing starlings in pursuit of self-interest to maximize chances of survival from predators follows the simple rules of (1) separation to maintain a short-range distance from their neighbors, (2) alignment to steer toward the average heading of neighbors, and (3) cohesion to fly the average position toward six or seven neighbors. These behaviors produce very complex, sudden maneuvering behaviors that optimize flying speed as well as protection from predators.

In these positive-feedback loops, any action taken by one agent is amplified by the positive feedback within the loop, much like those variables in Lorenz's simulation and similar to compound interest on your savings. Every interest payment adds to the principal, propelling even greater interest on the next payment and producing exponential growth.

Two things are noteworthy about this positive-feedback loop: (1) it takes a long germination time to build the momentum to hit the tipping point,[3] or chasm (in reference to Geoffrey Moore's *Crossing the Chasm*,[4] which is dubbed the bible for entrepreneurial marketing);[5] and (2) once past that critical inflection point, it can never revert to the original state and creates a spillover effect for others.

The underground germination time is what Lorenz noticed in his simulation results before the 1,650th iteration, after which the momentum swung above the surface. The same thing happens to every start-up company that reshapes the industry with radical innovation: when they appear on the radar screen, it surprises everyone because they "come from nowhere," but in reality, they have spent many years making small iterative improvements and building momentum under the surface. This is the same point Adam Grant, a social psychologist and Wharton professor, made in his book *Originals*: one of the patterns of those who change the world with radical innovation, whom he calls "originals," is that they are "late to the party."[6] While they are procrastinating, random ideas incubate in the back of their minds, which allows them time to consider divergent ideas, think in nonlinear ways, and make unexpected leaps.

A positive-feedback loop that creates amplification during the iterative process is particularly applicable in the information technology industry, creating a spillover effect to spawn other technologies. Some IT tools not only serve their originally intended purpose but create an explosion of new software and programming platforms, stimulating breakthrough ideas and opening doors for even more innovations. Users discover unintended ways to employ these tools, spawning a whole new ecosystem. These tools also open doors for the "adjacent possible,"[7] the term coined by Stuart Kauffman and expounded on by Steven Johnson,[8] referring to the area of possibility for innovation.

Complexity in the business ecosystem

Let's now take a business example of complex adaptive systems theory. What is the most popular, highest-revenue-grossing app in Japan, with a whopping 93 percent market share of a mobile internet population of 74 million people (60 percent of Japan's entire population), who use it an average of eighty-four minutes every day? No, it's not Facebook Messenger or WhatsApp (the instant messaging app Facebook acquired for $19 billion in 2014).

It's LINE, the most popular instant messaging platform in Japan, Thailand, Taiwan, and a few other countries in Asia. In fact, LINE has more than six hundred million downloads globally and over 218 million active users as of mid-2016—about 60 percent of WhatsApp's use. LINE generated revenues of over $1 billion in 2015, up 35 percent from 2014, whereas WhatsApp generated a paltry $19 million during the first half of 2014 before the acquisition. It's notoriously difficult to monetize IM apps, yet LINE went public in July 2016 with a market valuation of nearly $7 billion.

Media pundits and equity analysts were surprised at this newcomer and its astounding ability to monetize.

It actually took LINE more than fifteen years of trial and error to get there. LINE started in 2000 as Naver Japan, a search engine with a seed funding of ¥100 million (around $880,000). But business never took off and it closed in 2005. The following year, they spent about $30 million to purchase a search engine company and relaunched Naver Japan in 2007. They kept experimenting with different functions, such as blogging, searching, *matome* (a service allowing users to store similar information so others can find it more easily), *kuchikomi* (the ability to search user comments with a few keywords), and other services. Finally, in June 2011, they introduced LINE, based on the previous ten years of accumulated knowledge about the Japanese market and consumers. What the pundits and equity analysts see is the last four years of success, rather than the first ten years spent in germination, making iterative, incremental improvements under the surface.

How does LINE monetize its services when giants like Facebook Messenger are still struggling to do so? The answer lies in the vibrant network of services and products it has built in an ecosystem.

LINE turned its messaging app into a *platform* on which many services and products are sold. Most of its revenue comes from games, sticker sales from LINE characters, and character merchandise. These LINE characters aren't just static emojis; they have a life of their own. For example, the two most popular LINE characters, Cony and Brown, are married. Cony is an adorable but bad-tempered female rabbit who has a mean streak. Her best friend is Jessica, a fashionista cat who loves to cook. Cony was jealous of Jessica's fashion one day and tried to transform into her. Brown is a mild-mannered, stoic, reticent brown bear, much like the typical "salaryman" in Japan. But when he does blow up, he fights hard, exposing his claws and punishing his friends. If you're thinking this sounds like a sitcom scene, you would be right! LINE produces an animated TV sitcom titled *Salaryman*, much like *The Office* in the United States, using its cast of characters.

LINE also launched its Creators Market in which graphic artists from all over the world can submit stickers for approval and split the revenues from the sticker sales fifty-fifty with LINE. This arrangement has enabled LINE to create characters that are localized for individual markets, which designers at LINE headquarters can never do as it globalizes its business to more than one hundred countries. In the seven months after the launch, LINE Creators Market generated thirty thousand stickers from 145 countries.[9] Users bought 1.4 billion of these stickers for $30 million—not bad for LINE, which simply provides the platform.

LINE Game has introduced insanely popular games such as LINE Pop, LINE Disney Tsum Tsum, LINE PokoPang, and LINE Cookie Run, which are available only on the LINE messenger app. They are free to install but offer in-app purchases for lives and boosters and use the LINE characters. LINE Games capitalize on the network effect of its users by providing the ability to purchase coins and lives for their friends. LINE Play is a personal mobile homepage where users create and dress up avatars with items for free and for fee. Users can turn their mobile homepage into a party room or a flower garden, raise their pets by feeding them treats, and get ultrarare items only in the VIP castle (for fee).

LINE Music is a subscription-based streaming music service offered in partnership with Sony Music and Avex Group through which users can listen to and share music in the LINE messenger app. LINE TV allows users to watch full episodes of TV dramas and videos, become a fan of their favorite channels, and receive content available only on LINE TV, such as the *Salaryman* sitcom.

LINE also makes money by selling businesses access to LINE's users. LINE@ is a for-fee service for businesses and professionals to create official accounts and communicate with their clients using broadcast messages, one-on-one chats, and timeline posts, each of which has a price tag. Businesses can offer discounts and promotions to LINE users based on user profile information, which is much more effective than traditional advertising. LINE Business Connect allows businesses to build their own automated consumer experience, such as customer support requests handled via LINE, sending personalized responses to their requests using LINE character emojis, and collecting payments with LINE Pay.

LINE also offers online-to-offline (O2O) services such as payment, restaurant reservations for thirty thousand member restaurants, and taxi hailing. In partnership with VISA, MasterCard, and JCB, LINE Pay offers mobile payment services and money transfer services (think Venmo and iMessage combined or Facebook Messenger's payment option). LINE also has offline stores that sell plush toys of its popular characters and other merchandise such as shirts and hats and hold events where their fans meet LINE characters.

LINE has also launched supporting apps, such as B612 that helps its hundred million users edit selfies with filters, create videos and collages, and easily share them on popular social media sites. Another supporting app, Aillis (an acronym for "art is long, life is short"), allows users to customize their images with texts, stamps, and animated stickers. These supporting apps are connected to users' LINE accounts.

LINE Whosecall is an app for identifying and blocking calls and texts from those who are on the user's contact list, such as spams, robocalls, and telemarketers, based on a database of seven hundred million phone numbers. Whosecall encourages users to create collective intelligence and help each other by reporting the phone numbers of those unwanted calls to "create a reliable communication network for everyone." Users can create their personalized Whosecall card to use like a business card for caller ID.

These dizzying multitudes of interdependent activities in many-to-many relationships create the spillover effect among various LINE businesses as well as thousands of business partners, vendors, and corporate clients "grazing" from the positive-feedback loop in LINE's ecosystem, similar to how coral reefs support the entire ecosystem. In 2015 LINE was ranked the fourteenth most innovative company by Fast Company. These activities have resulted in exponential growth for LINE.

HOW TO CREATE THE NEW SUSTAINABLE COMPETITIVE ADVANTAGE

In 1985 Michael Porter, a professor at Harvard Business School, presented two frameworks on competitive advantage: one that enables a firm to outperform its competitors and the other on how a firm creates value. These frameworks are a standard part of every MBA education curriculum, and many common terms in MBA jargon, such as *five forces* and *value chain*, come from his frameworks. According to Porter, a firm's competitive advantage is what enables it to compete successfully, and is derived from either low cost (from the economies of scale) or differentiation, which allows a firm to charge a premium price. He believed that a leader's primary job is to build a sustainable competitive advantage, which

> *cannot be understood by looking at a firm as a whole. It stems from the many discrete activities a firm performs in designing, producing, marketing, delivering and supporting its product. Each of these activities can contribute to a firm's relative cost position and create a basis of differentiation . . . The value chain disaggregates a firm into its strategically relevant activities in order to understand the behavior of costs and the existing and potential sources of differentiation.*[10]

Can we understand how our consciousness works if we understand the workings of each neuron in our brains? Can we understand how termites build such a sophisticated structure by disaggregating each termite's activities? Similarly, can we understand how a firm can create a competitive advantage in today's complex world by disaggregating each component in the value chain, such as inbound logistics, manufacturing, marketing, and sales?

No. We no longer live in a predictable, reductionistic world that can be neatly disaggregated. The business environment and the world in general have become much more complex since the introduction of Porter's original ideas. Now we have many more factors entering the competitive landscape at breakneck speed, which are much more interdependent and blur the boundaries between firms. Each interdependent interaction creates a butterfly effect, so we cannot predict, let alone plan, a firm's future. This context breaks down the assumptions in his model and makes Porter's approach less relevant today.

Porter did touch on the concept of this virtuous interdependent synergy—what he calls the "fit" in his *Harvard Business Review* article "What is Strategy?"[11]—but in his view, it originates from sources *internal* to the firm. According to Porter, the fit creates a competitive advantage, which is as strong as its strongest link in the value chain and locks out imitators. Porter's idea of the fit has three types: (1) simple consistency between each activity (function) and the overall strategy, (2) second-order fit occurs when activities are reinforcing within the value chain, and (3) third-order fit goes beyond activity reinforcement to optimization of effort. But the world has crossed over the inflection point from complicated to complex. In the post–Industrial Revolution world where things were predictable and the environment was rather stable, leaders could just focus on the factors internal to the organization and make good decisions. Now leaders must consider the increasing variety and interdependence of environmental factors in order to make effective decisions.

If we agree with Porter's view that competitive advantage is what enables a firm to survive and compete successfully, and the sustainable competitive advantage is what makes it difficult for others to replicate that success, then the vibrant ecosystem LINE has established *outside the organization* illustrates how to create today's sustainable competitive advantage. The ecosystem for many hundreds of business partners, suppliers, and other symbiotic relationships that create adjacent possibilities, contribute to, and benefit from LINE's platform is much more difficult to replicate and less vulnerable to competitive attacks.

This emergent synergy is similar to the network effect formulated in Metcalf's Law: the value of the telecommunication network is proportional to the square of the number of connected users in the system (n^2), meaning the value of the network increases as the number of users increases. What is different is that the emergent synergy is much greater than Metcalf's Law, because the number of networks increases as the platform flourishes (n^n), each with its own ecosystem network, whereas the value of the network in Metcalf's Law is limited to one network.

For example, if we have three people connected to a telecom network, according to Metcalf's Law, the value of the network is $3^2 = 9$. In a complex system's emergent synergy, assuming each user is part of another ecosystem, the value is $3^3 = 27$. To account for redundancy, we divide this number by 2, maybe as large as 3 (this number depends on how much benefit you extract from the network and how useful these networks are). So, the emergent synergy of ecosystems is 13.5 or 9. As the nodes increase, you can see how quickly the value explodes: if there are 10 nodes, $10^2 = 100$ according to Metcalf's Law, but $10^{10} = 10$ *billion*. Even if we divide this number by 100 to account for redundancy, we come up with 100 million in the emergent synergy of complex systems, versus 100 in Metcalf's Law. This is the mathematical explanation behind the success of companies with an almost insurmountable first-mover advantage using platform-based ecosystems, such as Amazon with online commerce, eBay with peer-to-peer commerce, and Google with a search engine. I call this emergent synergy from creating a vibrant ecosystem of interdependent many-to-many relationships *ecosynergy*,* which is almost impossible for others to copy. Integral to ecosynergy is the concept of a platform, a radical innovation that provides a foundation for others to build their incremental innovation on. *This is the new sustainable competitive advantage.*

What conditions are required to promote a positive-feedback loop that creates ecosynergy? The consistent patterns of complex adaptive systems have massive business implications, because they lead to radical innovations that redefine the rules of the game for the succeeding era, creating this new sustainable competitive advantage. Let's go back to the termites and see how these concepts apply. Each of these patterns (and others not covered here) will be treated more in depth in later chapters.

Termites *self-organize* and self-heal when there is a breach in the system. If a group gets separated, they produce supplementary reproductives to start a new colony. They communicate the shortest routes to the colony and food sources by using pheromone trails. They build their mounds in the direction that minimizes the heat from the scorching sun in the afternoon. They do all these tasks without being directed, and yet they are in perfect harmony with the overall group goal.

Termites communicate with *simple rules,* such as "the shorter the route to food, the thicker the pheromone trail," and "when you see danger, alert others by banging your head." They produce vibrations by banging their heads on surfaces to alert the entire colony to a threat. These simple rules provide a loose structure to coordinate their activities to reach the common goal and also accelerate the speed of interaction among them.

These termites make incremental improvements through *profuse trial and error.* They constantly try to find faster routes to find food, more effective heat-protection strategies, and better ways to survive when they leave their colony to form a new one (the swarming termites fly through a mud tube to protect themselves from dehydration and predators). It took many, many trials and errors over millions of years to figure out the optimal solution. Perfection is not nearly as important as the incremental snowball effect of frequent, iterative feedback.

They also facilitate *differentiation* among the members. Each termite caste has its own specialized function and is anatomically distinct. Soldier

---

* Synergy refers to an emergent property where a system creates a whole greater than the sum of its parts and *eco-* means environmental.

termites have big jaws, sharp mandibles, and sometimes spray chemicals to protect the colony. Workers and soldiers secrete inhibitory pheromones to suppress reproductive functions, so they are solely focused on supporting the queen. Each role is highly differentiated with a specialized division of labor, and yet is flexible. For example, when a certain class of termite dwindles, they change the food given to nymphs to produce more of the dwindling class.

They *connect and collaborate with each other and the environment.* Termites live and work as a group (but they never sleep—too bad for Sanofi that they don't get to sell Ambien to termites!). They communicate with, take cues from, and adapt to the environment and each other. Their communication is frictionless because there is no hoarding of information, no political jockeying, and no fear of getting backstabbed. There is complete transparency for the good of the colony. Each termite is symbiotically part of a larger whole. The colony does not exist without individual termites, and the individuals cannot survive without being part of the colony. They influence and are influenced by each other because they are interdependent: changes in the environment change the individual termite, which in turn changes the environment, and so on. They are united under the common purpose of the colony: to protect the members and make more of them. They copy each other's behaviors in a self-similar pattern. All of them have distributed or limited intelligence, but when they pool resources, they achieve something far greater than what each can do as individuals.

Termites create an ecosystem of densely populated open networks in many-to-many relationships. Termites live in an open network and support other living systems surrounding the mounds in an ecosystem of ecosystems. They support denser tree populations around the mound, because when they decompose plant materials, they make more fertile moist ground—an optimal environment for the queen to lay eggs. In turn, these trees attract more herbivores, which attract more carnivores, the waste of which promotes more plant growth, which recursively benefits the termites in turn, and so on. In essence, they build a platform for others to build their own ecosystems. This is how they create holistic *emergence*, a signature pattern of complex adaptive systems where the whole is greater than the sum of its parts. Living these patterns has enabled them to be one of the most successful groups of insects on earth—one of very few species that have survived over 250 million years. Termites survived the Great

Dying at the end of the Permian period, in which some 70 to 96 percent of earth's species went extinct.

My purpose in this book is to examine how these complex adaptive systems achieve such sophisticated emergence and reveal a consistent pattern we can use to achieve organizational synergy resulting in radical innovation. All living things are complex adaptive systems, including humans, cities, and organizations. All complex adaptive systems share signature patterns, and we can greatly enhance our ability to lead organizations, and improve our chances of inducing radical innovation, by studying and applying those patterns. Since this book is not about biology but leadership competencies to produce radical innovation, the question becomes, How do we *apply* these principles? How does the success of artificial intelligence, coral reefs, and termites apply to people and businesses? I will show you how and share my own and others' research to substantiate the merits of such an approach.

Chapter 3

NEUROSCIENCE OF LEADERSHIP, OR THE LAWS OF HOW ALL LIVING THINGS WORK

THE INTERDEPENDENT AND UNPREDICTABLE QUANTUM WORLD

Imagine a cat sealed in a box with deadly radioactive material that has a fifty-fifty chance of decaying and killing the cat (please don't call PETA; this is just a thought experiment!). While the box is covered, the observer has no idea if the cat is dead or alive. Now imagine that the very act of opening the cover to see if the cat is dead or alive forces the cat to be either dead or alive. The corollary is that while the box is closed, the cat is both dead and alive at the same time. You see how absurd it sounds? This is the famous thought experiment Erwin Schrödinger devised in 1935, which illustrated the then-nascent concept of quantum superposition, which describes two opposite states existing at the same time indeterminately until they are measured—that is, the wave-particle duality of everything.

Fast forward sixty-seven years to 2002. *Physics World*, a magazine for the members of the Institute of Physics, took a vote among its readers to determine the most beautiful experiment in history (sadly, Schrödinger's cat didn't make the list, because it was not a real experiment). The criteria were that (1) it must have changed what people thought, (2) must not have been too complicated or expensive, and (3) must be within the reach of students to replicate. The prize went to the famous double-slit experiment applied to single electrons.

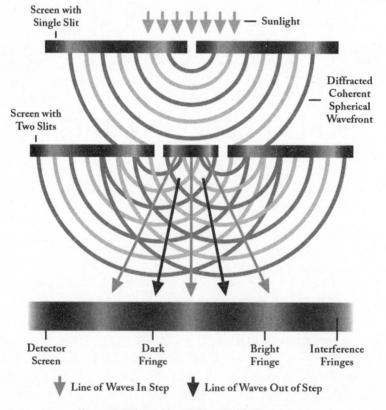

Figure 3.1 *Thomas Young's Double-Slit Experiment*

In the original experiment by Thomas Young in 1803, sunlight was passed through double slits and projected onto a wall of dark film. Young discovered that the back wall of dark film produced a zebra-like stripe. Dark bands were produced when the top of one wave met the bottom of the other wave, canceling each other. White bands were produced when the top of waves met, intensifying the brightness of light and exposing the dark film.[1] The amplitude of waves is additive, meaning when they have the same direction, + or -, the amplitude can be intensified in the same direction but when they have different signs, they cancel each other out. This experiment demonstrated the wavelike nature of light, which was a breakthrough finding at that time.

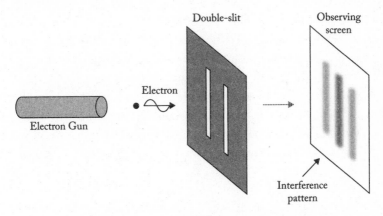

Figure 3.2 Double-Slit Experiment with single electrons
Wikimedia Commons

After a series of modifications by a few physicists, this experiment was later applied to single electrons, instead of sunlight. In this experiment, scientists shot thousands of electrons, one at a time, through a plate with two slits. When there was one slit, there was a single band on the observing screen behind the slit, as one would expect. When there were two slits, one would expect to see two bands with electrons going through one or the other slit, but instead, they saw an interference pattern akin to zebra stripes, which they recognized as wave patterns from Thomas Young's earlier experiment. What?! How does a particle produce a wave pattern? A particle was not supposed to be a wave! And how does one particle produce a wave pattern? Does it split in half or become a mist before passing through the slits?

Those zebra stripes meant that the single electron left the gun as a particle, passed through the two slits at the same time—which was only possible if the electron passed through the two slits as two waves—and then hit the wall as a particle. This result indicated that the electrons, which are particles, are also waves! Indeed, everything in the universe is a particle and a wave at the same time. What's more important for our discussion is that one can't predict where the electron will hit, because the electron's locations can be understood only as a probability distribution. What Schrödinger concluded was that electrons passed through the slits as a probability distribution, not as particles, sometimes through one slit and sometimes the other. The probability thus interferes with itself like a wave, producing the interference pattern.

Here is something even more bizarre about the experiment. The scientists installed electron detectors to observe which slit each electron actually went through. To their surprise, the electrons behaved like particles, going through just one slit at a time and producing two bands on the observing wall when the camera was turned on. But when the detector was not turned on, they behaved like waves (identifiable from the wave interference patterns captured on the observing wall). This result means that the very *act of observation* collapses the wave function to a particle; observation (or consciousness) determines the outcome. Think of a spinning coin that is both heads and tails until it is stopped and how the act of observation forces the coin to take a position—or Schrödinger's cat, which is both dead and alive until the observer opens the cover.

How does quantum physics inform our discussion on leadership competencies in the VUCA era? The double-slit experiment illustrates (1) the interdependent nature of our interaction with the environment, (2) the unpredictable nature of outcome (which can only be estimated as a probability), (3) the relative nature of reality, in which the very act of observation shapes our consciousness, and (4) that coherent vibration patterns void of a lot of noise is required before producing an interference pattern (more on this point in chapter 6 on differentiation). *The principles that govern quantum mechanics are also consistent with those that produce complexity.* In this era of increasing complexity, we cannot make decisions with certainty and must build tolerance for making decisions based on probability. The development of quantum mechanics in the twentieth century proved that the reductionistic, deterministic Newtonian physics doesn't apply to atomic (very small) scales and revolutionized the field of science.

In quantum mechanics, one can no longer neatly determine the outcome by understanding the input. This is a radical departure from the Newtonian framework, where one could, for example, predict force with certainty if mass and acceleration are known. Probabilities, not certainty, govern the complex quantum world. Our consciousness can influence the observation we make: the object being observed changes because it is being observed. From this perspective, nobody owns 100 percent of reality, because our perception, shaped by our past experiences, becomes our reality, which is different for every person. We each have a piece of reality. Unpredictability, interdependence, and relative reality are at the heart of quantum mechanics . . . and of leadership competency to succeed in this VUCA era and produce radical innovation.

THE MIND VERSUS THE BRAIN

The implications of quantum theory for understanding the human mind and behavior are huge. Eugene Wigner, who won the 1963 Nobel Prize in Physics and believed that the quantum theory applied to living systems,[2] said it is "not possible to formulate the laws of quantum mechanics in a fully consistent way without reference to the consciousness . . . It will remain remarkable, in whatever way our future concepts may develop, that the very study of the external world led to the conclusion that the content of the consciousness is an ultimate reality."[3]

Although some scientists disagree (because these principles are hard to test), advances in both fields have shown that the act of observing changes perception. Many assert that quantum principles apply not only to complex systems found in nature, such as coral reefs and termite mounds, but also to neurons, people, families, cities, stock markets, and organizations, with their interdependent relationships among self-organizing individual agents and nonlinear, dynamic nature.[4,5] Quantum mechanics provides the mathematical foundation for understanding the complex, interdependent, unpredictable behaviors of organizations and humans in them.

Daniel Siegel, a professor of clinical psychiatry of the UCLA Medical School, characterizes the *mind* as "a self-organizing, emergent process of a complex system that regulates the flow of energy and information" and the *brain* as "the neural mechanism shaping the flow."[6] Our mind is much more than just the sum of one hundred billion neurons in our brains. The *interactions* among the neurons, and our interactions with the environment and other people, give rise to something much greater than the collection of neurons, and make up our emotions, thoughts, beliefs, hopes, love, dreams, and selves: the essence of what defines each of us. It has an emergent property where the whole is greater than the sum of its parts. Our mind is an *organism* constantly reshaping itself in response to signals from others with whom we have relationships, whereas our brains are a *mechanism* that facilitates the process. We influence and are influenced by other people.

The logical next question, then, is how we can harness the power of our mind to develop leadership competencies to win in the unpredictable VUCA world, given that people, as well as the business environment we operate in, are complex systems.

NEUROPLASTICITY

What do London cabbies and birds have in common when it comes to neuroscience? No, not the size of their brains! Eleanor Maguire and colleagues studied London cab drivers' brains and discovered that the cabbies had larger posterior hippocampi, the part of the brain that stores spatial representation of the environment.[7] This same part of the brain is also associated with navigation in birds and animals. This study, and many more like it, show us that consistent use of specific areas of our brains stimulates neurogenesis in the hippocampus and strengthens specific synaptic connections. It also means we are no longer victims of our genes or our upbringing. When we change how we look at things, our emotions change, which changes how we respond, which changes how we look at things in turn, and so on. Our business environment is no longer deterministic, and neither are our brains.

Recognizing the nonlinear, dynamic nature of human genetics, Schrödinger made a prophetic prediction in his book *What Is Life?* (Cambridge University Press, 1944). He predicted that the structure of DNA is an aperiodic crystal, referring to the covalent bond (a bond in which one or more pairs of electrons are shared by two atoms) between the phosphate of one nucleotide and the sugar of the next nucleotide. This sharing of electrons results in a stable balance of attractive and repulsive forces between those atoms. It takes energy to change the stable bonds. His prediction about the structure of DNA turned out to be true.

Pioneering the field of neuroscience, Francis Crick and James Watson later credited Schrödinger's book as a source of inspiration for their initial research. Even though the four bases of adenine, cytosine, guanine, and thymine in DNA had been found earlier, the exact structure was not yet known in 1951. Two pairs of scientists were concurrently working on decoding the structure of DNA. Maurice Wilkins, physicist turned biologist, worked with Rosalind Franklin, an expert in X-ray crystallography, at King's College in London. At the same time, Crick, with backgrounds in math and physics, and Watson, in molecular biology, started working together at Cambridge. Crick and Watson were working on the idea that the DNA had to copy an exact replica of itself during cell division but didn't know the exact mechanics of the DNA.

One day, Wilkins, discontented with his working relationship with Franklin, showed Watson one of Franklin's X-ray pictures without her permission, which pointed to a helical structure. Watson describes this moment in his memoir: "The instant I saw this picture, my mouth fell open and my heart began to race. The black cross of reflections which dominated the picture could arise only from a helical structure."[8] With this discovery, Watson, Wilkins, and Crick went on to win the 1962 Nobel Prize in Medicine. Unfortunately, Franklin passed away from ovarian cancer at the young age of thirty-seven before she could be awarded with the same honor.

Despite their pioneering work on DNA, it is clear that Watson and Crick believed that information transferred from DNA to RNA to protein but such information flow between protein or from protein back to nucleic acid was not considered possible.[9] What this means is that the sequence of nucleobases of the DNA, the genetic instructions we inherit from our parents, determines our genetic makeup and cannot be changed. This deterministic view is ironic, given that Schrödinger's work, grounded on the principles of interdependence and probabilities, which could be the basis for neuroplasticity, had inspired them and guided their early work. But neuroscience research has now substantiated what Max Planck said earlier: "When we change how we look at things, what we look at changes." The perception of the observer depends upon the observer's own assumptions and cumulative life experiences. There are a few names for this phenomenon, which has been well-researched and substantiated: confirmation bias, self-fulfilling prophecy, the placebo effect, etc.

Recent neuroscience research has revealed the mechanism of how this change in our brains takes place: in response to changes in the environment (including other people), histone proteins alter which part of the DNA becomes accessible to be read, turning gene expressions on or off. According to Siegel, there are four pathways for neuroplasticity to occur:

- We can grow new neurons (neurogenesis).
- We can grow new neuronal *connections*, which allows learning and information storage.
- We can speed up the neuronal processing time (myelination— adding a myelin layer along the length of the neuron).
- We can make existing connections stronger or weaker using feedback from the environment, which ultimately updates our memories with new content to change the meaning.[10]

We are not a product of our past experiences or upbringing. We can use the epigenetic nature of our brains to harness the power of our minds and consciously choose how we react.

We are not a product of our past experiences or upbringing. We can use the epigenetic nature of our brains to harness the power of our minds and consciously choose how we react. This process changes the neuronal connections in our brains, changing our responses and emotions to that experience.[11] The recursive nature of interaction between a complex system (such as humans) and an environment means that the environment changes us—but we can change the environment as well. Although this principle has not been formally tested or accepted by most neuroscientists, we can see how principles of quantum mechanics can inform neuroscience. Neurons firing in our brains give rise to certain conclusions and emotions in our consciousness, coupled with physiological reactions in our body, but we can use our minds to change the firing patterns of our brains. We can change the focus of the mind to actually change the neuronal connections in the brain, which was shaped by our past experiences. We can use the focus of the mind to regulate how our entire nervous systems function, how our bodies react, how we balance our emotions, how we engage in relationships with others, and how we view ourselves. This is a foundational skill for effective leadership.

For example, your awareness of your tendency to overinterpret signs of threat can help you identify how you stress your team with overaggressive demands or rigid defensiveness. This awareness can help you change how you interpret incoming signals, which changes your emotional state.

Let's say you hear your employee saying, "I am not happy in my job," and you become aware of an immediate tightness in your gut. Then you trace the source of that tightness to a thought that flashed through your mind: "I am a bad boss. I am going to lose this employee. It'll be a pain to explain this to my boss and replace this employee." These thoughts flash through your mind in eight milliseconds and bring with them the fear-based tightness in your gut instantaneously. Reacting to that fear, you may try to rigidly convince the employee why he needs to stay, leaving him feeling unheard.

Alternatively, using your mind to manage your brain, you could choose to interpret what your employee said to mean "I need help," which generates empathy in you instead of fear, and gently ask what's going on so you can help him. *You can choose which emotions to feel by choosing how you interpret incoming signals.* This type of self-management is essential for effective leadership.

BRAIN STRUCTURE

Understanding our brain structure and how it works helps us capitalize on the full potential of our minds. The brain has three layers: the brain stem, limbic system, and cortex (which includes the frontal lobe and prefrontal cortex). Each layer is optimized for safety, connection, and learning, respectively. If that sounds familiar, it's because those are exactly the factors my survey respondents identified as most important in their leaders—in exactly the same order.

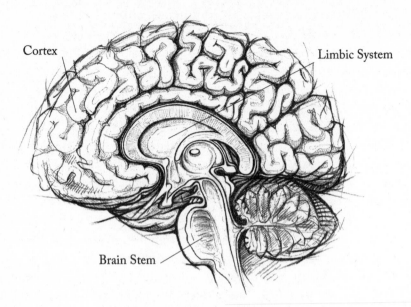

Cortex

Limbic System

Brain Stem

Figure 3.3 *Triune brain structure*
Shutterstock

Let's look at each of these elements more closely. Hang in here with me, because, as you will see in later chapters, understanding our brain structure and how it works helps us capitalize on the full potential of our minds and is crucial to effective leadership.

The brain stem

The brain stem is evolutionarily the oldest part of the brain, and we have it in common with reptiles—hence the nickname, the lizard or reptilian brain.[12] It controls the functions that are mostly beneath our conscious awareness in what is called the autonomic nervous system, which regulates activities that ensure survival such as breathing, blood pressure, digestion, heart rate, autonomic functions, and sex drive. It also works in conjunction with the amygdala in the limbic system to facilitate fight-flight-freeze responses. These functions must happen automatically in the subconscious (subcortical areas of the brain) for speedy, automatic reaction to threats. Otherwise, if we were to get distracted and forget to pump our hearts, for example, we could end up dead.

The limbic system

The limbic system is the next layer up, a structure we share with mammals. It governs attachment, emotions, nurturing the young, and memory. Because mammals have the limbic system but reptiles don't, dogs and cats feel attached to us, whereas snakes and turtles don't, even when we keep them for pets and take care of them. Human attachment is a mammalian heritage.

The limbic system has several components. The thalamus is the central hub of all the incoming sensory signals. The hypothalamus is our body's neuroendocrine and emotion processing center.[13] It controls our autonomic nervous systems. Procedural memory helps us perform repeated tasks efficiently, such as riding a bike, on autopilot. Conditioned memory is shaped when we step on a snake and get bitten and next time we see anything remotely resembling a snake, we process it as a snake automatically. Both types of memories are stored in the subconscious and referred to as implicit memory for our purposes. Working in conjunction with implicit memories, the hypothalamus evaluates emotional relevance and sends signals to the brain stem so emotions are expressed as bodily responses.[14] This is why I always invite my clients to scan their bodies and describe physical sensations, such as tightness in their throats or a sinking feeling in their stomachs, to help them identify what they are feeling. The emotions we experience are linked with physical sensations in our bodies, and can be located in specific places in our bodies.[15] This phenomenon turns out to be surprisingly consistent even across cultures.[16] We tend to be unaware of the physical expressions of our emotions because we are not paying attention.

The hippocampus is the episodic memory center of the limbic system, storing and recalling memory, similar to your computer's data drive. A 2006 study revealed that the hippocampus is smaller for those who have experienced acute stress,[17] which results in similar symptoms as when your computer's data drive is damaged, such as flashbacks or getting stuck in a loop, which means trouble with recall. A more recent study found that the hippocampus is the only place, other than the olfactory bulb, where adult neurogenesis occurs,[18] meaning if your hippocampus is damaged, new neurons are less likely to be regenerated. Older cells have more rigid preexisting synaptic connections and are less plastic, whereas new neurons can establish new connections with other neurons, which make it possible for us to be more flexible and develop new meaning and new behaviors. So, it is reasonable to conclude that those who have experienced chronic or acute stress in the past may be more rigid in their thinking; they are less open to new ideas and respond to current events with the same stress reaction they experienced in the past. This could explain some of the behaviors of jerk bosses who show a "my way or the highway" attitude, black-and-white thinking, or are overall inflexible and rigid. Before we assign persona non grata status to these intolerable jerk bosses and banish them to a remote island forever, we need to remember, however, this rigidity could be a result of past trauma, which helps us become more compassionate toward them.

Another part of the limbic system is the amygdala, which works with the brain stem to control autonomic responses that detect and respond to sensory stimuli in milliseconds; if it were a weapon, it would be a handgun. It also generates systemic endocrine responses, which are slower than autonomic ones but broader in scope, involving many parts of the body using hormones to environmental stimuli—like a tank, which is slower but more powerful than a handgun. Depending on the stimuli, the amygdala generates stress, fear, or anxiety responses to get us to take action to ensure our survival, coordinating fight-flight-freeze responses and the experience of pain. It also stores the emotional content or saliency of our memories that may be unconscious in nature, which have high emotional significance. Disorders that result from trauma, such as PSTD, often result from the dysfunction of the amygdala. We need to remember experiences that threatened our safety with associated emotions such as fear and anger, which activates our autonomic and endocrine systems, so we can mobilize our body more quickly next time.

The cortex

The most evolved part of the brain is the cortex located at the most outward part of our brains. This is part of the brain that controls logic, language processing, visual and auditory functions, and semantic memories. An example of semantic memory is remembering that Seoul is the capital of South Korea, which is different from the autobiographical episodic memories stored in the hippocampus, which helps you recall what happened to you in the past.[19]

The part of the cortex that is uniquely well developed among humans is the medial prefrontal cortex (MPFC). It performs such functions as attuned communication, emotional balance, response flexibility, empathy, self-awareness, fear modulation, and moral and ethical reasoning.[20] The combination of these functions provides a solid sense of self and healthy ways of relating to others. Imagine having a relationship with someone who doesn't have a healthy MPFC—you can see how difficult it would be, to say the least. Because we're built to connect with other people, when we don't have meaningful relationships, it's hard to feel happy and fulfilled in life. Now imagine working for a boss who has no empathy, self-awareness, emotional balance, attuned communication, or ethical reasoning skills. You would be either pulling your hair out or wishing you could be pulling out your boss's!

Because MPFC governs a secure sense of self and self-expression, this area of the brain is also closely linked to creativity. In 2008, Charles Limb, a neurosurgeon at Johns Hopkins School of Medicine, studied the brains of jazz players.[21] Through functional MRI scans, he and his colleagues monitored which areas of the brain had the highest neuronal activities. They discovered that when the jazz players played scales (very monotonous repeated sets of techniques to practice finger skills), the dorsal lateral prefrontal cortex (the part of the brain linked to self-monitoring and inhibition) was activated and MPFC was deactivated. But when they improvised, as most jazz players do, the opposite happened. What this experiment shows is that, to be creative and innovative, we must let go of inhibition, be willing to try different things, and be unafraid of making mistakes. It also calls for activating self-expression, solidly grounded in a clear concept of self. In essence, when you're a good relationship partner, you're likely to be a good leader, and you can promote a creative, innovative environment for your employees.

HOW THE BRAIN
PROCESSES SIGNALS

In 1959 David Hubel and Torsten Wiesel inserted a microelectrode into the visual cortex of an anesthetized cat and discovered that some neurons fired when they were exposed to lines at a certain angle and another cell at another angle. They concluded that different neurons recognized lines at different angles, shapes, and movements, a one-to-one relationship between a neuron and a movement or a line. Their pioneering work on how the brain processes perception won them a Nobel prize in 1981. What they didn't realize was that when each neuron is assigned to a certain angle and shape and movement for the millions of objects that we face in our life, we soon run out of neurons. This model was feasible under the assumption that there were only a few objects to process. Now we know a different model fits this reality better when it comes to how the brain processes perceptions: neural *networks* in multiple layers that recognize patterns and are connected to hundreds of thousands of other neurons where the activation of neurons in a layer determines the activation in the next layer, in *many-to-many* relationships. Again, it's consistent with how the principle of the many-to-many network structure in organizations can process more complex information better and faster, which we have reviewed earlier.

Now let's examine the six fundamental leadership competency groups my research has identified and consider how *you* can develop each one.

Chapter 4

EFFECTIVE SELF-MANAGEMENT: THE FOUNDATION OF QUANTUM LEADERSHIP

I n chapter 1 we reviewed how the business environment is changing into a much more complex one and the reasons behind the changing dynamics. We have also established how leadership competencies must change to adapt to the changing business environment and how to create the new sustainable competitive advantage available in this environment. In chapter 3 we examined the hierarchical needs of our brains and the concept of neuroplasticity—using our minds to rewire our brains for new meaning. Because of our brains' ability to change, we accepted that we are more than a product of our upbringing. Now, let's examine how that very brain structure can enable us, as leaders of teams, to facilitate radical innovation.

THE IMPORTANCE OF QUANTITATIVE MEASURES

Years ago, I observed a pattern. I watched my clients get paranoid about a new disruptive innovator making their business model irrelevant overnight. They didn't know how to develop their own capacity for innovation, and to say that this was stressful is putting it mildly. I set out to conduct global research on the leadership competencies that facilitate radical innovation.

As I mentioned in chapter 1, my research identified two distinct groups of leaders: Quantum Leaders and Mechanistic Leaders. This distinction defines the heart of the limitations of traditional leadership development approaches: most leadership development training provides no *quantitative* mechanism to help leaders understand the bottom-line impact of the necessary change. As a result, any change goal identified from 360-degree review is likely to take a backseat when other urgent matters arise. For instance, if leaders are given change goals to improve a certain leadership competency and they are up against a quarterly close, without a solid understanding of the bottom-line impact of the change they are trying to bring about, they are all too likely to fall into the trap of "Once I have met my quarterly goals, then I will . . ." (This is part of the reason why change is temporary, no matter how much we intend to change. More on this later.)

How turnover has an impact on your bottom line

What is the bottom-line impact of these two different types of leaders? Let's start with just one measure: turnover intent. The difference in turnover intent (employees' stated intent to switch jobs within one year) of the followers who work for these two groups is 37 percent: 61 percent of those working for Mechanistic Leaders intend to quit within twelve months, versus 24 percent of those who work for Quantum Leaders. This difference translates to a $448 million hit to operating expenses for a typical Fortune 500 company. In other words, each Fortune 500 company would have to generate an additional $8.7 billion in topline sales to make up for this hit to operating expenses—which is totally avoidable!

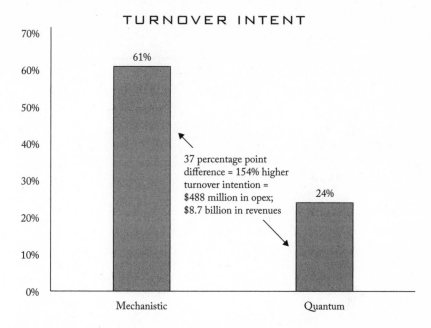

Figure 4.1 *The bottom-line impact of leadership on turnover intent for an average Fortune 500 company with annual revenues of $38 billion and the operating expense of 5.2 percent of sales.*

What radical innovation requires from you

I have also identified six distinct competency groups necessary to deliver radical innovation from my global leadership research. From the bottom up, they are self-management, providing safety, creating differentiation, strengthening connection, facilitating learning, and finally, stimulating radical innovation. The bottom two layers are about safety, the middle two layers are about connection, and the top two layers are about learning and innovation. Each preceding competency is a prerequisite for the next one. In other words, effective self-management is required for leaders to provide safety for others. Creating differentiation is a prerequisite for strengthening connection. Learning is a necessary condition for innovation. Safety must be satisfied before connection needs are met, and connection is needed before innovation.

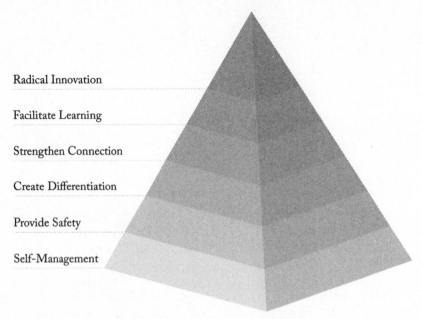

Radical Innovation

Facilitate Learning

Strengthen Connection

Create Differentiation

Provide Safety

Self-Management

Figure 4.2 Quantum Leadership competencies

WHERE MASLOW AND I DIFFER

Many people who read my research in *Harvard Business Review* connected my research to Maslow's hierarchy of needs. I would say there are similarities but critical differences. Maslow identified five hierarchical needs: physiological (food, water, shelter, etc.), safety, belonging and love, esteem, and self-actualization. Later, he augmented his model by adding three more needs: self-expression, knowledge, and transcendence.

The first difference is that my Quantum Leadership framework is based on complex adaptive systems theory, quantum mechanics, and neuroscience, emphasizing the importance of interdependence and the constructive shaping process of reality. Interaction with the environment is foundational for Quantum Leadership.

Second, Maslow starts with biological needs, whereas the starting point for the Quantum Leadership framework is self-management. When we use effective self-management skills, we create a stronger sense of safety and connection for—and attachment with—ourselves and others, meaning we can use the power of our mind to *overcome* the basic instincts of safety, which are often misplaced.

Third, the ultimate goal in Maslow's hierarchy is transcendence and self-actualization, whereas Quantum Leadership's ultimate goals are radical innovation and higher internal complexity.

Finally, Maslow's hierarchy is about one's personal needs (intrapsychic) whereas most of the Quantum Leadership framework is about leading others (interpsychic and systemic).

Bottom-line costs in compensation

Let's make this picture more real in terms of trade-off decisions. As I indicated in chapter 1, the leaders who participated in my research indicated that they are willing to forgo a whopping 39 percent of their compensation to work for a Quantum Leader, or they require 39 percent additional pay to tolerate working for a manager who does *not* demonstrate these competencies.

Let's examine how that 39 percent in compensation is distributed across the three major competency categories of safety, connection, and innovation. Survey respondents are willing to forgo the most pay in order to feel safe. They are willing to give up 22 percent of their compensation in order to work for a leader who provides safety; in other words, they demand an additional 22 percent to put up with working for a manager with whom they do *not* feel safe. This flies in the face of the "front stabbing" reported by the *Wall Street Journal* and the controversial management practices at Amazon as reported by the *New York Times*.[1]

Next, people are willing to forgo 12 percent of compensation for connection and belonging; in other words, they demand an additional 12 percent to put up with working for a manager who does *not* demonstrate these competencies.

Last, they are willing to forgo 5 percent of compensation for learning and growth; in other words, they demand an additional 5 percent to work for a manager without competencies to facilitate learning and innovation. Even though learning is the most important goal for organizations, we can't get there unless we satisfy our safety and connection needs first, and this is reflected in the research participants' responses of what they value most.

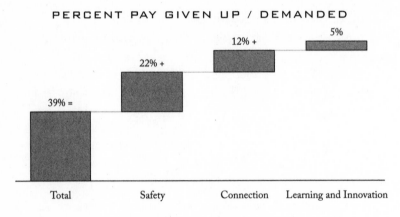

PERCENT PAY GIVEN UP / DEMANDED

Figure 4.3 *What safety, connection, and learning are worth*

While 39 percent might sound unreasonably high, it's not when you take into consideration that those who participated in my research are leaders themselves and their median annual compensation was $162,000. Even if they give up 39 percent of their compensation, it still leaves them nearly $100,000 per year, a lot of which is probably discretionary income, since they likely have a base of wealth accumulated over time. After a certain income threshold, demand for compensation is a lot more elastic, because people just aren't willing to put up with crap from their bosses: other factors matter more, such as a friendly working environment and good relationships with their managers. This point is corroborated in a 2010 study by Princeton researchers Daniel Kahneman and Angus Deaton, who found that people with a household income of $75,000 or more don't report a greater degree of happiness with increased income, no matter how much more.[2] They also report that after the $75,000 threshold point, other things matter more than money in the search for happiness.

Even though innovation is the most important goal for organizations, we can't get there unless we satisfy our safety and connection needs first. This is reflected in the research participants' responses of what they value most in very real dollar terms—and by the hierarchy of needs our brains have been optimized to fulfill by evolution over many millennia.

So, what specific leadership competencies make up the 39 percent of compensation people are willing to give up to work for you? Let's start with the foundation of the pyramid: self-management. We'll look at what it means to you, to those you lead, and to your organization, and make these points more concrete with a case study. Each of the six competency groups of Quantum Leadership will be covered in detail in the following six chapters, starting with this one.

COMPETENCY 1: SELF-MANAGEMENT

The most important foundational skill for any leader is effective self-management. In most of today's leadership frameworks, self-management (or personal leadership) is an afterthought. However, many studies, including my own, confirm that self-management is a foundational skill, required to provide safety for others. It emerges from my premise that the act of leading ten thousand people starts with managing one person successfully: oneself.[3]

This is your brain on fear

Effective self-management relies on understanding how our brains derive meaning from perceptions. Your sensory perceptions are first registered in the thalamus. The implicit memory bank deep in the amygdala becomes active if there is a conditioned response from previous experiences you perceived as a threat to your safety. Implicit memory is automatic and subconscious. This appraisal process is more about speed than accuracy. If there is even an approximate match, your body goes through the fear response of fight, flight, or freeze to handle the threat, automatically reactivating all the emotional, physiological, and cognitive circumstances surrounding those experiences, and bypassing the cognitive processing performed in the cortex in an effort to shave even a millisecond in response time (more on this in the next chapter). Our brains store all these sensory, emotional, physiological, and cognitive programs in the same neural network, activating them when any one of those elements is activated. This is our brains' way of creating redundancy, so if one element fails to respond, other elements still activate the appropriate fear response.

The programs stored in our autonomic, implicit memory in the amygdala help us avoid similar threats in the future. But the problem we run into is our brains' tendency to favor the type I error over the type II error. If you have taken a statistics class, you're probably familiar with these concepts, unless you were passed out at Baskin-Robbins every class period like Ferris Bueller. A type I error is a false positive, and a type II error is a false negative. Let's say you're going hunting and you hear a rustle in the bush. You think it's a tiger, and you make a beeline for safety. A few seconds later, you calm down a bit, look back, and realize it was just the wind. This would be a type I error.

What is the cost of a type I error? Maybe your mother's disapproval at the expletives you utter, a wasted elevated heartbeat, drops of sweat, sore muscles, and feeling dumb for running for nothing—but not that big of a deal.

Let's take a different scenario this time. Let's say you hear the same rustle but take no action because you think it's just the wind—but it really is a tiger. What is the cost of this type II error? Your life.

That's why evolution has favored type I over type II errors. But this safety feature comes with a heavy cost: we tend to overreact when there is no threat. Because our fear response (based on the implicit memory in the amygdala) prioritizes speed over accuracy, if an incoming signal remotely resembles a threat from past experiences, it activates a fear response. So, the next time you see a life-size windup Tigger toy bouncing over the bush, you're already making a beeline before your cortex gets a chance to process it fully and tell you to settle down.

As a leader, if you are not aware of your automatic fear responses and don't know how to manage them, you can easily be triggered by everyday stimuli into a fear response. You might not even be aware you're in a fight-flight-freeze response, but your body is already reacting to it, pumping out stress hormones and activating your sympathetic nervous system, all beneath your consciousness.

Research suggests that other people subconsciously detect your response, which sets off their own fear responses. Lilianne Mujica-Parodi, a cognitive neuroscientist at Stony Brook University in New York, and her colleagues obtained stress sweat from people during a first-time skydive, and sweat from people exercising routinely. Then they sprayed these samples of sweat on volunteers inside a brain scanner, which showed that their amygdalae lit up when exposed to scared sweat, but not when exposed to exercise sweat.[4] Not only that—other researchers found that sweat from aggressive men triggered anxiety in volunteers who sniffed it, even if they could not cognitively distinguish between sweat from an aggressive activity and a neutral one.[5] These studies show that detection of fear in others triggers our own fear response, well before we process it at a conscious level. As a leader, if you don't manage your own fear response, you *will* trigger others' fear responses, even without waving your sweat-soaked socks in front of them—people can smell them a mile away. Fear responses, as we know, inhibit higher cortex functions. And we need those higher cortex functions, because they stimulate innovation.

The following competencies are included in the self-management leadership competency group.

Open, flexible, and adaptable

Quantum Leaders are open-minded, flexible, and not opinionated. They accept that radical innovation requires elements of unchoreographed, accidental reconstitution of ideas and situations. They are open to new ideas and approaches, and can change views when presented with evidence. They are completely transparent, which expedites decision-making. Quantum Leaders courageously open themselves up to others. It takes equal measures of confidence and humility to be vulnerable. Vulnerability in turn creates safety, liberating the organization from battles for survival, and helping everyone unleash innate creativity, drive, and self-organization. Quantum Leaders refuse to hide behind polite discomfort, instead creating safety for others to openly offer differing views. They are courageous with their authenticity. Being open means being curious instead of judgmental. They don't make snap judgments about people, or snap decisions. When things get heated, they slow the process down and try to see the big picture of where each person is coming from, instead of getting caught up in the heat of the moment.

When communicating with others, Quantum Leaders are open to and curious about all possibilities. If a colleague comes across as irrational, ridiculous, or overreacting, they become curious, carefully exploring what might be behind his or her reality that they are perceiving as irrational, all the while suspending judgment. They know that judgment shuts off avenues of important discovery and learning. During this discovery, they can put aside their own emotions and pay focused attention. They can empathically imagine what must have happened for someone to create the reality that comes across as irrational, and can validate that reality for that person.

Quantum Leaders tolerate ambiguity and are comfortable with many shades of gray, instead of automatically closing their minds to other possible scenarios. Their flexibility and openness stems from their understanding that one's perception *is* one's reality, allowing others to own a different version of reality than one's own. They understand that exposures to previous experiences in cumulative life experiences lead to different experiences of the same reality. As a result, they show humility, knowing what they think they know might not be the only or full representation of reality.

Many studies have shown that the amygdala response compromises the higher functions of insight, rationality, and innovative thinking. Fear shuts the body down in defense instead of opening the mind to possibilities beyond one's perception of threatened safety.[6] This state of openness and flexibility is also important because it facilitates healthy debate over diverse points of views, inviting the power of collective intelligence, which is critical for innovation. Research has repeatedly shown that collective intelligence yields better outcomes than even the most intelligent experts. This point will be discussed in more detail in chapter 6.

Resilience

Rather than becoming flustered in the face of unpredictable obstacles, Quantum Leaders are adaptable and resilient. They accept that radical innovation requires failures, often over a long germination period. They embrace change, fluidly rolling with the punches because they don't equate their self-worth with their performance. This state of graceful openness is possible only when one is free from the fight-flight-freeze survival battles of the amygdala.

Agility

Quantum Leaders don't fall into the trap of perfectionism, but prioritize speed over accuracy. They understand that 80 percent accuracy today is better than 99 percent accuracy three months from now, because they know they will get to the answers they need more quickly by constant iterative attempts. They correct their course as they receive new information because *they are not committed to the outcome but rather to the process of constant iteration.* Note that agility is a conscious choice for speed, not driven by fear—it's not an automatic reaction as in a fight-or-flight response.

Self-awareness

The effort to manage emotion starts with an awareness of one's bodily sensations and the emotions that arise with an incoming perception. Do you know emotions can be traced to certain places in the body? Lauri Nummenmaa, a psychologist at Aalto University in Helsinki, and her colleagues showed that emotions are intricately linked to physiological sensations and can be mapped in our bodies. Quantum Leaders develop a high level of emotional awareness, and can correctly identify the sensation and location of an emotion in their bodies.[7] When we are unaware, our emotions and bodies are in conflict, which creates discomfort, confusion, and a general sense of unresolved uneasiness. Quantum Leaders recognize this discomfort and can trace it to the source to resolve the conflict. They recognize that self-awareness and regulation are essential building blocks to other skills, including communication. Relying on the wisdom of the body gives us cues about what we are feeling and helps us work through those emotions to regain a sense of serenity and confidence.

When leaders are in tune with their own emotions, they have insight into other's emotional maps. This ability for empathic attunement enables them to listen for the emotion behind the words others speak, as well as the content of the words themselves. Identifying the underlying emotion eliminates the defense or pretense and helps them quickly cut through all the noise that stands between them and the core issues at play.

Interestingly, a 2017 study revealed what most people work for a boss intuitively know: power causes brain damage. Interpretation? Bosses are brain damaged! Our cynicism about bosses with power had been justified after all. In all seriousness, Dacher Keltner, professor of psychology at University of California, Berkeley, termed this phenomenon the power paradox: people rise through the ranks on the basis of their good qualities such as empathy, but they lose empathy as they rise up the ladder. Keltner concluded that those under the influence of power "acted as if they had suffered a traumatic brain injury—becoming more impulsive, less risk-aware, and, crucially, less adept at seeing things from other people's point of view."[8] He reported that those feeling powerful showed less activation of mirror neurons, which means reduced capacity for respect for others, resulting in compromised rapport-building, trust, and collaboration. He cites many examples, such as the fact that drivers of luxury cars yield right-of-way only 54 percent of the time, whereas drivers of economy cars nearly always yield; and CEOs with MBAs are more likely than those without MBAs to engage in self-serving behavior that increases their personal compensation but causes their companies' values to decline.[9] Keltner concluded that power leads to empathy deficits and diminished moral sentiments and undermines the basic foundation of collaborative interactions with others.[10] This is why Google and many other Quantum Companies are taking power away from leaders and turning them into facilitators. At Google, bosses cannot make promotion, hiring, or firing decisions alone—these decisions are made in a committee with multiple people. This approach not only castrates leaders of the blinding effect of power but also minimizes errors by getting more heads into the pool of collective intelligence.

Then how do we avoid this power paradox? You must become self-aware first and use self-regulation skills, as noted in the following section.

Appropriate emotional and stress management

Quantum Leaders are aware and awake so they can detect others' emotions and take appropriate social cues. They are fully present, paying focused attention to the person with whom they are speaking. When you are self-aware and manage your own emotions appropriately, you in turn generate safety for others. In fact, a leader's effective self-management is essential for the team to feel safe.

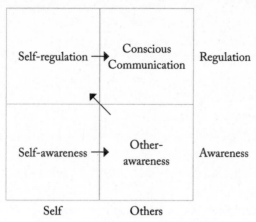

Figure 4.4 *Self-management skill domains*

Self-regulation

With this heightened awareness of themselves and others, Quantum Leaders regulate their emotions. They are a constant, much like a three-hundred-year-old oak tree that withstands the strongest of storms. When listening, these leaders don't get triggered by assigning their own meaning to what others say and reacting automatically. They can imagine what it must be like for the other person by stepping into his or her shoes. At the same time, they are comfortable in their own skin and do not attempt to please others. When others express their needs, Quantum Leaders don't turn it around and make it about themselves. When a team member says, "I don't feel fulfilled in my job," Quantum Leaders don't hear, "You are a bad leader." Instead, they hear, "I need help." This ability to be grounded creates safety for others and allows each person's reality to exist with equal merit.

Quantum Leaders are masters of all four quadrants of effective self-management, as seen in figure 4.4. On the foundation of self-awareness, they become aware of others, which enables them to regulate themselves, knowing how it affects others. Then they engage in transparent, open communication with others. Quantum Leaders take responsibility for their emotions, instead of blaming or dumping them on others. They've developed enough emotional awareness to recognize that the "You make me so angry" statement is a folly. As masters of their emotions, they consciously choose how they will feel and how they will react by consciously choosing the thoughts that precede emotions. By practicing focused awareness, Quantum Leaders avoid blaming and accusing others by not projecting their own left-over negative mental models from past experiences onto others.

Quantum Leaders manage their own stress appropriately, instead of letting the team feel the full intensity of the unfiltered stress. They provide a buffer between the upper management and their team by effectively managing expectations upward as well as downward. They are ever on guard about the power their leadership position brings. They do not extract compliance using power but reflect on what about the situation makes them want to resort to power. They know that open, collaborative decision-making that sincerely considers the merits of each viewpoint will yield the best outcome. They know they don't have to know all the answers. These skills to be aware of one's own and others' emotions, and to manage them effectively, are at the heart of emotional intelligence (EQ), which has shaped much leadership practice over the last two decades.[11]

To combat the power paradox noted previously, leaders can practice the 3Gs MESH model:

- **Gratitude.** Look for opportunities to say thank you for even little things and act on them.
- **Generosity.** Maybe indulge a random act of kindness; give credit to those who have helped you for your success.
- **Graciousness.** Let others speak first; write handwritten notes to people; remember what is happening with your team members' families and ask about them later.
- **Mindfulness.** Constantly check in with yourself; question if kindness and compassion are balanced with achieving goals.
- **Empathy.** Ask more questions to explore what others might be experiencing; imagine what it must be like and express sincere concern.
- **Sharing power.** Delegate courageously and use the eyes-on but hands-off approach.
- **Humility.** Remember nobody is irreplaceable; allow for the possibility that you could be wrong.

In my experience coaching many executives, most derailment comes not from technical deficiency but from poor situational judgment and relationship skills, which becomes more pronounced as executives gain more power. Remember, power can be intoxicating as you rise up the ranks, but you must be on the alert and manage yourself, conscientiously practicing these skills. Or else, you can be yanked down from it more quickly than your false sense of security might misguide you.

Positive mental models

Quantum Leaders understand how their choices of beliefs lead to their emotional experience of the world and their mental state. Thoughts and beliefs create emotions.[12] If you choose to believe you are a victim, you will feel helpless and alienate others by making them feel guilty. If you choose to believe you are inadequate, you feel depressed, disengage from others, and lose confidence. By choosing positive mental models about themselves, Quantum Leaders draw on the brain's extraordinary capacity to deliver on our beliefs. This is confirmation bias at its best. The principle of cognitive dissonance says that holding two conflicting messages at the same time creates mental stress and discomfort.[13] As a result, we come up with evidence to justify our beliefs, which can lead to a confirmation bias that breeds overconfidence in our decisions even when we are presented with contradicting evidence, and thus we ignore alternatives. We can harness this tendency in a positive way by channeling our brains' ability to justify our beliefs by coming up with evidence, hence delivering on our beliefs. *By choosing positive mental models, we direct our brains to come up with evidence to support our beliefs and create the reality we desire.*

Quantum Leaders also consciously choose positive mental models to trust others and give them the benefit of the doubt: you're innocent until proven guilty. Trust, in turn, enables them to let others self-organize, instead of hogging information or power.

Responsibility over reality

Quantum Leaders understand they are responsible for, and create, their reality—they are authors of their own destiny. They are agents unto themselves; they act rather than are acted upon. For example, if the reality is that the product marketing team they manage doesn't carry a lot of credibility in the company because it has frequently missed deadlines and broken commitments to other departments, they take responsibility for creating that reality, instead of looking to external explanations, such as the legal department that sat on the product release sheet too long before giving approval, or the vendor who didn't produce the prototype model in time. When something bad happens, they first reflect on what they did to contribute to or cause the situation. This is such an important concept to emotional well-being that many synonymous phrases have been coined in psychology to describe it: self-efficacy, free will, and internal locus of control.

Internal locus of control refers to attributing what happens to your life to what you can control. If you have an internal locus of control, you attribute your professional success to your actions and attitudes, instead of external factors such as your boss or industry. Studies show that those with a higher internal locus of control report higher job satisfaction and job performance,[14] better quality of relations with their managers,[15] lower stress,[16] and higher academic achievement.[17]

Even perceived (not actual) control has a positive impact on performance. In a study, subjects were exposed to loud noises while being asked to solve an insoluble puzzle and proofread for errors. Some were provided a kill switch to stop the noise if it became unbearable. Those who had the option of turning off the noise made almost five times as many attempts at the insoluble puzzle, and significantly fewer errors in proofreading, than those without a kill-switch option.[18] This study showed that just a perception of control improved performance. This is the reason Carol Dweck, in her book *Mindset*, encourages parents and teachers to compliment children on their efforts instead of their intelligence or looks.[19] Children have control over their efforts, but not over their IQ or natural appearance. Children feel helpless and, worse, conditionally loved when they feel they are judged by a factor they have no control over.

It turns out that an internal locus of control is important not only because it is an essential skill for effective self-management—and hence providing safety for others—but also because it has a lot to do with capability for innovation.[20] For example, CEOs of firms pursuing product innovation have been found to rate higher in internal locus of control than CEOs of firms involving little innovation. The relationship between innovation and an internal locus of control is a consistent pattern across cultures.[21]

Permeable boundaries

Every living organism has boundaries that separate it from its external environment. Cells have cell walls, which provide structural support and protection. We have a literal boundary of skin that separates us from the rest of the world. We also have invisible boundaries of space. In psychology, a differentiated person is a person who is not unduly influenced by others, and has strong boundaries. Differentiated people have a clear sense of self that is independent and separate from others. When people are less differentiated, others have more impact on their functioning, and they respond by trying more to control the functioning of others; that control might take the form of passive aggressiveness or being overbearing.

Here are some characteristics of people with loose enmeshed boundaries:

- They let others encroach on their space by not respecting their own feelings, or they expect too much from others.
- They define their self-worth through other people's opinions of them.
- They give too much to others until they are completely depleted, ignoring their own needs. Often, they don't realize they are letting others violate their boundaries; they justify their actions as being nice, charitable, or serving others.

People with rigid boundaries, on the other hand, exhibit these characteristics:

- They are distant, isolated, and withdrawn; they do not experience the rich joy that comes from feeling their emotions deeply and connecting with others.
- They don't let others influence them at all, adhering to their thoughts even when presented with contradicting evidence.
- They find it difficult to tolerate differences of opinion or different ways of doing things; hence, they tend to insist on "their way or the highway."

Neither form of boundaries is optimal, because neither can generate the highest level of complexity in our potential. The ideal form is the balance between the two: porous or permeable boundaries, so you accept yourself and at the same time allow others to be authentically themselves.

Here is how people who have strong yet permeable boundaries act:

- They do not try to increase their sense of self-worth through another's approval, validation, or praise.
- They don't look to others to fulfill their emotional needs to be happy or whole, because their self-concept is defined by a deep conviction that they are good inherently, not because of other people's opinion of them.
- They can clearly articulate who they are and what they like and dislike because their self-concept has not been subsumed into another's.
- They do not dispense advice to others unless they are invited to do so.
- They do not feel guilty about articulating and meeting their needs; they don't sacrifice their needs or self-respect to meet others' needs.
- They let others into their hearts and are open and flexible.
- They are not aloof but have a rich range of emotions.
- They don't withdraw from conflicts passive-aggressively but work through them even when confronting others is difficult.
- They are tolerant of differing opinions, rather than interpreting difference as rejection.
- They are flexible, adaptable, and balanced between compassion for others and their own self-respect.
- They freely exchange love and compassion while remaining firmly grounded in a secure identity and concept of self-acceptance.

In this type of integrated connection, you are not afraid of what others might think, or overconcerned about presenting just the right appearance. To be differentiated from others and at the same time allow true connection—the balance between differentiation and connection through permeable boundaries—is essential for a leader. It is a hallmark sign of a Quantum Leader.

CASE STUDY

David was vice-president of operations at a logistics company. His tall, toned body looked just as it did when he was in college. At forty-three, his face was marked with lines from life in the trenches, but his eyes were always alert, soaking in everything he observed. As one of the members of the executive committee, he was considered indispensable at his company because his highly analytical, quantitative approach to the company's most challenging problems had been very effective.

David had been trying to achieve a better balance between work and the rest of his life. He wanted to work out and spend more time with his family, but he worked sixty hours a week. When he wasn't working, he worried about not working. As his company geared up to go public, they were under a lot of pressure to generate a steady stream of increasing revenues every quarter. He couldn't quite completely delegate a task and let his team self-organize. He felt very stressed, emotionally distant, and at times made unreasonable demands of his team and family. This is when he came to me asking for help.

David's effectiveness as a leader was compromised because he was so depleted. His stress created a crisis-driven culture in his team and also took a toll on his relationships at home. He didn't engage in small talk because he felt rushed to get to other, more urgent things. He didn't know his team members on a personal level—didn't know what their interests or their kids' names were.

I invited David to observe himself and become curious about the patterns running his life. He discovered that a deep-seated fear of personal failure stemming from past experiences was interfering with his performance at work and his ability to be fully present with his family. His lack of emotional awareness, created by years of repressing his feelings, resulted in a vaguely disconnected quality of relationships with his family and work colleagues. He lacked confidence that his work was good enough to earn the trust of his colleagues.

In the process of coaching, he discovered the source of his lack of confidence. David excelled in everything he attempted because of his meticulous attention to detail and analytical approach. He earned an MBA from Harvard and was recruited by McKinsey upon graduation. To his great surprise, he received a negative review after his first year. He was put on probation and was let go during his wife's first pregnancy. It took him six months to find another job. They had no insurance when she delivered the baby, and they had to borrow money to maintain their home.

This was a very scary experience for him, and he told himself he would never let it happen again, thus developing paranoia about excellent performance. This experience taught David that "relaxing results in a threat to survival." So, when his cortex—his logical brain—told him to relax and enjoy his family because now he had enough money in the bank, his (much more powerful) subconscious brain was still firing on all cylinders out of fear. Once he made the connection that his past experiences were interfering with his performance and fulfilment at work and in life, he made a conscious evaluation of the costs and benefits of this belief and made a conscious choice to let go of the old belief, replacing it with a new belief: it's okay to relax. By recognizing the obstacles to his full potential, David was able to lead his team more effectively and show more empathy with their challenges.

David's team has since doubled in size, but now he can allow his team to self-organize and create an environment where they can grow, experiment, make mistakes, and learn from failure. Now, when interacting with challenging colleagues, he is quicker to recognize his anger and frustration, pause, and work through it productively, self-managing his emotions. He can clearly articulate his needs and expectations instead of resentfully brooding inside. His work-life balance has much improved and he is more "present" when he is at home with his family. Overall, he now reports that he feels less stress, sleeps better, and is happier at work and at home. He is one step closer to fulfilling the maximum complexity in him and achieving greatness.

CONCLUSION

Measuring effective leadership must be tied to business results and leaders must be fully aware of the bottom-line impact of their leadership skills. Quantum Leaders produce 37 percentage points higher team retention than Mechanistic Leaders, which translates into a $448 million savings in the operating expense line.

People are willing to give up 39 percent of their compensation to work for a good manager who provides safety, connection, and learning, in that order. These priorities confirm hierarchical evolutionary needs as well as the incoming signal processing order in the brain. To provide safety, connection, and learning, leaders must be able to effectively manage themselves. Some of the specific competencies in the self-management competency group include being open, flexible, and adaptable; appropriate emotion management; appropriate stress management; taking responsibility for one's emotions and the reality one self-creates; and exercising an internal locus of control. Effective self-management not only improves performance as a leader but often increases the overall quality of life and relationships because these all stem from the same source.

In the next chapter, we will review the first building block of Quantum Leadership for radical innovation: providing safety for others.

Chapter 5

PROVIDING SAFETY

L et's briefly return to our hunting scenario from the previous chapter. One day you go out hunting for food for your family. Suddenly, you feel a whiff of warm air on the back of your neck. Those sensors on your skin send a signal to your central nervous system, conveying data about the warm air. Then your cortex sends a signal to your neck muscles to turn, so you can see the source of the warm whiff of air. You turn your neck, and lo and behold, there is a roaring saber-toothed tiger about to chase you down for dinner. Your brain immediately sends a signal to your legs to run. All this processing takes less than a second, but for the subcortical structure in your brain in charge of your survival, that processing time is too long. When sensory input is relayed to the thalamus in the limbic system, the signal reaches the amygdala in eight to ten milliseconds.[1] It takes forty milliseconds to reach the cortex and up to ten seconds to be fully processed, which means the limbic system processes information a thousand times faster than the cortex region.[2]

Then it processes all this information—well below our conscious brain—pertinent to the dangerous situation, including the perception (warm air), emotion (fear), situation (hunting), and cognition (warmth equals danger). The amygdala processes and stores information pertaining to this episode in a single neuronal network, combining sensory perceptions of warmth, physiological response of adrenalin, emotions of fear, and the mental frame of a threat to your survival and forms associative conditioned memory. Then, when a new sensory perception is received, the amygdala activates the neural network of fear related to this episode based on the associative conditioned memory when something is even remotely close to it.

Fast forward a few months. Now you're getting ready in the bathroom and your kid shoots a blast of warm air from the blow-dryer at your neck for fun. Your fists immediately tighten, your heart is pumping at 180 beats per minute, and your legs take off running before your cortex even has a chance to process that it's just your kid playing around with you. Again, we have been evolutionarily programmed to favor a type I error, so we tend to overreact to threats to safety. Speed is more important than accuracy when it comes to ensuring safety.

Our body processes perceptions of threats in hierarchical steps. According to Stephen Porges's polyvagal theory, our body has three hierarchical response steps to sensory input, where the most primitive systems are activated only when the more evolved structures fail.[3] Richard Boyatzis's research on resonant leadership also points out that when the incoming sensory input is safe, a higher substrate of the social engagement system gets activated, eliciting a more evolved response of nurturing and connection with others.[4] According to Porges, when an incoming signal is not safe, our social engagement system fails and activates a less evolved response. We then ask the next question: Is this something I can take on and have a fair chance of winning? If the answer is yes, then we activate the fight response. If the answer is no, then we ask the next question: Can I outrun this threat? If the answer is yes, we activate the flight response. If the answer is no, we resort to the least evolved response: our body activates the freeze response, in which we become paralyzed and sometimes defecate, in effect playing dead and hoping our predators won't want to eat rotten meat.

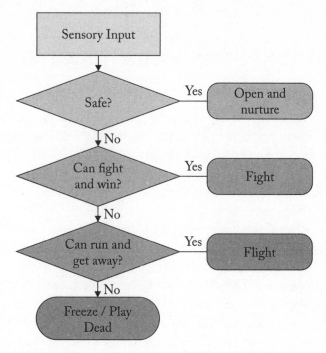

Figure 5.1 *Hierarchical perception processing of the brain*

RESPONSE TO SAFE SIGNALS: SOCIAL ENGAGEMENT

If an incoming signal is deemed safe (i.e., no fear activation from the implicit memory), the social engagement system, along with the parasympathetic nervous system, is activated. Our bodies relax, pupils narrow, and saliva and mucus production increase to facilitate digestion. The gastrointestinal tract activates the immune system, and we approach the source of safety to form a closer connection. This is where we nurture each other, have sex, digest, touch, connect, and love.

DEEP DIVE: RESPONSE TO THREATS—STRESS REACTION

When incoming sensory information is deemed a threat to survival, our bodies activate the sympathetic nervous system and a whole chain reaction called the hypothalamic–pituitary–adrenal axis (HPA axis), to deal with the incoming threat—whether it is real, perceived, or even subliminal. When the sympathetic nervous system is activated, our pupils dilate to let more light in to see what is happening better, all digestive functions diminish, heart rate and blood pressure increase, the immune system is inhibited, and higher levels of glucose are produced, anticipating higher energy consumption. In the HPA axis, the signal from the amygdala travels to the hypothalamus at lightning speed (eight milliseconds), which then secrets corticotropin-releasing hormone (CRH), which signals the pituitary glands to produce adrenocorticotropic hormone (ACTH), which in turn signals adrenal glands to release glucocorticoid hormones such as cortisol, epinephrine, and norepinephrine. Epinephrine is better known as adrenaline. Acute stress, when accurately placed, helps us to avoid danger, but the problem is that some or even most of the stressors in life are type I error responses.

Enough false positives from acute stress accumulate and form chronic stress, which activates the stress hormone cortisol that inhibits neurogenesis in the hippocampus (so we can focus on the immediate task of securing survival). That compromises our brains' ability to produce new neurons and make new neuronal connections. When new neuronal connections for new meanings can't be made, we become rigid and closed to new ideas, being stuck in the old synaptic connections.

Another factor that exacerbates rigidity is that epinephrine and norepinephrine are vasoconstrictors, meaning they constrict blood flow to capillaries in order to increase blood flow to large muscle groups such as arms and legs.[5] This response gears our bodies up for fight or flight. But more blood in the arms and legs must come from somewhere: our brains and guts. Researchers found that when we are exposed to threats to our safety, the blood flow to our frontal cortex dramatically decreases.[6] One of the functions of the medial prefrontal cortex is rational decision-making, such as conflict monitoring, error detection, executive control, and assessment of risk and reward.[7] In short, we are not as intelligent when we experience stress from threats, because we are only thinking with our instinctual reptilian brain.

Other researchers found that when the stress of threats reduces blood flow to our brains, the range of peripheral vision diminishes to thirty degrees (from the normal range of 180–230 degrees).[8] They measured the level of stress and peripheral vision in athletes within two hours of competition, and found that the athletes experienced significantly reduced peripheral vision and higher stress before competition.[9] Richard Boyatzis at Case Western Reserve University describes the medical term for this condition: tunnel vision—the loss of peripheral vision while retaining central vision, resulting in a constricted circular, tunnellike field of vision. When you have tunnel vision, you are literally too inflexible to be open to new ideas or approaches.

When we perceive a threat, the stress hormone cortisol generated by chronic stress hardens our blood vessels, and eventually calcifies our arteries.[10] Chronic stress also increases blood coagularity, because of the resulting imbalance of pro- and anticoagulant modules.[11] Smaller blood vessel diameter, combined with more viscous blood from stress reactions, renders our body more susceptible to cardiac arrest. Boyatzis explains the impact of stress in depth in his book *Resonant Leadership*.[12]

When our brains are exposed to stress, they also release a stress-induced analgesic called dopamine, which helps us tolerate pain.[13] Using functional MRI, researchers scanned participants' brains as they applied a mildly painful stimulus to the participants' fingers. At the same time, they were asked to perform mental math while experiencing increasing levels of noise to produce stress. The researchers found that pain tolerance increased as stress increased.

This makes sense since our bodies cannot be distracted with the discomfort of small cuts or aching leg muscles when we need to fight or run for our lives. But this adaptation becomes damaging when the dopamine level increases from chronic stress.[14]

HOW ADDICTION TO STRESS HAPPENS

Dopamine is a neurotransmitter that runs the brain's reward and pleasure center. It enables us to see rewards and pushes us to go achieve them. It is also highly addictive—all addictions cause a powerful surge in dopamine. When we achieve goals, dopamine makes us feel pleasure. Our brains develop tolerance for dopamine, meaning that as time goes on, increasingly higher levels of dopamine are needed to get the same level of pleasure. Addictive, novelty-seeking behaviors are the result of high levels of dopamine. This is how one gets addicted to achieving goals. The neurons that fire together get wired together in our brains, meaning stress and the dopamine rush that goes along with it get connected. This might explain why some chronically stressed people don't celebrate achieving goals—they are constantly looking for the next goal to get their next fix of dopamine. Their employees might feel discouraged because their achievements go overlooked or unappreciated. These managers may artificially create crises to justify the elevated level of stress and dopamine their brains have gotten used to.

Under chronic stress, our bodies are constantly hyperaroused. The amygdala is kept in a highly primed vigilant state where stress hormones such as adrenaline get released. Our brains associate stress with pleasure (albeit a mild form), which is addictive. Those who are used to an elevated level of stress hormones might also rely on the adrenaline rush to finish projects by waiting until the last minute. When they become leaders, the members of their teams suffer higher levels of stress as well. The leaders don't see that their own tolerance of stress hormones is higher than others', and expect others to be at that level by imposing unreasonable deadlines or workloads.

IMPACTS OF STRESS

Under chronic stress, our brains adapt by elevating the amygdala's vigilance level with enhanced memory and emotion about the threatening situation so they can detect potential threats more quickly next time.[15] This hypervigilance for harm is an adaptive response to increase our chances for survival. Again, natural selection favors committing false-positive type I errors in life-threatening situations. However, it can have unintended negative consequences if it fires too readily when there is no actual threat.

When this pattern of fight, flight, or freeze in response to stress is repeated over time, it carves a neural highway in the brain, and can shape our dominant coping strategies and leadership styles. These leaders tend to make snap judgments, as they are used to making quick threat appraisals. They tend to be black-and-white thinkers who are opinionated and rigid, as the subcortical appraisal function is apt to sacrifice accuracy for speed and the neurogenesis function in the hippocampus gets compromised, which we reviewed earlier. Implicitly accepting the intrusive initial thoughts wound with more threats to safety than warranted, their emotions are volatile, which makes it difficult for them to trust others and allow them to self-organize. With only the chronically primed, hyperaroused state to deal with similar future threats, they are snappy and controlling so as to avoid threats to safety. The huge surge in neuronal activities during the HPA axis and sympathetic nervous system arousal also render them more irritable.

Now, to make our discussion more relevant to you, I invite you to think of the worst boss you've worked for and select the top three reasons why you disliked working for him or her.

STRESS AND MECHANISTIC LEADERSHIP

Let's review the list of competencies the Mechanistic Leaders fail to demonstrate, as discussed in chapter 4 on self-management. Mechanistic Leaders are not open, flexible, or adaptable. They don't manage their emotions or stress appropriately. They don't choose positive mental models, and as a result, they don't trust others. They believe you're guilty until proven innocent. This lack of trust makes it difficult for them to let others self-organize, and they hog information and power. They blame others for how they feel and the reality they themselves have created. Their locus of control is external.

Now I would like to remind you of the impact of stress on our brains and invite you to assess how many of the symptoms Mechanistic Leaders demonstrate are similar to stress reactions. How many of the reasons you disliked working for your worst boss were related to stress reactions? If you are like a typical participant in my innovation and leadership training programs, most of the bad leadership characteristics you dislike about your worst boss are a result of mismanaged, repeated exposure to safety threats from past experiences.

When you don't manage yourself effectively and let your stress reaction to perceived threats dominate your leadership style, your fight-flight-freeze reaction takes over and makes it impossible to provide safety for your team. I am not talking about OSHA-style safety regulations; I'm referring to psychological safety. When your team members don't feel safe, their own fear reactions will take over, triggering their fight-flight-freeze responses, which jeopardize the higher functions of their cortex where innovation can be unleashed.

QUANTUM LEADERSHIP COMPETENCIES: PROVIDING SAFETY

Safety is a primal human need, and it's imperative that leaders ensure their team members feel safe, first and foremost. Simon Sinek confirms this point in his book *Leaders Eat Last* that creating a circle of safety in which people feel safe is a foundational requirement for them to deliver good performance.[16] The following section covers Quantum Leadership competencies necessary to provide safety.

Ethical, authentic, and congruent
Leaders often think that the importance of upholding high ethical standards is self-evident, so they rarely spell out why. In my research, "high

ethical and moral standards" was ranked as *the most* important leadership attribute, hands down, across geographies, genders, and positions. It is ranked so highly because when our leaders have high moral and ethical standards, we expect that they will play by the (fair) rules of the game, and that creates a sense of safety. We can relax and invoke our brains' higher capacities for social engagement, innovation, and creativity. We can deal with losing the game a lot better than we can deal with not knowing what the rules of the game are. If the incoming signal is unsafe, we activate a fight-flight-freeze response, and we lose access to the executive function of the cortex. For these reasons, creating safety should be the number one job for leading others.

At the macro level, studies have shown that countries with higher levels of corruption have lower levels of human development, as measured in terms of education, health, and gross national income.[17] An increase of corruption by one index point dampens GDP growth by somewhere between 13 and 90 basis points (0.13–0.90 percent) and lowers per capita GDP by $425.[18] These are important indicators that call for organized development programs to strengthen moral and ethical behaviors and improve transparency in business dealings.

Along with high ethical standards, Quantum Leaders practice authenticity and congruence. They are an open book. They courageously open up and share their feared outcome, instead of having a conversation about another person in their heads and thinking of ways to manipulate that person into their views. Their values, feelings, thoughts, words, and actions are congruent. This transparency creates safety for others.

To provide a greater sense of safety, leaders must first think about the systemic, interdependent nature of human relationships. What I do has an impact on you, which in turn has an impact on me, which then affects you again. When one person does the right thing, it creates a ripple effect that reverberates through and positively changes an entire system. When one person does the wrong thing, the same thing happens in the opposite direction. Quantum Leaders look several steps ahead to consider the consequences of their actions and decisions on their families, organizations, and others who share the same ecosystem (e.g., suppliers, business partners, customers, and even future generations and environments). This concept of interdependence originates from quantum mechanics (the act of being observed changing the observation itself) and is the foundation for strong ethics.

CASE STUDY

"I just don't know what to do—it has taken a life of its own. I need your help," muttered the COO with a deep sigh.

I was brought in to resolve a conflict between two executives in a company, which was tearing the entire company apart. The company had become a leader in the industry with a technology and relationship platform that generates residential mortgage leads to sell to real estate companies with tens of thousands of realtors.

Dennis was the head of operations, responsible for lead generation, and Matt was the head of sales for the Western region (though they could go after any accounts in the United States). Dennis took pride in his strong work ethic and was highly regarded by the executive management team. His team members started coming to him with complaints that some of the sales reps in Matt's team were rejecting their leads, which lowers Dennis's team's key performance metric. Upon further investigation, Dennis found out that Matt's sales reps were trying to strike a shady deal with some of Dennis's team members: Matt's reps were asking for more highly qualified leads than those sent to other regions in exchange for accepting all of the warm leads from Dennis's team. Dennis's team was measured on the percentage of leads accepted by the sales team, with the goal of producing high-quality leads. Matt's team was measured on the number of deals closed and the sales revenue generated from them. So Matt's reps pressured Dennis's lead generation team members for higher quality leads in exchange for accepting all the leads, creating a "win-win" solution between them.

Obviously the problem was that it was not fair for the other four sales regions, since they would get lower quality leads, lowering their performance. Dennis thought just a few of Matt's team members were trying to game the system and started digging to

---

get more information. He was appalled to find out that Matt was the one that actually told his reps to go strike deals with Dennis's team members. He became furious.

"It's a matter of principle," Dennis said. "Nobody should get away with cutting corners and unethical behavior. They should work just as hard as other regions and they must be fair." He created a PowerPoint document detailing evidences of Matt's shady deals and went to various leaders on the executive committee, making a case for why Matt had to be fired.

Matt gave the impression that he was innocent and took the high road by not attacking back. Then Dennis went to his peers and their team members to create a bottom-up pressure on the executive team. The entire company was divided on the issue. The angrier Dennis got, the less credible he came across and the more invalidated he felt, which fueled his anger even more, creating a vicious cycle. That was when I was brought in.

I could see that if Dennis had just presented the facts and left the decision on what to do with Matt up to the executive leadership team, they would have seen the picture and would have taken corrective measures. Instead, they felt put off by Dennis's pushy arguments to fire Matt and actually questioned the validity of the facts he was presenting.

I worked with Dennis to get him to become curious about the intensity of his indignation. He then discovered the driving force behind his anger. His father was a narcissistic, habitual gambler and kept promising his family that he would bring in money. He thought he was too good to get a regular job. Every bit of money went to support his gambling dream to "strike big" one day. In the meantime, his mom and siblings had to move into his grandparents' basement and Dennis had to get a job at age fourteen to make money for the family. He had deeply seated resentment about his dad. When he started seeing that what he was really angry about was his dad, not Matt, he took a big breath, speechless.

I curated a meeting between Matt and Dennis, and Dennis shared with Matt why he had been so venomous about what Matt had been doing and owned his anger. Dennis took a risk in trusting Matt and becoming vulnerable about his painful childhood experience. He then presented to Matt the facts that led Dennis to his conclusion for the first time, which he had done tens of times with others in the company. Matt owned his part frankly and they both sat down and came up with measures to prevent the same thing from happening in the future, including some changes on how each team got compensated, which they both took to the executive team. Matt lost part of his performance bonus that year as did his team. Their teams started meetings again and they began to heal the distrust between the two teams and in the company. Through a very difficult experience, they both learned that vulnerability builds trust, which is the foundation of any relationship and organization.

Clear expectations

Quantum Leaders communicate expectations clearly so team members do not get blindsided with bad news. They also communicate with the specific intent to create safety. This type of proactive communication necessitates skills such as preempting any potential threat others might feel by specifically neutralizing a feared outcome before starting the conversation, which I call "clearing the air." For example, in a difficult conversation with a team member, you can clear the air by declaring your intent directly but with empathy: "I am not trying to blame you—whatever the challenge, we can make it through when we put our heads together. I am just curious and trying to understand what happened." This type of clearing the air, transparency that makes the implicit explicit, makes it a lot safer for the team member to engage with you to analyze the situation and come up with a suitable game plan to address the issue at hand.

Trust and advocacy

Quantum Leaders do not manage through fear, so their team members can trust their leaders not to harm them. Quantum Leaders praise others in public and coach them in private, protecting their ego. They go to bat for their team members, advocate for their teams and their projects, and protect them from potential outside sabotage. They also separate coaching from performance evaluations, so genuine learning can take place without the fear of consequences. By fearlessly and authentically protecting their team, Quantum Leaders solidify a sense of safety. This protection of others engenders an intense sense of loyalty.

This "employees first" philosophy is the driver behind the success of Costco, the second largest brick-and-mortar retailer behind Walmart. As of December 2016, the S&P 500 ten-year stock return was 57 percent. Walmart's was only 46 percent, but Costco's was a whopping 189 percent. Both Costco and Walmart have a no-frills approach, but somehow Costco managed to also carry the perception of high quality. The hourly starting pay at Costco is $13.50;[19] Walmart's is $10.[20] The average top-scale hourly wage for Costco is $23, which a full-time employee can expect to make after putting in about four years;[21] Walmart's overall average hourly wage is $13.69.[22] How has Costco managed to create more shareholder return when its stated first priority is employee welfare and its average wages are a lot higher? When employees feel valued and trusted, they live up to the expectations. They take more initiative, act more like owners instead of hirelings, and are nicer to customers. As a result, they are more efficient with their time, do things faster and better, and do the right things because they are more conscientious. Costco hasn't had labor disputes in decades, whereas they are a common occurrence at Walmart, diverting management focus and sapping energy.

Another important angle of trust is sharing information. Knowledge shared is knowledge squared: hoarders of information become the primary cultural barriers to learning.[23] When information is shared, trust is created, and that trust encourages a bidirectional flow of information critical to organizational survival.

Distribution of power

Quantum Leaders distribute power, control, and decision authority down to where information resides: frontline employees. They do not approve; instead, they facilitate and coach. They do not play favorites, and they distribute projects and awards fairly (not necessarily equally). They do not bully others and don't tolerate bullying in others. On every front, they make an intentional effort to provide safety to their teams.

CONCLUSION

Safety is a primal human need. The human brain has evolved over millions of years to increase our chances for survival as a species. In today's organizations, leaders must first provide a sense of safety and order for their employees to feel connected and free to pursue innovation. When people don't feel safe, they activate a stress reaction of fight, flight, and freeze, which compromises their ability to access the higher-functioning part of their brains. Many of the undesirable attributes of Mechanistic Leaders are a result of learned responses to chronic stress from their past.

Ensuring others' safety is possible only when leaders feel safe first and open themselves up to connect with other people by activating the social engagement network in the limbic system of the brain. Grounded in the foundation of self-management, Quantum Leaders provide safety for others by demonstrating high ethical and moral standards, being authentic and congruent, setting clear expectations, engendering trust, advocating for others, and distributing power. Quantum Leaders then create safety for their teams so that everyone's innate creativity, drive, and innovation can be unleashed to achieve his or her full potential.

Chapter 6

CREATING DIFFERENTIATION

WHAT IS DIFFERENTIATION?

So far, we have reviewed the Quantum Leadership competency in the bottom two layers of the pyramid: effective self-management and providing safety for others. Once we feel safe, we can open ourselves to others and form connections. But there is another prerequisite to connection. It might sound contradictory, but *differentiation* is required for meaningful connection, which increases internal complexity of a system. Differentiation is a process of producing variation, separate and distinct from others and from the environment. As a human species, differentiation evidenced by strong boundaries is a necessary condition to form meaningful and fulfilling connection.

Applied to leadership, differentiation among the members of an organization is required to form meaningful team cohesion, which allows your company to kick-start radical innovation. Implementing differentiation means

- establishing permeable yet strong personal boundaries, as we have reviewed in chapter 4, and establishing the same at the team and organization level;
- facilitating collective intelligence by drawing on the wisdom of the crowd, a culmination of individual learning from trial and error;
- valuing and nurturing each team member's unique skills and talents and promoting diversity of thoughts; and
- allowing team members to self-organize.

In this chapter, we'll look at these factors one by one. First, let's examine why we should pursue differentiation as a leader and as an organization and its impact on radical innovation.

THE BENEFITS OF DIFFERENTIATION

Differentiation is a necessary condition for connection

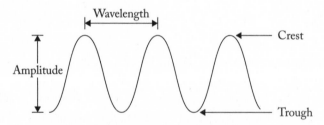

Figure 6.1 *Structure of a sine wave*

According to quantum mechanics, coherence is a necessary condition for entanglement,[1] the condition where two particles are so connected that they can influence each other across great distances. It is an ultimate state of deeply forged connection. There are two sources of waves: coherent and incoherent. If the atoms in a light source vibrate with the same wavelengths (the distance between two crests or troughs is the same), same speed, and almost the same amplitude, they are said to be oscillating in single frequency, vibrating in phase (constantly maintaining the same distance between two crests). Then they become a coherent light source, having no internal wave interferences. Laser light is coherent but candle-light is not. A laser, unlike a candle, produces a clean beam vibrating in single frequency with no other internal noise. When two coherent light sources with the same wavelength meet *in phase*, they can produce a constructive interference pattern, with the amplitudes greater than they can produce on their own. Stable interference patterns by two waves, which we reviewed in chapter 2, are produced *only if they are coherent*.[2] This is the reason why Thomas Young had to pass the sunlight through a slit: to produce a coherent light source with single frequency before he could study the interference pattern in the double-slit experiment.

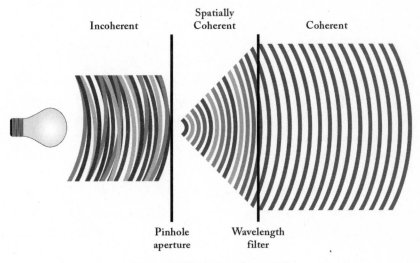

Figure 6.2 *Producing coherent light*

The same principle applies to relationships and teams. When we are differentiated as individual persons and teams, we become a blend of coherent lights that create a synergy that is greater than what we can do as separate individuals.

Differentiation increases complexity

According to complex systems theory, differentiation increases positive (internal) complexity. By allowing more variation, each differentiated agent in a system can make different connections with other agents and systems, which adds more variety and strength to the quality of connection. This additional connection increases the probability of natural selection and evolution because the organism's variations (i.e., mutations) facilitate better adaptation to the environment. *Complexity increases when differentiated parts are connected.* This increased internal complexity, in turn, enables an organism to respond even more effectively to unexpected challenges from the environment and increases its chances of survival.

My church choir provides a simple example of how differentiation increases complexity. When we learn a new song, the soprano, alto, tenor, and bass voices practice their parts by themselves. When each part is sung in unison, the resulting music doesn't sound very rich or complex. When the four parts are finally combined, they produce a rich tapestry of beautiful, complex music.

Let's take another example. Fruit flies and humans share 60 percent of their DNA—a surprisingly high number. One would be right to question how the remaining 40 percent could account for the much higher complexity of humans. The key is in the number of *interactions* in many-to-many networks among the genes. Humans have about twenty-five thousand unique genes; fruit flies, about fourteen thousand. The number of protein interactions among the genes in humans is about 650,000—ten times as many as that of fruit flies.[3] Each additional differentiated gene produces exponential growth in the number of genetic interactions. The network effect, which we discussed in chapter 2, resulting from the interaction among genes explains how a small difference in the number of genes can create an enormous difference in the complexity level between humans and fruit flies. The same pattern of exponential growth applies in the relationship between the number of genes and the gene interactions.

The highest level of internal complexity can be achieved by developing optimal differentiation, connecting the differentiated parts, and replicating that connection on multiple levels. If you have just undifferentiated parts, there is nothing to integrate, which results in suboptimal complexity. Once the foundation of safety is in place, Quantum Leaders facilitate differentiation in each of their team members, as well as the whole team as a unit, maximizing each member's unique talents, skills, and perspectives.

Differentiation is so important to the optimal functioning of the human race that a differentiation mechanism is inherently built into the human development phase—it's called pruning, and it takes place in the teenage brain. At birth, neuronal synapses in a child's brain are more numerous than in an adult's. Synapses multiply rapidly during childhood, soaking up knowledge like a sponge. This is why it's much easier for children to learn foreign languages, musical instruments, and sports. As a child matures into a teenager, the brain prunes away underutilized synapses, so the synapses used most often can work more efficiently. The long body of the retained neurons get myelinated in a myelin sheath, which accelerates the conduction speed of the ions between neurons a hundredfold. This increased speed is made possible through the process of saltatory conduction, in which ions jump between nodes instead of steadily traveling along the axonal length of the neuron. In addition, myelination accelerates the resting period between neuronal firings—the refractory period—thirtyfold. The combination of these functions makes pruned synapses three thousand times more efficient than unpruned ones.[4]

The pruning process produces unique patterns of neuronal synapses manifested into unique strengths and talents. This evolutionary mechanism highlights the importance of differentiating individuation before integrating with another differentiated person (e.g., a spouse or a team). Once parts are fully differentiated, connecting differentiated parts and replicating these connections to the next level (in this case, raising the next generation of children or leaders) increases internal complexity. All complex systems strive to increase internal complexity by nature because higher complexity means better chances of natural selection.

Differentiation introduces randomness

Another important concept is that differentiation in the form of environmental perturbations helps produce radical innovation. This dynamic can be illustrated by modern communication devices. In some situations, white noise helps produce a more coherent, clear sound. Recall the constructive interference pattern of the double-slit experiment from chapter 2. When the peaks of two waves meet, it produces a constructive interference, with an additive peak higher than either of them. When the peak of one wave meets the trough of another, they cancel each other out: destructive interference. According to the mathematics of complexity theory, when an adequate (not too small or too big) level of random perturbations from the environment and the complex system's periodic adaptations to these perturbations happen to meet and amplify the peaks of their waves, it can result in radical change. It is counterintuitive to think that adding noise produces clearer sound, but the laws of physics make it possible. This is the principle that scientists from Sogn og Fjordane University College, Norway, demonstrated when they treated children with ADHD with background white noise to improve their cognitive functions, including memory.[5]

Inbreeding produces an opposite effect of random perturbations. A 2015 study published in the journal *Nature* identified the effects of inbreeding: marrying your first cousin produces offspring that generally have lower cognitive ability, smaller lung volume per second, and ten months' less education and are 1.2 cm shorter.[6] Inbreeding has also been associated with some devastating diseases such as Mendelian disorders. *Biodiversity produces better fitness for survival.*

What do white noise and biodiversity teach us about stimulating radical innovation? When our ongoing efforts coincide with the random perturbations of the environment, it can result in radical innovation, an accidental anomaly in the process of profuse experimentation in search of a better fit with the environment. This is why differentiation or diversity that introduces elements of randomness is important for radical innovation.

Differentiation increases robustness

Differentiation, in the form of mutation, is what has sustained the earth's evolutionary history. If genes preserved 100 percent fidelity to the original DNA in the cell replication process, meaning if there were no mutations, all species would have died during the extreme periods of unrest in the earth's history—ice ages, solar flares, and meteorites. But some of the genes that underwent mutation—a failure in the DNA copying process—produced features that were better fit to survive in the new extreme environment. This should sound an alarm bell to those infected with the disease of perfectionism—failure is a necessary condition for radical innovation.

**Failure is a necessary condition
for radical innovation.**

Another benefit of differentiation is that it can create functional redundancy, which in turn improves system robustness and resilience. When a system is robust, it means it is not susceptible to threats from the environment. Similarly, our body becomes more robust when it has developed immunity to germs from being exposed to them in small doses, which is the principle behind immunization. An immunized body that can more easily fight off invasions of pathogens is a more robust body.

Similarly, differentiation in the form of diverse skill sets, perspectives, and mental models in an organization creates a form of a bet-hedging or functional redundancy. For example, if one part of the organization is under severe stress from high turnover, or showing signs of vulnerability to competitive attacks, other parts, albeit not an intuitively perfect match, can step in to fill the space.

Differentiation fosters exaptation

In this case, filling in doesn't require an identical copy—only one similar enough, which creates an opportunity for innovative mutations to occur. Steven Johnson refers to this as "exaptation" in his book *Where Good Ideas Come From*. Exaptation describes a trait that served one particular function and was subsequently co-opted to serve another, such as feathers, which were initially evolved for heat, then co-opted for display of power, and later for flight.

One example of exaptation is the invention of the tractor (as presented by Stuart Kauffman, a medical doctor turned complexity theorist).[7] In 1889 the Charter Gasoline Engine company produced the first tractor by combining a steam traction engine with an internal combustion engine—a radical departure from horse-drawn farm equipment. But the heavy weight of the engine buckled the tractor chassis. Subsequently, the engineers thought to use the heavy engine with an equally heavy gear box and drive axle components as the chassis of the tractor. The front axle, ancillary equipment, and driver's seat were attached to the engine/gearbox/chassis, and the separate chassis was eliminated, which reduced the tractor's weight significantly. In the example, the chassis of a tractor was an exaptation of the engine—which became widely popular once launched into the market.

This type of exaptation-based radical innovation requires different perspectives and different heuristics from a diverse pool of people. So how do you foster differentiation as a leader?

FOSTERING DIFFERENTIATION: SETTING BOUNDARIES

The first skill for Quantum Leaders to foster differentiation is establishing strong boundaries, which prepares teams to differentiate and pursue their maximum potential. We have reviewed why and how to establish strong, permeable *personal* boundaries in chapter 4. Here, we focus on how to establish the same at the team and organization levels.

Strong yet permeable boundaries at the team and organizational level

When an organization has strong boundaries, everyone is clear on its reason for being, what is on strategy and what is off, what behavior is expected, and how each person and team fits into the big picture. Everyone respects and seeks out the diverse perspectives and unique contributions others bring to the table. There is no preferential treatment or deification of the revenue-generating department over others. Quantum Leaders keep strong yet permeable boundaries for their teams. To improve your differentiation skills for the team, try the following:

- Never engage in discussions about the *substance* when the *form* is in violation. For example, let's say you are the head of a legal team and just found out that an attorney on your team habitually sits on a document to review instead of turning it around quickly because the document comes from someone who is competing with his spouse in another department in the company (based on a true story!). If he admits he has done that, the *form* is clearly in violation. When you approach him to discuss the matter, he says it's only been three weeks. In this case, do not get confused and go down the path of discussing the substance of whether three weeks was an excessive time, as opposed to one week.

Whether it is one week or three weeks is not relevant because the *form* is already in violation before the substance of "how long" can be discussed. Clearly set the expectation that his practice is unacceptable and ask him to develop a game plan to never repeat it, followed by repairing the damaged trust with the person who sent the document to him.

- Never let one member of your team complain to you about another in his or her absence. Allowing this dynamic to occur is a boundary violation called triangulation and is very damaging to the team dynamics, and destructive politics are likely to ensue. Do not engage in discussing the merits of the complaint; doing so legitimatizes the team member's right to break boundaries. Invite him or her to resolve the issue with the other person directly. Offer to mediate if it doesn't work. Such mediation must be facilitated in the presence of both of them.

- Clearly establish and regularly communicate your team's unique value proposition and purpose to other teams, as well as to your team members. This requires clarifying what is included and what is not. It means understanding, communicating, and practicing your company's (or team's) core values.

- Clearly define roles and responsibilities for each member in your team. At the same time, adaptively and flexibly pull in different skill sets from your team, outside the regular job description, depending on the situation.

- Respect others' boundaries. Let others self-organize, yet hold them accountable for their self-organized efforts. Resist the temptation to impose unreasonable deadlines or demands on other departments just because you have urgent requirements.

- Start and end meetings on time. Match the content of the meeting with the format of the meeting, and table issues inappropriate for the format of the meeting. For example, use ten-minute daily huddles to cover routine progress check and hurdle clearance, and use quarterly off-sites for developing strategic direction and crafting competitive responses. If the latter topic surfaces during the daily huddle, table it for the next off-site.

At the same time, the strength of the boundaries must be balanced with permeability of the boundaries because *boundaries regulate the flow of information*. If boundaries are too rigid between teams, the information doesn't flow freely, which is detrimental to rapid information processing an organization needs to facilitate radical innovation, which we will cover more in depth in chapter 7 on learning. Therefore, leaders must strive to create boundaries that are strong enough to hold the integrity as a team and yet maintain free flow of information with other teams.

DRAWING ON THE WISDOM
OF THE CROWD

The second major skill to facilitate differentiation means acknowledging the power of collective wisdom, resulting from diverse heuristics.

Wisdom of the crowd: Reducing errors

Differentiation reduces collective errors via the wisdom of the crowd: the phenomenon that the opinion of a group of individuals almost always produces better results than a single expert.

Several research studies and stories substantiate this concept. In June 1968 the USS *Scorpion* and its ninety-nine crewmen were declared lost after failing to return to port at Norfolk, Virginia, from a tour of duty in the Mediterranean Sea.[8] The navy's immediate search-and-rescue mission to the *Scorpion's* last known location yielded no success, because the search area extended into the depths of the Atlantic Ocean near the Azores Islands, over 1,300 square miles. Later that year, naval officer Dr. John Craven, chief scientist of the US Navy's Special Projects Division, pulled together a team of experts and asked them to make a best guess at where the sunken submarine might be. The team included sailors, mathematicians, and salvage and submarine specialists. Their guesses were averaged into a single number, drawing on a Bayesian statistics technique. Although none of the experts' guesses was right, the average of the experts' guesses was amazingly accurate, placing their guess within two hundred yards of the actual location of the sub.

Fast forward to 2005 for another example. *Nature* led a peer-reviewed investigation to compare the accuracy of Wikipedia, a disruptive innovation, as compared to the *Encyclopaedia Britannica*.[9] The study chose fifty entries from both Wikipedia and *EB*, which were reviewed for accuracy by experts who didn't know which source their article came from. The study concluded that Wikipedia articles contained an average of four errors per article and *EB* three. This observation shows that the collective intelligence from many "average Joes" is comparable to one or a few experts who probably have PhDs in the field, having spent a lifetime of study on the topic; and all the examples above demonstrate the power of drawing upon collective wisdom.

When to call on the wisdom of the crowd

Scott Page of the University of Michigan presents three conditions for the wisdom of the crowd to work:[10]

- Problem-solvers must be smart, as measured by being able to take derivatives in calculus.
- Problem-solvers must have diverse heuristics and perspectives to be able to improve on a solution.
- The problem itself must be hard to solve (or one smart person could just solve it).

To improve the quality of your decisions, rely on a diverse pool of problem-solving techniques (heuristics) and ways of thinking, because the wisdom of the crowd yields the most accurate results. Our combined intelligence is almost always better than that of one genius superstar—much like blind men touching an elephant, each with different descriptions of the part of the elephant he is touching, especially when things change constantly in the environment.

As we can see from these cases, harnessing the collective intelligence of people from diverse backgrounds can solve seemingly impossible feats. To curate various interdisciplinary functions within an organization—or even across diverse organizations—and produce extraordinary results, leaders must be open to divergent views, and flexible enough to consider the merits of opposing views seriously. With enough quantity, you can get quality.

Therefore, each element that contributes to the quantity matters. We can make better decisions when each of our perspectives is valued and explored.

How to tap into collective intelligence

For an organization to truly tap into the power of collective intelligence, leaders must relinquish control and decentralize their decision-making authority—difficult to accomplish when they have gut-level resistance to doing so. Where does this resistance come from?

Almost all of us have experienced a threat to our safety because of loss of control. To tap into collective intelligence, we must develop the leadership competency of self-management and trust others whom we may believe to be inferior in education and judgment. Some of us might think that we have worked very hard for our education after all and are paid higher wages than the average worker to make decisions as leaders.

But those who are on the front lines know better than anyone else about the realities in the external environment. The cashier in the Costco checkout line knows what products are popular because customers express their disappointment when they stop carrying a product. (I regularly voice my opinion at my Costco checkout line.) An assembly-line operator knows better than anyone else how to tell if a machine is about to fail. Leaders must provide a platform to tap into this collective intelligence (many software platforms are now available for enterprise collective intelligence management, providing tagging and searching functions).

UTILIZING DIVERSITY

Quantum Leaders' third differentiation skill is fostering diversity.

Diversity of thoughts raises complexity

As we have seen, harnessing the collective intelligence of people from diverse backgrounds can solve seemingly insurmountable feats, impossible to solve by one super expert. To curate various interdisciplinary functions within an organization, or even across diverse organizations, and produce extraordinary results, leaders must initially generate as many different views as possible and evaluate the merits of every view. Valuing diverse opinions requires asking questions more than issuing orders.

Collective error is equal to the average of individual errors minus diversity (variance) of the group.

Scott Page also mathematically explains that collective error is almost always smaller than individual errors, because collective error is equal to the average of individual errors minus diversity (variance) of the group.[11] From this equation, we can surmise that there are two ways to decrease collective error: reduce the average individual error, by hiring smart people; or increase the diversity of thoughts from many people. It also highlights a potential risk: if we adopt other people's opinions or mental models too much, we might reduce individual errors, but the diversity (variance) of the group goes down, resulting in higher collective error. This is a mathematical explanation for what happens in groupthink; people make irrational or dysfunctional decisions in an effort to conform to each other (as was the case in the space shuttle *Challenger* disaster). Everyone on your team must be valued and given credence to minimize collective error. This, in turn, raises collective complexity.

The reason diversity lowers collective errors is that people bring different heuristics and perspectives shaped by their unique life experiences. Those who grow up in the Siberian tundra have a much richer vocabulary and perspective on cold weather, ice, vodka, and caribou, and see the world through those lenses. Those who grow up in a thatch-roofed house built on Rio Dulce in Guatemala have a completely different perspective on rivers, boats, fish, swimming, and tropics, and see the world through those lenses. Life experiences from different environments provide different heuristics, or simple rules, to handle daily challenges in life. When two engineers from these two completely different environments are put together on a team to solve a problem about how to design space meals optimal for weight and reuse, the resulting output will be much richer than if the two engineers had both grown up in Titusville, Florida. For challenging problems, we need a team, ideally made up of people from diverse backgrounds and with diverse heuristics.

Diversity as a strategic issue

How do we structure a team optimal for diversity of thoughts? Researchers from Northwestern, Kellogg, Columbia, and Stanford business schools shed light on this issue. They wanted to find out what impact the diversity and information sharing of a group had on the quality of group decision-making. They set up groups of three people who were told to solve a murder mystery. Groups were composed of (a) three individuals familiar to each other, (b) two familiar individuals and a stranger, or (c) three strangers. Before group discussion, clues were either fully shared, so all members possessed identical information, or partially shared, so each member possessed several unique clues to which no other member had access. The results indicate that all-stranger groups were most likely to identify the correct suspect when information was fully shared.[12] Two conditions for optimal decision-making are (1) diversity of heuristics and (2) transparency of information, which we will discuss in the next chapter.

Quantum Leaders pull their team members from various races, genders, religions, and cultures to expand the pool of heuristics and increase the chances of generating diverse ideas.

In this sense, diversity is a strategic issue, not a compliance issue. Since there aren't objective, tangible ways to measure diversity of thought, Quantum Leaders pull their team members from various races, genders, religions, and cultures to expand the pool of heuristics and increase the chances of generating diverse ideas. The exponential growth of fluctuations (errors, failures, or diversity) are a necessary condition for radical innovation. This idea will be explained in more depth in chapter 8.

How to improve diversity of thought

To increase diversity of thought, review the self-management competencies in chapter 4 first, to ensure you and others feel safe. Then try the following:

- Introduce a fresh outsider's perspective. GYK Antler is a creative service company based in Boston. They have a program called Exec Exchange, in which they temporarily exchange their CEO with that of another company. Travis York, GYK Antler's CEO, has exchanged roles with Matt Bonner, NBA player for the San Antonio Spurs; Jeremy Hitchcock, ex-CEO of Dyn, a cloud-based internet infrastructure-as-a-service company; Mark Bollman, CEO of Ball and Buck, a sportsman-themed fashion company; and Kent Devereux, CEO of the New Hampshire Institute of Art. They attend regularly scheduled meetings, make decisions (except those related to HR), and interact with customers. This kind of practice infuses fresh outside perspectives that are completely different from their familiar context and greatly expands diversity of thinking.
- Ask questions more frequently than you express opinions.
  - "For X to happen, what would be the assumptions, and in what situations would those assumptions break down?"
  - "What evidence supports the *opposite* conclusion?"
  - "What do we make of what we see, and how else can we interpret it?"
- Run meetings explicitly aiming to increase the diversity of thought.
  - Let others speak first, encouraging everyone to take a turn and speak their minds. This will make it safe for even the shiest members on your team to express their opinions. Give your opinion last.
  - Designate the devil's advocate role to one of your team members for each meeting.
  - Have people shadow those with different perspectives for a day.
  - Rotate the role of facilitator among your team members.

CAPITALIZING ON
SELF-ORGANIZATION

We've examined three aspects of differentiation: creating strong but permeable boundaries; utilizing the wisdom of the crowd; and valuing diversity. Let's look at the fourth necessary nexus of differentiation: self-organization. My global leadership research found that allowing self-organization was the second most important when evaluating bosses, surpassed only by strong ethical and moral standards. It's not only a universal human need to be self-directed and determine our own fate but also an essential driving force behind innovation. Self-organization—autonomy—is what Daniel Pink identified in his book *Drive: The Surprising Truth About What Motivates Us* as one of the three fundamental aspects of human motivation.

When 195 global leaders were asked to rate 74 qualities, these rose to the top.

Percentage of Respondents

Strong ethics & safety	67%	Has high ethical and moral standards
Self-organizing	59%	Provides goals and objectives with loose guidelines/direction
Strong ethics & safety	56%	Clearly communicates expectations
Efficient learning	52%	Has the flexibility to change opinions
Nurtures growth	43%	Is commited to my ongoing training
Connection & belonging	42%	Communicates often and openly

Figure 6.3 The top 10 leadership competencies, grouped into five themes
Sunnie Giles, "The Most Important Leadership Competencies, According to Leaders Around the World," Harvard Business Review, *March 15, 2006.*[13]

Self-organization: An autocatalytic process

Self-organization is a necessary condition for radical innovation, which is equivalent to the spontaneous higher order that takes place in natural complex adaptive systems. Self-organization in a complex system enables *spontaneous order*, in which the whole is greater than the sum of its parts: higher order at the global level emerges out of seeming chaos observed at the local level. Individual termites don't know what the entire colony looks like and how they are building the intricate system, complete with temperature control and ventilation. But the self-organization of each termite, based on feedback from the environment through profuse trials over millions of years, has fine-tuned each element of the colony, giving rise to a higher level of complexity as a colony than in each termite.

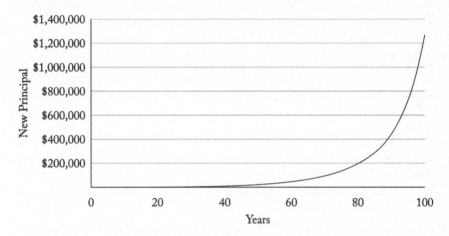

Figure 6.4 Autocatalysis in compounded interest

Agents in a complex system interact with and get feedback from the environment in an *autocatalytic* process. Autocatalysis is like compound interest: the growth from the principal gets added back on to the principal, exponentially accelerating the growth of the principal. As you can imagine, growth is negligible in the beginning because the principal is too small to fuel much growth. Let's say you started with $100 and each year you earn 10 percent interest. Without contributing any more to the principal, after the first year, your principal will grow to $110. During the second year, you will now be earning interest on $110, not the original $100, yielding a new principal of $121 at the end of the second year. After the fifth year, $161.05; after the tenth year, $259.37. For the first five years, the growth in the principal is $61.05; but in the next five years, $98.32. The following five years yield $158.35 more in interest. During the five years between the ninety-fifth and hundredth years? $522,393.63. Your $100 initial investment will have grown to nearly $1.4 million. The rate of change accelerates exponentially because the interest you are earning is added back to the principal. This concept illustrates the principle behind autocatalysis.

In chemistry, autocatalysis refers to the process in which the reaction product is catalyzed by one of the reactants, creating a self-sustaining pattern. This process creates exponential growth, amplified by the positive-feedback loop between the reaction product and the reactant. Similarly, when agents in a complex system adapt to the environment's perturbations, experimenting to see what works the best in many iterations and incorporating the results of each experiment, they create a positive-feedback loop, amplifying the speed of change in an exponential fashion. The agents become part of the result of the experiment, since they are interacting and interdependent with the environment and incorporating the change into their next iteration of the experiment. This process is characterized by a long, slow germination time during which the change is negligible. But after the critical inflection point, the change is radically accelerated. This is self-organized criticality applied in business. It takes a long initial germination time to build the initial momentum in the autocatalytic process, but this germinated growth explodes into radical innovation, catching everyone by surprise—"They just came out of nowhere!" Thus, the history of radical innovation (as well as evolution) shows the same pattern of punctuated equilibria, characterized by a slow initial phase, exponential growth, and leveling off.[14]

Self-organization speeds the iterative process

The hierarchical model of the Industrial Revolution was designed to maximize efficiency and standardization while minimizing errors and variance. However, the increasingly more complex business environment rendered this efficiency model ineffective; today too many variables can create too much unpredictability too quickly. As mentioned in chapter 1, the decoupling of information, decision-making authority, and responsibility created by higher VUCA in the environment results in a situation in which one smart leader with decision-making authority and responsibility can no longer take all the variables into consideration, anticipate all possible outcomes, and develop game plans to effectively and quickly deal with each outcome because the agents in the front lines have more information. In many companies, the intimate and rich intelligence from the front lines gets muddled as the situation report ascends through the hierarchy of the organization over time. As a result, decisions made by those in higher ranks often do not accurately reflect the reality in the front lines because (1) the opportunistic time to respond is already gone and (2) the information has lost its original salience.

Therefore, it is critical to distribute power to the lowest levels of the organization and rely on the input from those on the front lines, because that's where intelligence about the environment is highest, freshest, and most accurate. Self-organization allows agents to detect the random perturbations in the environment and correct their behavior to effectively deal with it quickly. How much power to give to lower levels? Google's simple rule is to distribute power until the leader starts feeling uncomfortable. Allowing self-organization of employees facilitates full differentiation.

Instituting the principles of self-organization is important for companies, partly because satisfying our innate yearning to be self-directed and express creativity results in higher employee satisfaction and decreased turnover. But more important, self-organization is a *necessary condition* to create the critical inflection point beyond which lies spontaneous order: a game-changing radical innovation.

How Zappos improved self-organization

Self-organizing teams are characterized by distributed control, resilience with self-healing, and adaptation. At Zappos, an online shoe and clothing company founded in 1999 that Amazon bought for $1.2 billion in 2009, employees take pride in excellent customer service. At the Zappos call center, reps don't have any call scripts or limits on call lengths (the longest one was over ten hours!). They are encouraged to go beyond the traditional role expected of a call center rep, to the point where they will order a pizza for you if you are too inebriated to make the call yourself!

What is less known about Zappos, but more important for students of leadership (like myself), is that it has instituted and practices *holacracy*, the concept of viewing employees as self-organizing, autonomous wholes that are interdependent parts in an organization. Tony Hsieh, the CEO of Zappos, used holacracy to turn Zappos into an organization where top-down hierarchy is replaced by fluid work circles (similar to departments in the traditional sense but focused on a defined scope of work instead of a permanent place in an org chart) made of self-organizing people with roles they opt in to. Instead of an org chart, they have a work chart. These circles are nested within larger teams and guided by over 350 lead links and 500 circles. The lead links of circles have little formal authority but are responsible for finding the best talent for each role in their circles.

They have a constitution: a living document defining the rules by which circles form and operate. Roles are defined and assigned collectively. Technology plays a key role in tracking these rules and ensuring implementation of these processes. They use enterprise software, such as GlassFrog and holaSpirit, to clarify the purpose, accountability, and decision rights of every circle and role.[15]

Employees are assigned a hundred points they can spend to be part of a circle posted on the Role Marketplace. They fill 7.4 roles on average, and there are 3.5 distinct responsibilities per role, producing more than 25 responsibilities per person.[16] Each circle gets a certain number of points to spend on recruitment. This type of free-market structure provides a clearing function, where supply for work streams matches demand. They make environmental perturbations explicit by calling the items on a meeting agenda *tensions*: the difference between where they are and where they need to be. There are no performance evaluations. Employees are paid according to the skill badges they earn, such as Java and C++, or certifications like the Certified Information Systems Auditor (CISA). When deciding where to channel their self-organization efforts, they use the simple rule "Go for it if it's safe to try." Like Quantum Leaders, Zappos employees set clear expectations about the global *what* and *why* of the work (rarely *when* and *who* and never *how*) with team members.

Holacracy dramatically reduces the multiple layers of red tape in a bureaucratic organization. Decisions are made by those closest to the situation. In this structure, leadership is distributed among roles, not individuals. The role of a leader changes into that of an empowerer, enabler, facilitator, and connector. Because these circles are formed modularly around a specific work scope, they can be quickly formed or disbanded as the situation dictates.

This type of organizational structure creates functional redundancy, which increases the robustness of an organization in the face of environmental perturbations. At the same time, some practitioners of holacracy report some deleterious effects, mostly coming from the lack of cohesive direction and structure. Self-organization of employees must be bounded by cohesive direction and connection, the topic of the next chapter.

CONCLUSION

Choreographing employees' differentiation in the form of self-organization is a crucial competency for today's leaders, and empowers organizations to quickly adapt to environmental signals in real time. In turn, profuse experiments and iterative adaptations based on self-organization can kick-start radical innovation beyond the critical inflection point. In the process, corporate culture and values should balance the self-organization efforts of employees to prevent chaos. Once sufficiently differentiated based on principles of strong but permeable boundaries, diversity of thoughts, collective intelligence, and self-organization, we can start the work of connecting these differentiated parts.

Chapter 7

STRENGTHENING CONNECTION

O rganizations in pursuit of radical innovation, and the wild success it brings, need to generate higher internal complexity. For maximum internal complexity that leads to radical innovation, both differentiation from self-organization *and* connection that provides cohesion are necessary. The leadership competency we reviewed in chapter 6 was how to maximize differentiation; this chapter is about how to facilitate connection.

We will address how to strengthen and harness the power of interdependence and connection. We will explore the topic of connection in both of our now-familiar contexts:

- From a quantum mechanics point of view, when different particles (remember, everything, including people, is made of particles *and* waves at the same time) vibrate "in phase," combining them creates constructive interference where the amplitude gets greater than what they can create alone. The resulting connection among the members of a team or a community fuels critical momentum for mass adoption of radical innovation. When two or more minds with differentiated perspectives meet, synergy is created with much greater and better output than they can create on their own, at the macro, organizational level.

- From a neuroscientific point of view, connection facilitated by the limbic system prepares the way to unleash the functions of the higher-level brain, the cortex. In addition, secure attachment among team members helps them become more resilient, which they need in the process of profuse iteration, much of which is bound to yield failure, at the micro, individual level.

A MACRO VIEW: INTERDEPENDENCE IN MANAGEMENT TOOLS

In the 1990s and 2000s, the dominant management tools included Six Sigma and total quality management. Many flagship companies, such as GE, Motorola, Toyota, and Samsung implemented these tools to improve their manufacturing efficiency, and they were later adopted by intangible industries, such as financial services. Motorola reported cost savings of over \$16 billion from the Six Sigma initiative[1] and GE over \$4 billion in the span of just four years (1996–1999).[2]

However, Six Sigma has three major limitations relevant to the scope of this book.

Limitation 1: Making efficiency the goal

The first limitation is its assumption that problems can be defined and controlled. The major phases of Six Sigma (define, measure, analyze, optimize, and control) are designed to improve *efficiency*. It assumes problems can be clearly defined and controlled in a stable environment. Today, in the face of so many new and interdependent variables creating too much unpredictability too quickly, the basis of competition has evolved from the industrial era (efficiency and accuracy) to the digital era (adaptability and innovation).

In the VUCA era, effectiveness trumps efficiency: doing the right things (creating an environment conducive to radical innovation) is more important than doing things right (driving cost out, eliminating variances, or improving efficiency). What good does it do to spend years trying to elimi-nate variances in the manufacturing process to produce defect-free products 99.99966 percent of the time—the goal of Six Sigma—if a competitor in someone's garage totally changes the rules of the game overnight, rendering your product obsolete? What good does it do when you spend hundreds of millions of dollars to develop a state-of-the-art supply chain and warehouse management system, complete with robotics and refrigerated trucks, and minimize the delivery cost in the last mile, when Amazon comes out with a drone technology that totally obliterates your business model?

Limitation 2: Eliminating variance

The second limitation is that Six Sigma is designed to *eliminate* variances. Variances are the reality of the VUCA world and cannot be eliminated—it is the essence of the game. A better approach is to *harness* them, as dis-cussed in chapter 1.

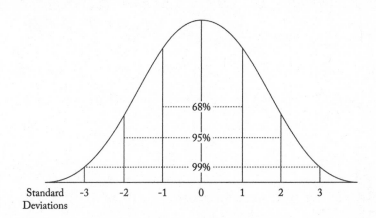

Figure 7.1 *Normal distribution bell curve*

Limitation 3: Assuming variables are independent

The third limitation has to do with Six Sigma's statistical analysis, which uses normal distribution for most of its analyses. One view of statistics is that it tries to use small samples to predict true answers of a phenomenon in the real world. Six Sigma's relentless pursuit of efficiency to drive out variances relies on a statistical analysis method called ANOVA (analysis of variance). The familiar bell shape of a normal (Gaussian) probability distribution used in ANOVA assumes that events are randomly distributed, independent of each other. It also assumes that the variances behave in a homogeneous fashion.

By now, you know that today's VUCA environment is nothing like the assumptions made for the ANOVA analysis. Events are becoming increasingly more *interdependent* on each other, as we reviewed in the Brexit and Ebola cases in chapter 1. From this perspective, Six Sigma deals ineffectively with today's complex business environment. The whole notion of controlling and eliminating variance assumes that variances follow a normal, random distribution, assuming they are independent of each other. Variances rarely follow a normal distribution in a complex world because they are *interdependent*. When this assumption of independence breaks down, normal distribution no longer applies.

COMPLEX SYSTEMS PRODUCE POWER-LAW DISTRIBUTIONS

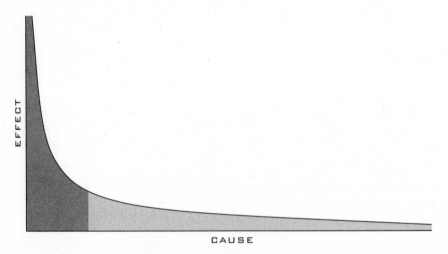

Figure 7.2 Power-Law Distribution

The interdependent nature of today's complex world calls for a different framework to make sense of what we see and to predict answers. When events are interdependent, as is the case in complex systems, we are in the world of power-law distribution,[3] not normal distribution. Power-law distribution is an asymmetric pattern in which the majority of adoption takes place in the beginning, followed by a long tail trail. Most of us are familiar with the Pareto concept, or the 80-20 rule, in which 80 percent of the effect comes from 20 percent of the cause. That is a simple representation of the power-law distribution.

Power-law distribution is a result of interactions among interdependent agents in complex systems, such as neurons, people, cells, organizations, stock markets, animals, plants, weather, and solar flares.

Complex systems influence and are influenced by the environment and each other. The iterations of environmental perturbations and a complex system's adaptations to them create positive-feedback loops that are sensitive to and amplify small changes in the process. Being social animals, we are influenced by each other.

As we reviewed in chapter 6, this is an autocatalytic process analogous to compound interest. Autocatalytic processes can build a huge momentum over time, reach a critical inflection point, and spontaneously turn into a huge social phenomenon. Agents in a complex system are interdependent, which is consistent with the quantum mechanics principle that the act of being observed changes the observation itself (as we reviewed in the double-slit experiment in chapter 2). This also explains why phenomena in which interdependence is not a factor—such as a person's height or body temperature—follow a normal distribution, not a power-law distribution.

The autocatalytic process holds lethal power to fuel and be fueled by interdependence *among the agents* as well as *with the environment* in which they operate. In the process, constructive interference of additive amplitude from connection and interdependence kick-starts critical momentum for mass adoption of radical innovation.

There are many examples of power-law distribution, including the frequency of family names or words in a given language, the sales figures of blockbuster CDs or movies, and the salary of popular athletes, which have all been extensively covered in Laszlo Bock's book, *Work Rules!* This is also what Malcom Gladwell's *The Tipping Point* is about: how a few trends cross a threshold to become a huge social phenomenon. Because we are all connected and interdependently influence each other, the arenas of interest to business and governmental leaders display power-law distribution far more commonly than a normal distribution.

THE MECHANISM BEHIND THE POWER-LAW DISTRIBUTION

When we connect with people, we expand our networks to catalyze the virtuous synergistic process that starts radical innovation. Kleiber's law, discovered by Max Kleiber in the 1930s, provides a mathematical explanation of connection among people that scientists could not explain at the time. It states that an organism's metabolic rate, r (heat produced per day in calories), is the mass of the organism, M, raised to the power of three-quarters ($r = M^{3/4}$). What this means is that the higher the mass of the organism, the less efficient its metabolism. An adult who is twice as large as a child cannot metabolize twice the energy—his body runs more slowly because more energy and resources are used to deliver the nutrients than to process nutrients. This relationship holds true across all organisms with very few exceptions; as life gets bigger, it slows down.[4] This same scaling law applies to plants and trees: the number of branches scales to the radius of the tree trunk.

Geoffrey West is a theoretical physicist who was president of, and still works at, the Santa Fe Institute in California, which is known for cross-disciplinary research on complexity. West extended this model to cities, and found that the infrastructural quantity of the city (the number of gas stations, the surface area of the roads, electric cables, etc.) always scaled to the population of the city raised to approximately the power of four-fifths, similar to the three-quarter power law in the relationship between body mass and metabolic rate found in living organisms. The bigger the city is, the less infrastructure per capita you need, representing economy of scale.

West found something amazing when he looked into creativity and innovation. The same concept applies to cities, but the exponent was about 1.2: since the exponent is greater than one, that means that as cities get bigger, the more innovative they become, displaying increasing returns. Steven Johnson, in his book *Where Good Ideas Come From*, explains that a city ten times larger than its neighbor isn't ten times more innovative; it is *seventeen* times more innovative. A metropolis fifty times bigger than a town is 130 times more innovative.[5] This implies the *rate* of patenting is a scaling function of the urban size: the number of new patents generated by a city of ten million will stand in the same proportion to those generated by a city of one million, as the number of patents generated by a city of one million relative to those created by a city of hundred thousand and so on.[6] The rate of patenting as a function of city size is *scale-free* wherever you look on the spectrum of city size, but the total innovation is disproportionately greater for bigger cities.

Creative synergy gets generated when people with their own networks run into each other and connect. West explains that the structure of this network of relationships could be analogous to the behavior of the networks of blood vessels in the body: living things are sustained by the transport of materials through linear networks that branch to supply all parts of the organism, just as cities are sustained by human networks. But when you double the size of the city, you get *more* than double the amount of both good (e.g., innovation and creativity) and bad (e.g., crime and venereal diseases) socioeconomic quantities, because of the network effect we discussed in chapter 2.

CONNECTION AT THE MACRO LEVEL: ECOSYSTEMS OF NESTED SYSTEMS

Because no man is an island in complex systems, our decisions influence each other's decisions to show power-law distributions. Each life form is delicately balanced within a larger system, interdependent with all others who share the same environment. Cells, neurons, organs, respiratory, circulatory, and digestive systems, our bodies, families, organizations, societies, nations, earth, and the galaxy are all intricately connected nested systems, interdependent with their environments and others who share the same ecosystem.

In chapter 2 we discussed that everything in the universe is made of particles and waves. In mathematical terms, the amplitude of the waves determines the amount of energy they emit: the higher the amplitude, the higher the energy. In this sense, *waves are an energy transport medium*. For this reason, when we bring stress home from work, our loved ones instantaneously and unconsciously pick up on it through the mirror neurons in our brains, and our loved ones get anxious and grumpy in return, which reinforces our negative response to them. The next morning, we bring this negative energy back to work, which our coworkers pick up and take to their families, and so diffuses the ripple effect. Positive energy works the same way. This is why the self-management skills discussed in chapter 4 are such an important foundation and prerequisite for leading others.

An organization is part of a nested system

The word *organization* comes from the Latin word *organum*, meaning "system or instrument." You might wonder how one word could have such seemingly different meanings. An organization is a complex system. It works like an instrument that needs to be tuned to other instruments in the same orchestra. In the beginning of every classical orchestra concert (much to my daughter's boredom, I often try to take her to Utah Symphony concerts), the concertmaster, the leader of the first-violin players, always signals to an oboe, an instrument with a constant pitch, to play the A note as a standard to all the musicians in the orchestra to tune their instruments to the same pitch, no doubt an effort to produce coherence. Members of a system must be tuned to each other to achieve its maximum potential.

In much the same recursive way, an organization's response to change brings about another change in the environment and in people, which induces yet further change in the organization. Organizations are living systems made of people who are complex systems themselves. Members of an organization must be attuned to one other so that an optimal response can be given to signals from another, maximizing the constructive interference of positive energy that builds connection.

Interdependence and corporate responsibilities

This interdependent nature of complex systems highlights the importance of corporate social responsibility and doing business in a sustainable, ethical manner within the context of the system's environment. An organization must be conscious of the environment in which it operates, as well as other subsystems that share the same ecosystem (such as customers, suppliers, and business partners), which in turn influence and are influenced by the organization.

PepsiCo has a corporate strategy consistent with this principle. It's called "Performance with Purpose" and has three cornerstones: human sustainability for how to *nourish* people with healthier, more nutritious snacks; environmental sustainability to *replenish* the earth by conserving water and reducing waste and environmental impact; and talent sustainability to *cherish* and develop its people. Of course, it is focused on delivering financial results as the number one goal, but CEO Indra Nooyi clarifies that PepsiCo wants to achieve its goal "in a way that is sustainable over time and in a manner responsible and responsive to the needs of the community all of us share."[7] Its philosophy is encapsulated in its belief that doing the right thing for society is the right thing for business.

Another example is Overstock's Worldstock Fair Trade. In the thirteen years since it began the program, Overstock, an online outlet megastore, has purchased more than $120 million worth of inventory directly from artisans living in very poor countries. By cutting out the middleman, 60 to 70 percent of the sales price is returned to the artisan, making a huge difference in the quality of the lives of the artisans, their families, and their communities. Overstock has used net profits generated from this program to fund philanthropic causes in several countries. Furthermore, Worldstock sends all items through carbon-neutral shipping, contributing to sustainability of the earth. We thrive when we create symbiosis with the environment, because we are interdependent with all other living organisms who share the same ecosystem with us. Corporate greed without regard to coevolution with others is not only bad for PR and brand image but produces suboptimal results for radical innovation.

THE ROLE OF CORPORATE MISSION, VALUES, AND STRATEGY

What are corporate mission, vision, values, purpose, and strategy supposed to do, other than serve as sitcom raw materials for cynical *Office* episodes, *Dilbert* comic strips, nice catchphrases for the annual report, or decorations for spartan office walls? In an organization with an eye focused on radical innovation, shared vision serves as an ignition switch for passion, which provides boundaries within which people can self-organize, using their creativity. It also forges a sense of connection as members of the same community.

Gary Hamel, a management expert, describes how the basis of loyalty comes from a common purpose, not economic dependency.[8] When you ascribe to the same purpose as your organization, it ignites your passion, which produces better results. Jim Whitehurst, CEO of Red Hat, describes the relationship between a common purpose, passion, and results: a purpose inspires people to do the right things, and passion motivates them to extraordinary performance—to go the extra mile.[9] Some Red Hatters are so passionate about their calling to change the world through open-source technology that they have gotten tattoos of the Shadowman logo.

Creativity *needs constraints* and shared vision. Common purpose provides the constraints within which diverse employees can self-organize in their own way. Tom Spahn, an ex–McKinsey consultant turned president and COO of TIKD, analyzed how the Grateful Dead improvised to create legendary rock music.[10] Each member of the band brought individual expertise in different musical instruments and techniques. They improvised without written music, but the music did not descend into chaos because they were constrained by a few simple rules: one band member would function as the leader; a fixed number of chords would be allowed for each member; and the tune had to have a clear beginning and ending. As the music progressed, each member would constantly explore new frontiers in response to the ever-evolving tunes. Each member coevolved with the harmony created by every other member. The net result was neither rigid monotony nor chaotic cacophony; it was dynamic, vibrant creation, brimming with life and creativity.

Shared vision and purpose provide the global boundaries for local employees' self-organization and creativity, so the organization as a whole can march in the same direction even as individual employees are self-organizing and pursuing their own interests. In addition, shared vision and strategy can activate a state that synchronizes the emotional wavelengths so people feel connected.

HOW ACTIVATING A CORPORATE BRAND PROVIDES CONSTRAINTS NECESSARY FOR UNITY AND CREATIVITY

While corporate vision and strategies provide answers to "what" and values provide a *big picture* perspective of "how," a corporate brand provides the "how" of a perfect platform for a CEO to galvanize an entire organization with specific boundaries and unified direction. Leaders must first clearly define (or communicate internally, if there's already a clear definition) what the brand stands for, and correlate the brand values to corporate values. They must set clear expectations about what is on-brand and off-brand.

Quantum Leaders often reiterate team and company goals, strategies, and brand promise so the team is clear on the direction they need to go. They use the brand promise as a rallying cry, a common goal for everyone to march toward, a glue that connects everyone in the organization. They translate company goals, strategies, and brand promise in practical terms to help their teams in day-to-day decision-making. Most important—and this is where the majority of companies fail—the customer must experience the brand consistently across geography, over time, and spanning the entire customer-experience spectrum at every touch point. When what customers experience is consistent with the brand promise communicated in the form of advertising and marketing, the customer experiences the brand as authentic and feels safe engaging with it. If you are an airline company and your brand promise is "fun," every aspect of your company must consistently communicate fun in all touch points *and* internal departments. The customer experience from this culture is fundamentally different than a company that just plays a funny safety video when the rest of the organization is not consistent with this promise—it feels inauthentic, hence unsafe to do business with. Everyone in the organization must live and breathe the brand promise, or it never becomes clear enough to be translated into a salient, consistent brand experience.

Brand

Strong branding and effective leadership inform each other to lead companies to great success. A brand is a promise. To create a strong, enduring brand that consistently delivers profits and engenders customer loyalty, companies must take the following four steps. The first three are about making a brand promise, and the last, about keeping it. From a neuroscience point of view, to connect with the customer and secure loyalty, keeping the promise must precede making the promise, and requires effective execution of the promise made. This is the RCDC (relevant, credible, differentiated, and consistent) framework for effective corporate brand management, which integrates the three Cs of business strategy (customer, company, and competition) and four Ps of marketing (pricing, promotion, product, and placement).

1. Make a brand promise **relevant** to the core segment it serves. This requires knowing whom the brand is serving and what is important to them. For example, Apple is about innovation. A leader's role here is to align the brand to the core *customer* base who value innovation.

2. Make a **credible** brand promise. If the promise extends too far away from the customer's permission, the brand becomes too diluted and weak. Ferrari doesn't have the customer's permission to extend its core promise of speed to durability. Hence, if they were to advertise durability, the promise is not credible and would weaken the brand. A leader's role here is to align the brand with the *company's* core competency, knowing itself.

3. Make a **differentiated** brand promise. Focus on what you can do better than anybody else. Even if you make a relevant and credible promise, your brand will not endure if everybody makes the same promise. A leader's role here is to align the brand with the firm's competitive advantage to beat *competition*.

4. Implement the brand promise **consistently** across time and geography, throughout all touch points in the entire spectrum of customer experience: from TV commercials to call centers, emails received, the website, services or products experienced, customer service attendants, and even to the news coverage about the company. It must be communicated consistently across the company's pricing decisions, placement (distribution) strategy, product (features and packaging), and promotion (marketing messages).

The first three steps are about creating and communicating the *perception*; the last step is all about *reality*, where the rubber meets the road. This is where you need to actually make the customer experience consistent with the brand promise—evidence of promises kept. This is how consistent culture drives everything you do and say (perception management) and everything customers experience at the touch point (reality management). Window dressing (talking the talk by communicating what sounds good but not walking the walk with what the customer actually experiences) never works because it's not authentic; reality inevitably catches up with you. Inauthentic brands are not safe. They are rejected at the level of the reptilian brain, and hence cannot be moved to the next stage of engagement, connection, facilitated by the limbic system. Because of the far-reaching impact of the customer experience on the brand, this step goes far beyond the chief marketing officer. *Managing the brand is everyone's job.*

What does the HR department have to do with the brand? They are not at a customer touch point. Oh, but they have a huge impact on those who are. The kinds of hiring criteria they set, behavior they incentivize, and people they promote or terminate send clear messages to the organization and set behavioral norms, which customers experience at the touch point. Every point at which the customer experiences the brand is an opportunity to strengthen or weaken the brand. When the entire organization focuses on keeping the brand promise tenaciously, customers experience the brand as authentic and congruent. They see the brand promise in the messages communicated through advertising, experience the brand at actual touch points, and can easily determine whether the company keeps its promise. This is where most brands fail. When the brand promise is kept consistently, the amygdala in the customer's brain registers the brand as safe, allowing the brain to form connection with the brand in the limbic system, a higher place in the brain. This is how brand loyalty is formed: keep the promise first. Using the brand to fuel the vehicle of culture can be very effective.

The brand is a powerful platform that provides the boundaries and constraints that people need to guide their day-to-day self-organizing decisions and express their creativity. These efforts create strong, enduring brands that pay off huge dividends, with profits generated by loyal customers year after year—a source of competitive advantage in the crowded world of brand proliferation.

CONNECTION HARNESSES COMPLEXITY

The power of independence through self-organization and differentiation must be bounded and harnessed or else it will result in chaos. A lack of differentiation leads to rigidity, where uniformity robs vitality, as we have reviewed in chapter 6. But a lack of linkage leads to chaos. Where there is no unifying direction or purpose, forward momentum is brought to a standstill. Creating connection provides the unified direction and cohesion necessary to catalyze the network effect and positive autocatalytic momentum essential for radical innovation. Now we move on to the topic of connection at the micro level, among individuals.

A MICRO VIEW: ATTACHMENT AS THE SCIENTIFIC ACKNOWLEDGEMENT OF CONNECTION

As mammals, we are built for connection. Effective learning and radical innovation cannot take place unless the needs of the lower layers of the brain are met: safety and connection. If an incoming signal is deemed safe, our social engagement system, along with the parasympathetic nervous system, is activated. We approach the source of safety for closer connection. As mentioned earlier, this is when we nurture each other, have sex, digest, touch, and love.

Oxytocin and mirror neurons

The main hormone that activates this attachment state is oxytocin, which gets released during climax in orgasm, hugging, touching, and kissing in both men and women, and during delivery and nursing of babies in women. Oxytocin, often called the love hormone, also increases trust,[11] generosity,[12] and empathy—not only for those with whom we have secure relationships, but even for enemies during war.[13] Oxytocin is also released when we feel empathy and trust for others.

When research participants playing a social game were administered a nasal spray of oxytocin, their trust level and willingness to take social risks with people went up, and the amygdala activation level went down significantly.[14] As you might recall from chapter 3, the amygdala gets activated with fear, which jeopardizes one's sense of safety. Oxytocin has also been found to produce higher levels of self-control in obese men, resulting in lower food intake.[15] Oxytocin, and the resulting sense of a stronger connection among people, improves both self-regulation and a sense of safety, greatly enhancing leaders' ability to provide safety for their team. Oxytocin can soothe the overactive amygdala so we can connect with others more easily. The resulting sense of cohesion and connection improves team performance. A 2010 study of NBA players demonstrated that small, early-season touches, such as fist bumps, high fives, hugs, and team huddles, predicted greater performance for individuals and teams later in the season.[16]

Many other mechanisms maximize our chance of building solid connection with others. Mirror neurons in our brains—an evolutionary design to increase our social interactions with each other, which in turn increase the chances of survival as a species in a world full of predators—help us detect and copy others' emotions and intentions. Using functional magnetic resonance imaging, researchers found a mechanism that enables individuals to detect the intentions and emotions of others. They named it the *mirror neuron system*. The discovery of mirror neurons started when researchers noted that when a macaque monkey picked up a raisin to eat, the same motor region of a second monkey's brain lit up observing the first monkey, detecting the first monkey's intention to eat it.[17] Since then, a similar mirror neuron system has been discovered in humans. These mirror neurons help us unconsciously understand others' intentions and emotions within milliseconds, so we quickly tune in to or mimic them. Attachment—and the mirror neurons that facilitate it—serve an evolutionary purpose. This attunement with one another improves our chances of secure attachment with others, which increases our chances of survival.

Many studies affirm that emotions are contagious. Employees feel emotionally depleted just by watching unpleasant interactions of others at work.[18] One's happiness is related to the happiness of one's friends, one's friends' friends, and one's friends' friends' friends, incorporating people well beyond one's own limited social horizon.[19] Researchers even quantified that each additional happy friend increases a person's probability of being happy by about 9 percent.

From this perspective, "getting on the same wavelength" is not just a figure of speech. A group of people behaves as one organism that can intuitively feel and detect each other's intentions. More relevant to radical innovation, emotional attunement also speeds up communication, because common meaning can be instantly communicated.

Although it has not been tested in empirical studies yet, we can see the quantum mechanics principles in our brains. Brain waves in two different people pulsating synchronously with another creates a condition in which two particles are so inexorably connected that they cannot be described independent of the other, even when separated by a great distance, creating a state called *quantum entanglement*, as discussed in chapter 6. When our neurons fire synchronously with those of other members of the team, we feel a magical sense of connection, which enables us to achieve seemingly impossible feats with almost instant and intuitive communication, which increases the speed and accuracy of execution.

In his book *Team of Teams*, General Stanley McChrystal describes one such feat by the team of Navy SEALs who rescued Captain Richard Phillips and his crew from Somalian pirates. The rescue plan required three perfectly placed shots delivered in unison to rescue the crew without jeopardizing their safety. The sniper waited for hours until a pirate got up to take a breath of fresh air. Then, aiming at targets on a bobbing lifeboat seventy-five feet away, three SEAL snipers simultaneously shot each of the three pirates in the head, killing them instantly. This kind of unison requires almost instantaneous coordination over a fraction of a second. General McChrystal identified the source of this coordination: "SEAL teams accomplish remarkable feats not simply because of the individual qualifications of their members but because those members coalesce into a single organism"[20]—a state the SEALs forge methodically and deliberately.

How the electromagnetic energy of the heart produces connection

Researchers at the HeartMath Institute studied the impact of the human heart on performance and attachment. They posit that the human heart produces a significant electromagnetic field. Each contraction is due to the coordinated depolarization of myocytes, which produce a flow of electric current.[21] The magnetic field extends three to four feet outside the body. Researchers found that an exchange of electromagnetic energy produced by the heart occurs when people touch, or even are in proximity.[22] They found that one's electrocardiogram (ECG) signal is registered in another person's electroencephalogram (EEG), and elsewhere on the other person's body, which changes the other person's ECG. This electromagnetic energy creates coherent resonance with another—the constructive interference we discussed in chapters 2 and 6. When our hearts beat on the same wavelength and in the same coherent resonance pattern, we sense a connection in which we feel felt and seen by each other. Although the science behind their research is still nascent, it is an area worthy of further examination.

Other studies also show just how interdependent we are on each other. A 1971 study published in the journal *Nature* explained the McClintock effect: that menstrual cycles of female college dormitory residents tend to synchronize through pheromonal mechanisms.[23] The same dynamics apply to attachment among members in organizations. No, it doesn't mean all the female employees will have their periods on the same day! It just means that when they are inexorably connected with each other with bonds of trust and affection, their hearts and minds can work synchronously to create an extraordinary result. This is the type of connection the Navy SEALs had with each other when they rescued Captain Phillips by taking three simultaneous shots in a split second.

The Maharishi effect: The power of collective consciousness

John Davies from the University of Maryland and Charles Alexander from the Maharishi University of Management set out to test their hypothesis that if the square root of 1 percent of a local population gather to practice Transcendental Meditation (TM), it would significantly reduce violence in that locale. TM was developed by Maharishi Mahesh Yogi, a spiritual leader from India, whose practitioners believe that all occurrences of violent conflict arise from the accumulation of collective stress. TM is an "effortless procedure for allowing the excitations of the mind to settle down until the least excited state of mind is reached . . . a state of inner wakefulness with no object of thought or perception."[24]

Davies and Alexander studied the twenty-seven-month period from 1983 through 1985 during which TM practitioners meditated together in a collective coherent manner in a series of seven assemblies, including a war-ridden Israel-Lebanon area; Fairfield, Iowa; Yugoslavia; the Hague, in the Netherlands; and Washington, DC. They recorded daily data derived from nine international and regional news sources during these periods. Levels of conflict, cooperation, and casualties were scored. What they found was shocking: a 71 percent reduction in war fatalities, 68 percent reduction in war injuries, 66 percent increase in cooperation, and 48 percent reduction in conflict during the assemblies.[25] Researchers throughout the world replicated the study and produced similar results in hundreds of studies, and named this astounding phenomenon "the Maharishi effect."

What the Maharishi effect shows is how powerfully coherent collective consciousness can change the world in a positive way. When we are connected, we can achieve something extraordinary, far beyond what each of us can do alone. We are social beings, and nature has built many features into our brain structure and hearts to facilitate connection with each other. I summarize this observation on attachment in close relationships in an aphorism: "God didn't give us fangs or claws but a need for attachment and mirror neurons." As a species without fangs or claws, interdependence and connection is crucial to our survival. We are built for deep connection with each other and with the environment around us—not from a tree-hugging, New Agey perspective but from a scientific perspective.

Benefits of secure attachment

As we have reviewed all the mechanisms built in us, which facilitate connection or attachment among us, what are the benefits of secure attachment, other than a catalyst for radical innovation? There are many benefits to secure attachment, including healthy physical, emotional, intellectual, and social development. There is a classic procedure studied by every student in the mental health field: a strange situation devised by Mary Ainsworth in 1969 to categorize types of human attachment.[26] In this scenario, the infant and parent enter the room equipped with some toys. A short while later, a stranger enters the room, talks to the parent and the infant, and the parent conspicuously leaves the room. Ainsworth and colleagues identified four attachment patterns based on how the infant behaves when the parent returns. The first one is a secure attachment pattern and the other three insecure attachment patterns:

- Secure attachment: A child with secure attachment to its mother will explore and play freely while the caregiver is present, using her as a "secure base" from which to explore. The child will engage with the stranger when the caregiver is present and will be visibly upset when the caregiver departs. Those toddlers in secure attachment with their parents would quickly return to exploring after having been left by their parents. And they are happy to see the caregiver on his or her return and resume play and exploration after reuniting. The child feels confident that the caregiver is available, responsive to their attachment needs, and engaged in communications. The implication here is that strong connection with people we care about provides a secure basis for exploration and learning. A hallmark of secure attachment is freshness of response and freedom from prescribed and proscribed behaviors, as differentiated individuals.[27] In essence, secure attachment and healthy differentiation mutually reinforce each other as necessary and sufficient conditions for happiness.

- Insecure attachment—avoidant: A child shows no separation distress from his or her parent and ignores or avoids the parent upon return. The child won't engage in play or exploration regardless of who is present. These symptoms are a result of repeated past interactions where the child came to believe his or her needs won't be met and communication of needs has no influence on the caregiver.

- Insecure attachment—ambivalent: A child shows this pattern of insecure attachment when he or she is clingy or difficult to comfort even before the parent's departure and after return. It is a response to unpredictably responsive caregiving. The displays of anger or helplessness toward the caregiver on reunion can be regarded as a conditional strategy for maintaining the availability of the caregiver by preemptively taking control of the interaction.[28]

- Insecure attachment—disorganized: If the behavior of the child is not coordinated in a consistent way, perhaps alternating between clinging and ignoring (approaching and distancing), it indicates a disruption or flooding of the attachment system, perhaps activated by fear, hopelessness, or desperation.[29]

In essence, when we feel safe and a secure connection with each other, our parasympathetic nervous systems kick in, by which our immune systems get a boost, and endorphins that make us feel pleasure and satisfaction get released. When endorphins lock into the opioid receptors, they are immediately broken down by enzymes, unlike what happens when dopamine is released. As a result, we don't develop dependence. We feel happy and content with secure attachment.

Secure attachment also increases resilience to help us deal with vicissitudes in life. Jim Coan from the University of Virginia and his colleagues conducted a clever experiment showing just how important secure attachment is in modulating threat and physical pain. Wives underwent a stressful situation by having electrodes tied to their ankles, which shocked them occasionally.[30] Before the shock was administered, they were given one of two signals: (1) a safety signal that they would not be shocked or (2) a threat signal that there was a 20 percent chance that they would be shocked. During the experiment, the women were permitted to hold a stranger's hand, their husband's hand, or nobody's hand. The researchers monitored their brain firing patterns under both situations with functional magnetic resonance imaging (fMRI).

What they discovered is that hand-holding reduced both the perception of threat and pain. The wives holding the hands of their husbands in highly satisfied marriages reported the least amount of pain perception and threat as shown on fMRI activations of their brains. Interestingly, for those women in less happy marriages, the threat and pain levels were higher when holding the husband's hand than holding a stranger's hand. The upshot is that those women felt safer with a stranger than with a husband who was not a secure attachment figure. As we can see from this experiment, secure attachment, which activates our social engagement system, can be a powerful mechanism to modulate fear and can even reduce the intensity of pain one feels, making us more resilient.

Resilience is important for radical innovation because radical innovation requires profuse experimentation, which means a lot of our trials will result in error and failure. Resilience from secure attachment with our teammates and our bosses provides a secure base for us to keep venturing out, trying the untested, and exploring new opportunities, in the face of repeated failures, without the fear of punishment and rejection. The pain of rejection is so great that it actually elicits physical pain. Naomi Eisenberger from UCLA and her colleagues organized an online game of catch with two other players while in the fMRI brain scanner.[31] When the two throw the ball only to each other excluding the study subject, the subject showed an increased level of activity in the same regions of the brain that would be activated in response to physical pain. Our brains perceive a broken heart and a physical pain just the same.

Here is a radical concept: it is imperative for leaders to provide secure attachment to their team members; yes, I am saying you need to *love* them! If I may get on my soapbox for a minute (I have resisted doing so throughout much of this book, so bear with me), one of the most egregious errors modern organizations have made is eliminating all elements of emotions at the workplace, turning us into sterile facades. Sure, I see why companies, facing the threat of astronomical damages in lawsuits, wanted to reduce liability as much as possible. What was your reaction when I said we need to bring more emotions at work and love the people we work with? Something like, "Yikes—emotions at work?!" Yes, emotions at work can be messy, but they are also the raw materials that create connection and attachment. You simply cannot connect with a robot. Without emotions, we cannot feel connected and close. Instead of eliminating emotions at work, as leaders you need to actually increase emotions and love those who work for you.

We spend more time with our colleagues at work than with our families. If you pretend to love the team you lead only because you want to maximize your chances of radical innovation or get more results out of them, you will fail because your team will pick up on your lack of sincerity (remember the mirror neurons that pick up on subliminal signals?). Love them first and results will follow. But loving them doesn't mean you let bad performance or laziness slide. You must care about them enough to find out what's really happening, help them improve, get reassigned, or find another opportunity in some cases. *Loving them means helping them reach their maximum potential.* And you must love them more than your pride, political ramifications, or your own advancement.

This perspective highlights the dangers of turnover: if you recall, my research quantified the impact of turnover intent difference between a Quantum Leader and a Mechanistic Leader as 37 percent, which translates into a $448 million hit to operating expenses and an additional $8.7 billion in topline sales to make up for the difference for a typical Fortune 500 company. These numbers don't even include the hidden cost of the time and energy we have to spend to build trust, upon which we can provide safety and secure connection for them, before we fully tap into their medial prefrontal cortices' power to produce radical innovation. It takes time to build trust and losing people means you need to start the trust-building process over with new people. Reducing turnover and maintaining safe and secure relationships is crucial for radical innovation.

How Quantum Leaders harness connection and interdependence

Quantum Leaders facilitate connection and interdependence by loving the people in their teams, modeling transparent communication, increasing the speed of communication, often reiterating and reinforcing the direction they are headed as a company, and facilitating a sense of belonging and community.

Increase speed—increase transparency

Quantum Leaders remove friction in communication and increase transparency by sharing as much information as possible. Transparency is crucial because it increases the speed of communication. Also, everyone on the team needs to know what those in their network are doing, so they can recalibrate their own actions based on others' feedback. Without transparent communication and feedback among members of the same network, self-organization is impossible; people don't know what they need to adapt to.

Many tech giants in Silicon Valley practice this principle with weekly all-hands meetings where all employees call in or attend in person all over the world, a bona fide balkable move in a traditional company with tens of thousands of employees. These meetings include everyone. Typically, participants review OKRs (objectives and key results, metrics to gauge how the company is doing), updates on important initiatives such as an organizational change program, celebrate big wins from customers, address major issues (e.g., issues in M&A or PR issues like sexual harassment lawsuits involving company executives). And they take questions from the audience, remote or present. There are ways to make this a lot more manageable. For example, Google's employees vote on the questions in queue raised by others so the questions with more votes rise to the top. Invariably, these meetings involve food for those attending in person and some element of fun, against all odds in reviewing charts and numbers. For those sticks-in-the-mud who are not fully converted to the merits of these all-hands meetings, the benefits of direct communication and transparency of information with no friction or distortion from bureaucratic layers far outweigh the opportunity cost of the employee time and real cost of providing the communication platform.

Reiterated direction

Quantum Leaders reiterate the organization's goals, strategy, and direction frequently. When we are caught in our self-organized cycles, it's easy to get off strategy or off brand. Frequently repeating the direction we need to head grounds us and provides cohesion.

Sense of belonging

Quantum Leaders build team cohesion with songs, chants, symbols, colors, or logos that uniquely identify the team. They create an environment in which members feel a strong sense of connection—like they "have each other's backs." Interdependent, connected team members initiate the momentum necessary for mass adoption of a radical innovation, create an advantage to sustain the momentum, and satisfy an evolutionary need to unleash our brains' full capacity to learn.

At the same time, Quantum Leaders can also *dismantle* the power of interdependence that builds momentum for something hugely disruptive. For example, if you are the director of planning for a large metropolitan city faced with high crime rates among the homeless, breaking up the homeless population into smaller units and distributing them throughout the city would stifle the power of interdependence that produces the negative social phenomenon of crimes. This is exactly what Salt Lake City is planning on doing—under the direction of Mayor Jackie Biskupski, the city plans to break up a big homeless shelter into smaller neighborhood centers, to be completed in 2019.

Mindful of the interdependent nature of complex systems, when solving a problem, instead of addressing the symptoms manifested in one side of the system, Quantum Leaders try to identify the recursive pattern of interdependent parts. They are on the lookout for the recursive autocatalytic pattern, and approach the problem from a systems perspective—the more A happens, the more B happens, which results in more of A—because the amplifying mechanism in the autocatalytic process can produce a huge phenomenon that can quickly get out of control.

For example, huge amounts of greenhouse gases (carbon dioxide, methane, and nitrous oxide) are resulting in global warming. Over 90 percent of the excess heat trapped by greenhouse gases is absorbed by the sea, which then expands because of the higher temperature of these gases. The resulting rise in the sea level is breaking up large masses of glaciers in Antarctica and Greenland. Without the white glacier to reflect the sunlight, the sun is absorbed by the darker-colored ocean, and the temperature of the sea rises even more, creating a (dangerous) autocatalytic situation we discussed in chapter 6. The oceans and plankton cannot absorb as much carbon dioxide as the water temperature rises, trapping more greenhouse gases in the atmosphere. The higher carbon dioxide concentration level produces higher temperature, which in turn produces more carbon dioxide in a vicious recursive autocatalytic cycle, which could spiral out of control once it hits the inflection point (and no, global warming is not a hoax invented by the Chinese!). Quantum Leaders understand that to address this issue, the whole system needs to be addressed, not just a symptom of the issue.

CONCLUSION

To increase today's level of complexity and harness the complex nature of the new business environment, maximizing an organization's capacity for radical innovation, Quantum Leaders must strengthen interdependence and connection among the members of the organization. Organizations benefit from analyzing situations with the power-law distribution and paying attention to the interdependent nature of an organization as part of coevolving nested complex systems. They also need to provide boundaries and constraints to guide the self-organization of individual members, using corporate shared values, mission, and brand promise.

The preceding competencies of self-management, safety, differentiation, and connection all build up toward the next competency: learning.

Chapter 8

FACILITATING LEARNING: THE PINNACLE OF LEADERSHIP COMPETENCIES

Learning is the pinnacle of leadership competencies, and directly contributes to radical innovation. All the previously discussed competencies of self-management, providing safety, creating differentiation, and strengthening connection prepare you to achieve this competency. Radical innovation is a serendipitous by-product of profuse fearless experimentation and learning that simply does not come about in an atmosphere where people don't feel safe or connected. On the foundation of safety and connection, correcting errors in reading signals from the environment and adapting accordingly (my definition of learning) powers good decisions and is a sufficient and necessary condition for radical innovation.

THE SECOND LAW OF
THERMODYNAMICS

Left unattended, atoms inherently tend to become randomized, disordered, decayed, and disorganized: dead animals rot, iron rusts, hot water cools, houses lapse into chaos (those of you with children know what I am talking about!). Iron rusts when iron atoms react with oxygen. Bodies rot when bacteria break down barriers among and within proteins, carbohydrates, lipids, nucleic acids, and bones. The concept of entropy was first discussed by Robert Clausius in 1850. Ludwig Boltzmann then formalized the theory after a few iterations into what is recognized today as the second law of thermodynamics: entropy in a closed system increases over time if left unattended, and you always end up with less energy at the end of a physical process than what you started with. This is why some of the early physicists reached the erroneous conclusion that the universe is headed toward a catastrophic "heat bath" where everything will be all mixed up.

But a peculiar phenomenon is noted in nature. How does spontaneous order arise from disorder, as we saw in the termite colony? How has the human species not fallen victim to this law, avoiding the seemingly inevitable fate of decay and disorder? Why didn't we disappear eons ago as just another species in a chapter of evolutionary history? Instead, our species reigns supreme in the earth's food chain, and we create higher order and internal complexity as time goes by. Why does the second law of thermodynamics (the law of entropy) not seem to apply to us?

Two conditions are necessary for this law of entropy to work: "left unattended" and "in a closed system." Being left unattended means no external intervention. Work can reverse the process from decay into order at the local level. Applied to organizations, leaders must (1) create an open system and (2) curate learning interactions with an environment (work) by correctly reading signals from the environment and making necessary adaptations. In other words, learning reverses the process of decay or disorganization.

This is the definition of learning I have repeated throughout this book: correcting errors in reading signals from the environment and adapting accordingly. In this sense, learning is not a passive transfer of knowledge. Learning is a two-step process: it must involve correcting errors in reading the signals *and* adapting to them—a change in behavior. When it comes to complex adaptive systems like humans and organizations, the ability to learn is vital to avoid the inherent tendency for decay and disorder. Indeed, learning and coevolving with the environment is what enables complex adaptive systems to produce spontaneous order at the global level out of seeming chaos at the local level. Learning is the defining feature of complex adaptive systems compared to all other simpler systems and other complex systems found in nature. Our superior capacity for learning is what has enabled us to become the most dominant species in the food chain, despite our physical inferiority.

Leaders must be able to learn effectively because reading signals correctly enables them to make the best decisions when they have to act on imperfect information. As more information becomes available, effective learners correct prior beliefs. Therefore, learning requires remembering previous information, processing incoming signals based on prior information, and using the results to adapt to the situation. This type of adaptive learning requires constant profuse iterative experimentation, incorporating the experiment's results back into the next iteration of the experiment, creating a positive feedback loop. The process of rapid iterative experimentation builds an autocatalytic momentum that can produce a spontaneous phase transition to a huge social phenomenon or radical innovation.

There are five requirements of learning:

1. Creating knowledge from profuse trial and error
2. Storing gained knowledge
3. Updating prior knowledge in response to feedback from the environment
4. Using heuristics (simple rules) for rapid processing
5. Adapting behaviors through effective feedback

We'll look at each of these requirements to see how Quantum Leaders incorporate each step to optimally facilitate learning in themselves and their organization.

CREATING KNOWLEDGE FROM PROFUSE EXPERIMENTATION AND ADAPTATION

Our first requirement for learning in organizations deals with the importance of profuse experimentation. We must create a culture of accepting failure as an essential ingredient to produce radical innovation.

Geology sheds some light

In the late 1970s Italian theoretical physicist Roberto Benzi was baffled by the recurrent pattern of ice ages, which have occurred every one hundred thousand years in the earth's geological history. Then he came across fifty-year-old research by Serbian geophysicist and astronomer Milutin Milanković, who identified several of earth's cycles, including the earth's axial tilt every 41,000 years, orbital eccentricity every 96,000 and 413,000 years, and axial precession every 26,000 years. Milanković theorized that these variations resulted in large variations in climatic patterns, but his theory still didn't explain the hundred-thousand-year cycle of ice ages.

After calculating countless variables to explain this phenomenon, Benzi finally identified the mechanism: stochastic (noise) resonance. When the random white noise of short-term solar radiation coincided with the earth's very small periodic orbital variations (0.1 percent of the solar constant), it produced a constructive interference of huge peaks in climate change, resulting in periodically recurrent ice ages.[1] This is similar to the mechanism behind how white noise produces a clearer sound, as reviewed in chapter 6, and the constructive interference we reviewed in chapter 2. This model perfectly explained the hundred-thousand-year pattern mathematically.

Three things are noteworthy from Benzi's seminal paper:

1. The variation in earth's orbital pattern alone is unable to produce the major peaks, nor can the white noise of solar radiation; it takes both of them at the same time to amplify the effect and produce major peaks in climate change.
2. Very small changes in the earth's orbital pattern can produce a very large change in the climate.

3. If the noise is too weak or too strong, it doesn't produce the periodic change in insolation.

Stochastic resonance is analogous to the random perturbations or variations that are necessary for radical innovation. Radical innovations are marked by the exponential growth of fluctuations (errors, failures, or diversities). Radical innovation *requires* random, moderately sized perturbations and noise, as we covered with the white noise concept in chapter 6 on differentiation. These random perturbations could include unexpected challenges from the environment, failures in our efforts, and sparks of diversity of thoughts among our team members. Each iteration in profuse experimentation adds momentum toward radical innovation. What this means for effective leadership promoting radical innovation is the importance of

1. providing an environment where employees can freely experiment and serendipitously come up with their own ideas (self-organization);
2. facilitating moderate (not too hard or too easy) challenges they need to work through; and
3. tolerating—indeed, embracing—failures as a necessary input to radical innovation and providing a safe, fast way to fail.

Recognizing this important role of moderate errors and challenges in innovation and evolution, Steven Johnson, in *Where Good Ideas Come From*, identified Darwin's greatest error as his failure to understand the protean force of error in the DNA replication process.[2] In a similar context, Johnson also explained that moderately intense ocean waves are necessary for a thriving coral reef colony. The waves must be strong enough to stir up the microorganisms at the bottom of the sea for fish and corals to feed on, but not so strong as to destroy the delicate coral structure. Again, providing a moderate level of challenge for teams creates an ideal environment in which radical innovation can be spawned. Creating knowledge from profuse experimentation and adaptation is a fundamental building block in learning.

STORING KNOWLEDGE

The second requirement of learning is a key characteristic of complex adaptive systems: their ability to store knowledge and utilize accumulated experience and learning in the present. Our capacity to store information allows us to accumulate experience about the kinds of feedback that improve our odds of survival and facilitate radical innovation. The ability to conserve information based on past experiences is vital. Let's say you hear a rustle in the bush as you are taking a walk in a forest, which turns out to be a cougar that attacks you. Remember the definition of insanity: doing the same thing and expecting different results. You would be perpetuating Bill Murray's *Groundhog Day* insanity if every time you hear a rustle in the bush you (1) wonder what that might be, (2) turn around and open up the bush to check it out, (3) discover the two staring eyes of a giant cougar, and (4) turn around and run for your life while it effortlessly pounces to feast upon you.

We learn from the initial experience and run when we hear the rustle, bypassing all the intermediate steps because our neurons have organized themselves to store all pertinent information about the situation in the same neural network—a rustle, a forest, a pine smell, a large cat, and a threat to your life—and created an associative conditioned memory. Contrary to our moms' beliefs about us (remember the familiar refrain: "If I said it once, I said it a thousand times before!"), we do learn, and our learning does stick, because of our ability to conserve information as complex adaptive systems. This stored knowledge, however, must be constantly updated as new information emerges.

UPDATING PRIOR KNOWLEDGE IN RESPONSE TO FEEDBACK FROM THE ENVIRONMENT

Let's examine the third component of learning: using feedback to update what we know. In fact, updating prior knowledge is *un*learning what you know (or what you thought you knew) to be true. To illustrate this process, we'll compare the two major approaches in the field of statistics: frequentist and Bayesian.

The frequentist approach is most familiar. It calculates the likelihood of an event, using the information available at that time, given a level of error we can tolerate. Let's say that the European Central Bank (ECB) mints a new coin in celebration of Pope Francis's inauguration. But the ECB uses da Vinci's newly discovered secret method to use more silver on the heads without making it appear semi-3D, so the coin looks as though it is weighted fairly when the heads actually weigh more. To figure out if the coin is fair or not, the frequentist would first determine the level of confidence and the tolerable margin of error to determine the number of times the coin would be tossed. With a confidence level of 95 percent, the frequentist might say, "If I repeatedly toss the coin so many times, in 95 percent of these cases, the confidence interval will contain the true value."

The Bayesian approach is somewhat counterintuitive and not as commonly practiced. Its name originates from Thomas Bayes (1701–61) who instituted an inference method that updates probability for a hypothesis as more information becomes available. It uses the prior knowledge that most coins are fairly weighted, since this particular coin doesn't appear to provide any reason for us to believe it's not fair, and have a fifty-fifty chance of falling on either heads or tails. After each coin toss, a Bayesian statistician would update prior knowledge with the result of each new coin toss, asking the question, "Given this result, to what degree do I believe that this coin is fair?" This is the basis of Bayesian thinking: *Given this new knowledge, how do I need to adjust my prior thinking?* A Bayesian constantly updates prior beliefs as new information is absorbed.

What does that tell us about effective leadership in the VUCA era? Let's illustrate this point with an example. Say you're vice president of sales for a large logistics software company. While accompanying reps on customer calls, you hear a customer talk about a potential competitor as a viable, cheaper alternative to your solution. What is the probability that this new competitor is a threat worthy of your attention? To take a Bayesian approach to this problem, we need three pieces of information:

A. Prior probability. What is the probability you would have assigned to a new entrant being a credible threat *before* you heard about it from a customer? Let's say you define a credible threat as taking more than 5 percent of market share within a year. You have no statistics specific to your company, but you figure that, because of the high entry barriers, a new entrant turns out to be a credible threat one out of ten times in your industry. So, we will use 10 percent for the prior probability.

B. Conditional probability. Assuming it is a credible threat, what is the probability that you hear about a potential competitor? Let's say from past experience, 50 percent of the time.

C. False-positive probability. What is the probability that you hear about the potential competitor and it is NOT a credible threat? What are some other reasons why it could be happening, other than your assumption that it is a credible threat? It could be that the customer is neighbors with an executive of the competitor, and he is trying to feed you bogus information about their products to distract your management focus. Or your customer volunteers on a nonprofit committee that solicits donations from companies to fight global warming, and he is trying to get your pledge by citing your competitor as another company pledging donations. Pretty far-fetched, but viable nonetheless. Let's assign 5 percent probability that you heard about the potential competitor but they do not represent a credible threat.

With these three pieces of information, we can now figure out D, the posterior probability. This is what we want to know—the probability that the competitor is a credible threat, given these observations. We can figure out the probability of the new entrant being a credible threat by incorporating the new information that you heard about using Bayes' theorem:

$$AB / (AB + C(1 - A)) = D$$

$$(.1 \times .5) / (.1 \times .5 + .05 \times (1 - .1)) = 53\%$$

You're about half confident that the new entrant is a credible threat.

Now, let's say next week you hear about this competitor again from a *different* customer. Last time, you gauged prior probability at 10 percent, but now you can use your updated prior probability (53 percent) to figure out the new posterior probability using the same formula:

$$(.53 \times .5) / (.53 \times .5 + .05 \times (1 - .53)) = 92\%$$

Now you're almost positive that the new entrant is a credible threat. This is the power of Bayesian inference.

Bayes' theorem provides a framework to think more methodically when new evidence emerges. You are less likely to get worked up by your emotions, causing a false positive, or dismiss a credible signal of threat, resulting in a false negative. Taking feedback from the environment and rapidly adapting to new situations is an important skill for leaders who face a deluge of new information coming at them at an increasingly faster speed with unpredictable interdependent consequences—the essence of complexity.

The Bayesian approach also alerts us when we need to revise the heuristics with which to understand a phenomenon and guide our behavior and is a lot more effective in today's constantly changing VUCA world than the static frequentist approach. This is the very definition of learning: correcting errors in reading signals from the environment and adapting accordingly. Updating prior knowledge requires openness and flexibility in thinking and incorporating signals from the environment.

Unlearning

Although information conservation is critical to maximize chances of survival when it comes to life-threatening situations, it can also represent a liability to us as leaders. Our current information processing is constrained by our past experiences, which means we are not completely neutral or open to new possibilities or ideas. This limitation becomes a huge liability for leaders in these VUCA times, when unpredictability dominates. To overcome this limitation, *Quantum Leaders ask questions designed to expand the team's spectrum of prior experiences.* Many leaders get stressed that they don't know all the answers, but providing answers as an expert is *not* one of the effective leadership competencies in the VUCA era. Mechanistic Leaders feel insecure and threatened when their team members know more than they do. On the other hand, Quantum Leaders ask the right questions to enable others to *un*learn what has become automatic for them, and be open to finding answers in unconventional places. The leader's job is not to provide answers, but to ask the right questions to help others unlearn and expand their horizon of thinking.

Framing questions in a new light

Max Planck, the Nobel Prize–winning pioneer of quantum physics, said, "When you change the way you look at things, the things you look at change."[3] This view is consistent with the quantum principle of interdependence between the observer and the observed in the double-slit experiment: the observer is part of the observation, and hence changes the observation.

In the words of paleontologists Niles Eldredge and Stephen Jay Gould, "Theory dictates what one sees . . . The expectations of theory color perception to such a degree that new notions seldom arise from the facts collected under the influence of old pictures of the world."[4] This is why it is so important to frame a new theory, propose a new way of looking at things, and pose questions from outside the box. The tricky but important part of leadership is asking questions that open possibilities in all directions, instead of narrowing avenues of exploration because they seem improbable. *What one determines to be improbable is a product of one's life experiences*, which are different for each individual. As a leader, you must see that your truth might not be *the* absolute truth, only your version of the truth.

To help you practice the curiosity and nonjudgmental exploration that promotes learning, it's helpful to ask the following questions:

- Alternatives: When is this not true? (How else can I interpret what I am seeing? What else could be happening other than my automatic assumption?)
- Counterfactuals: What would make it not true? (What evidence supports the opposite conclusion?)

Ask questions out of curiosity, instead of being judgmental

In facilitating learning, being curious about what is really happening is a powerful alternative to prescribing, telling, or fixing. *Your curiosity as a leader can guide where your team members look for answers because the question is part of the answer.* Approaching others with curiosity rather than judgment or criticism also provides safety. People are fully capable of coming up with solutions themselves, as evidenced by the Pygmalion effect. In a study conducted by Robert Rosenthal and Lenore Jacobson, teachers were given the names of a random selection of 20 percent of their students and were told those students were "intellectual bloomers." These randomly chosen students showed superior academic performance at the end of the school year. The researchers concluded that teacher expectations can influence student achievement.[5] As a leader, when you believe in your team members, they will rise to your expectations. When you use curiosity, you can help others use curiosity to explore the situation and come up with their own solutions.

Challenge each other's thinking

All the hard work you have put in for self-management, providing safety for your team, creating differentiation, and strengthening connection shines through when you challenge each other's thoughts, which is essential to make the best decision possible. When you don't have safety and connection in your team, your team members won't challenge your or each other's thinking. They will either retreat to passive aggression (agreeing in front of you but not implementing the decisions), waste precious time, disengage, or, worst of all, sabotage the decision.

There are two familiar stories about aircraft that illustrate how crucial it is to create environments in which it is safe to question one another.

On January 28, 1986, the space shuttle *Challenger* exploded seventy-three seconds after liftoff. Seven crew members were on board, never to return to their families when the shuttle shattered in the sky. The temperature was too cold (in the lower twenties Fahrenheit) for the O-ring, which required a minimum temperature of fifty degrees Fahrenheit to function properly. The O-ring failed to expand in the solid rocket booster to form a seal critical to preventing pressurized burning gas from reaching the hardware and external fuel tank. Further investigation revealed that multiple conditions led to the disastrous failure:

- "Go fever" was palpable; NASA engineers were under enormous pressure to launch the space shuttle.
- Christa McAuliffe, the first civilian member of a space mission team, was a schoolteacher who would have conducted live educational broadcasts from the shuttle and transmitted them to classrooms throughout the world. She had created huge public interest.

- The public disappointment from the previous six failed launches pressured NASA managers to favor launching and to ignore warning signs earlier that morning that it was too cold to launch.
- Within NASA, managers were trying to satisfy several conflicting goals: the government's expectation to be financially self-sustaining, the scientific community's specific mission requirements, and the global community's unity in friendship.
- The pressure around cost also created a culture to cut corners and deliver a quick result, bypassing proper germination time for development before operationalizing the shuttle.
- Similarly, the managers at Morton Thiokol, the subcontractor of the project, excluded its engineers from the conference call with NASA, trying to quiet their concerns about the low temperature. They were afraid of losing the NASA contract after so many delays.

All these factors prevented decision makers at NASA from voicing dissenting opinions to launching the shuttle. They silenced the engineers in both organizations from weighing in on the final decision.

There were many opportunities that could have prevented this tragic outcome, but this situation, in which signals from the environment couldn't be accurately read—a learning failure—led to the disastrous result. This incident serves as a case example of *groupthink*, a situation in which people make bad decisions because of the pressure to conform—a shining example of what *not* to do, taught in almost every MBA curriculum.

Let's fast forward to 2009 to look at another aircraft incident that happened in a different culture. On January 15, 2009, US Airways flight 1549 took off from LaGuardia. Shortly after takeoff, it struck a large flock of birds, which disabled both engines. Captain Chesley "Sully" Sullenberger worked with his copilot and the crew to reach the decision quickly to land the aircraft on the Hudson river, saving all 155 lives on board. Every second counted during the crucial moments after the impact. Sully considered returning to LaGuardia and landing in Teterboro in New Jersey but realized he would not have enough time to safely land the plane at either location. In a split-second decision, they decided to land on the Hudson. All the conditions spelled disaster—so what made the outcome different from the *Challenger* incident?

A subsequent public hearing by the National Transportation Safety Board attributed the successful decision to crew resource management. According to the NTSB:

> *The captain indicated that, because of time constraints, they could not discuss every part of the decision process. Therefore, they had to listen to and observe each other. The captain stated they did not have time to consult all of the written guidance or complete the appropriate checklist. So he and the first officer had to work almost intuitively in a close-knit fashion. For example, the captain stated that when he called for the QRH [Quick Reference Handbook, an aviation manual], about seventeen seconds after the bird strike, the first officer already had the checklist out.*[6]

Leaders must invest time and energy to build safety and create connection with their teams so they can be intuitively in sync with each other and *challenge each other to make the best decision possible.* This incident, dubbed the Miracle on the Hudson, now serves as a case example of teamwork and collaboration in almost every aviation safety training course.

Being open to new ideas and information

Being open to new ideas means being ready to be persuaded and willing to change your prior set of beliefs. Such openness enables learning. When a team member throws out an idea, before immediately deciding it is far-fetched or irrational, ask, and encourage others to ask, the following questions while debating and clarifying your ideas:

1. *What would have to be true for this idea to be true?* This question forces you to examine your prior beliefs. Remember, we all interpret incoming perceptions based on our brains' simple rules of signal processing, which are shaped by our cumulative life experiences. A scenario might be unfamiliar to us, but *unfamiliar* doesn't mean improbable. As Arthur Conan Doyle said, "Once you eliminate the impossible, whatever remains, no matter how improbable, must be the truth."[7] If an idea measures up to the conditions thrown at it, no matter how unfamiliar it might seem to you, it is probable.

2. *How complete is our set of prior beliefs?* In a similar vein, asking this question to your team helps them look beyond what *seems* logical, which is constrained by their past experiences, and identify if there are any holes in the information you have.

USING SIMPLE RULES FOR RAPID PROCESSING

Our fourth requirement for learning is to use simple rules for rapid processing. As we discussed in the AlphaGo case in the introduction, simple rules facilitate a rapid feedback loop that speeds up information processing. Malcom Gladwell wrote a whole book on how people use simple rules to make decisions "in the blink of an eye."[8] In chapter 7 we reviewed how simple rules provide the cohesive direction and constraints necessary for self-organization and creativity of employees. In this chapter, we discuss yet another important aspect of simple rules: an optimization mechanism from iterative learning.

Here is an interesting question to consider: How would you fit a surface area the size of a tennis court into the volume of two footballs? Or another daunting question: How would you design a system that circulates blood on a journey that passes no more than five cells away from every one of the thirty *trillion* cells in your body—*and* takes up less than 5 percent of the body?

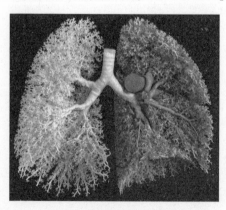

Bronchial tubes of human lungs
Courtesy of Professor Ewald R. Weibel, Institute
of Anatomy, University of Bern, Switzerland

A simple rule for the bronchial tubes of our lungs, specifying when to bifurcate to the next level of branches, gives rise to the extraordinarily complex organ our lungs are. The alveoli are tiny air sacs within the lungs where the exchange of oxygen and carbon dioxide takes place. Each lung contains three hundred million alveoli—if stretched out they would span a football field. The total surface area of the lungs is equal to a tennis court. Our circulatory system uses Koch snowflake fractals to create lungs that have a maximum amount of surface area while taking up little space. This fractal design makes it possible for oxygen transportation that passes no more than five cells away from every one of the thirty trillion cells in your body (the adjacent four cells can transmit nutrients to each other) yet takes up less than 5 percent of the body.

That's no accident: lungs need to fit into the confined space of our chest, so they need to have a small volume, yet have as much surface area as possible in order to diffuse a maximal amount of oxygen through their surface. Being crinkly like a fractal makes that possible, and the crinkliness results from a simple rule that determines when to bifurcate to the next level of bronchial tubes and blood vessels, all the way down to capillaries. These simple rules determine how local interactions take place at the individual cell level, as well as what the global structure looks like in the end. The global shape cannot be predicted from simply observing local interactions, because it is an emergent property. Because of the exponential autocatalytic effect of local interactions and the feedback loop, rapid implementations of these simple rules and iterative adaptations give rise to extraordinarily complex global patterns.

Local rules are the criteria individuals use to determine what to do given a certain feedback from the environment: if A, then do B. The global shape will look very different if there is even a slight change in local simple rules. Developing a strategy based on simple rules and executing it with rapid feedback builds the necessary momentum for radical innovation.

Strategy as simple rules

Professors Kathleen Eisenhardt from Stanford Business School and Don Sull from MIT Sloan School of Management make a convincing case that using strategy made of simple rules brings about competitive advantage in high-velocity markets. They identify three approaches to strategy:[9]

- Choose a position and defend it—best suited for stable industries.
- Nurture and leverage unique resources—useful for moderately changeable industries.

* Flexibly pursue fleeting opportunities using simple rules—best for rapidly changing industries, which every industry is certainly becoming in this age of complexity. The speed of interaction and learning today will continue to increase in all industries because that is the nature of complex adaptive systems.

What is the role of Quantum Leaders in executing strategy based on simple rules? They recognize patterns correctly, develop simple rules to expedite the feedback process, and create a network effect to kick-start radical innovation. They manage the simple rules and change them when necessary. Again, because of the autocatalytic nature of complex systems, a small change in how simple rules are implemented among employees at the local level dramatically changes how global patterns appear at the organizational level. It is crucial for leaders to monitor how simple rules work, maintain them long enough to build momentum, and replace them when they no longer reflect the changing environment.

Facilitate rapid execution

Execution based on simple rules increases speed and hence is much more effective in the dynamic VUCA environment businesses encounter today. Things are changing too rapidly, and the timing of management feedback is too far removed from real-time action, robbing companies of opportunities for vital feedback. The purpose of feedback is to facilitate rapid learning. In executing simple rules, feedback must be provided as close to real time and as frequently as possible. Simple rules are not meant for accuracy but speed. Hence, a certain amount of error in execution is inherent. But developing and implementing simple rules for innovative core processes that expedite processing time can enable an organization to accumulate enough errors and failures to reach a critical inflection point and explode into radical innovation.

For example, in new product development, one can institute a simple rule that says, "When 5 percent of customers ask for a feature, conduct a cost-benefit analysis to evaluate the economic impact. When it reaches 10 percent, incorporate it into an existing product. When 20 percent of customers ask for it, develop a new product focused on delivering that solution." This type of execution not only brings speed but also provides a coherent direction and a drum beat for the organization to march to.

Simple rules about simple rules

Another important job of leaders is to keep one eye on executing the simple rules and the other on evaluating the simple rules. Quantum Leaders quickly identify when those simple rules do not accurately reflect the situation on the ground and replace them with improved ones. Quantum Leaders institute mechanisms to constantly measure the effectiveness of these simple rules and occasionally update them. In the process, they use simple rules to decide when to change them (for example, when the error rate of the simple rule exceeds 30 percent, change the simple rule), constantly making trade-off decisions about the benefits of the momentum from the coherent direction that the simple rules provide versus the cost of the errors of those rules.

ADAPTATION THROUGH EFFECTIVE FEEDBACK

Creating new knowledge from profuse experimentation, storing knowledge, updating the knowledge by unlearning old knowledge, and using simple heuristics for rapid signal processing leads to the final requirement of learning: changing behaviors to adapt to the new environment. In this sense, learning is action, not just a transfer of knowledge or information. The most challenging barrier to this type of action-oriented learning is our own prior beliefs. When our new knowledge propels us to take action contrary to our prior beliefs, it can generate subconscious resistance, especially if the prior belief was formed in the context of what our amygdalae believed to be threatening to our safety.

Change the traditional annual performance review

The purpose of feedback is to aid learning, adapting to the new situations from the environment. From this perspective, as I mentioned in my *Forbes* article,[10] annual performance reviews are becoming irrelevant. In fact, they're a hindrance to success because they interfere with the rapid learning cycle that organizations need to survive in the era of volatility, uncertainty, complexity, and ambiguity. One of the most important skills for leaders in the VUCA age is providing effective performance feedback that facilitates the iterative learning cycle. But most performance reviews are conducted suboptimally. Aside from the anxiety that we are all familiar with when it comes to annual performance reviews, they're also costing companies a significant amount in tangible terms. Deloitte identified that its annual reviews cost two million hours a year.[11] That translates to over $1 billion in revenues, using the average daily associate rate of $5,000 and probably an additional $2 billion for partners. Most of that time is spent completing forms, holding meetings, creating ratings, and discussing outcomes among the partners. These numbers don't even include the opportunity costs of not taking action on rapidly emerging situations on the ground.

Recognizing these inherent limitations, some companies are beginning to implement a real-time solution. Adobe, Gap, Goldman Sachs, GE, Microsoft, IBM, and Accenture have all changed or abolished their annual performance ratings in favor of providing ongoing feedback.[12] Deloitte changed from issuing performance ratings to focusing on performance improvement by implementing weekly check-ins, quarterly or end-of-project feedback, and annual compensation decisions. The annual meeting merely formalizes what has been discussed all year, and hence can be completed much more quickly. Team leaders "set expectations for the upcoming week, review priorities, comment on recent work, and provide course correction, coaching, or important new information."[13] Similarly, in 2016, IBM ditched its ten-year-old annual review system based on the survey results of its 380,000 employees.[14] The program was replaced with one that gives more opportunity to shift employee goals throughout the year and includes more frequent feedback. IBM employees now set shorter-term goals, and managers provide feedback on their progress at least every quarter.

In this rapidly changing VUCA era, learning and adapting to the environment produces a much more accurate and relevant result than fine-tuning the same thing to the nth degree, during which time what you are fine-tuning might become irrelevant. This is why Google's product launch philosophy is "ship and iterate" through soft launches instead of the traditional approach of "iterate, iterate, iterate, and ship." The constant interplay between feedback from the market and adaptation of features, products, and marketing provides a much greater impact during the same period than refining close to perfection. This is how *speed means quality*. When you roll a fistful of snow down the hill, it gains momentum as it rolls, gaining more snow on each roll. So it is with the dynamics leading to radical innovation. Building a collective body of intelligence from iterative learning and providing rapid feedback overcomes the inherent limitation of the annual review process: the timing of feedback is too far removed from real-time action, and doesn't contribute to learning (adapting to the signals from the environment).

Give, solicit, and encourage effective feedback

Radical innovation is a serendipitous result of rapid iterative feedback and learning. Given the vital importance of updating prior beliefs and adapting to new information, one of the most crucial skills for today's leaders is providing effective feedback—yet this is one of the most difficult tasks many leaders face. They are afraid to hurt team members' feelings, or they are uncomfortable to be in a position of authority over them. Here are six simple guidelines to accelerate the learning process that facilitates the adaptation of what we learn. To get the most out of feedback in this VUCA era, leaders can do the following to give, solicit, and encourage effective feedback among their team.

Tolerate failure

This is what empowers employees to self-organize and unleashes their innate creativity, a primordial soup for radical innovation. Annual budgeting, annual performance reviews, five-year strategic planning, and contingency planning are common practices in most organizations today. These tools worked well in the more predictable, linear business environment of the industrial era, but trial-and-error-based profuse experimentation and iterative corrections are much more effective in the dynamic VUCA environment. To facilitate the iterative experimentation necessary, the organization must create a culture of *accepting failure as a necessary input* for radical innovation. Learning is essential for radical innovation, but failure is required for learning, which means failure is *required* for radical innovation. To resolve this apparent conflict, today's organizations must provide a culture of safe risk-taking, rapid feedback loops, and a platform to build collective intelligence from failure.

As an example, the Agile software development approach, in an effort to embrace complexity, facilitates learning through rapid iterations, continuous integration, and failing quickly. In this sense, perfection is an enemy of radical innovation.

Another example is how many consumer product companies—including L'Oréal, Philips, Nikon, and of course Samsung and Hyundai[15]—use South Korea as a testing ground for their products because

- Seoul and its surrounding areas have a concentrated population of about twenty-five million in 835 square miles, producing the third-highest populated metropolitan area in the world;[16]
- South Korea has just the right sample size—fifty million people—to test a consumer product;[17]
- the average annual income of Seoulites is nearly US $40,000;[18]
- South Korea has the cheapest, fastest average internet speed in the world,[19] which helps spread consumer trends quickly, and Seoul in particular has the highest broadband penetration rate among all cities in the world;[20] and
- satisfying the needs of Korean consumers, with their discriminating eye for details, trains companies to become competitive in consumer service in the rest of the world.

Finding out your product is a flop in a smaller market and either making quick iterations until it succeeds or cutting your losses is much better than launching it after many years of perfecting the product, by which time your product could become obsolete.

Leaders must facilitate fast and safe failure using smaller tests such as what these consumer products are doing in Seoul. They can use web analytics tools such as A/B testing, lead source tracking, and conversion funnel tracking to reveal what works best, what doesn't work, and why. Make sharing the findings of these profuse experiments a regular part of meetings to build collective intelligence in your team.

Embrace speed and flexibility

Build tolerance for ambiguity and favor speed over accuracy. Avoid black-and-white thinking and be open to all possibilities, using the tools provided in the effective questioning section in this chapter. Allow the possibility that you could be wrong.

Be prompt

Feedback must be immediate to prevent a loss of salience and relevance to what is happening on the ground right now. Don't wait for your one-on-ones and definitely not for an annual review. Feedback doesn't have to take a long time; a quick two- or three-minute conversation in the hallway walking to a meeting will do. This is when all the efforts and energy you have spent to build safety, trust, and connection with your team will pay big dividends. When they know you care and they trust and like you, you can give feedback that maximizes learning.

Be safe

Performance reviews should be about creating a platform for trial and error—feedback and adaptation—not evaluation. All too often, managers provide performance feedback in an annual review with a list of positives and negatives (often sandwiched between positives), which culminate into a rating, which often determines the raise for the following year. This is suboptimal. As we discussed in chapter 5, learning cannot take place when our brains perceive a threat and our amygdalae get activated. By combining feedback with performance evaluation, the feedback session is anything but safe. Any meaningful feedback must take place in a safe setting, fully removed from evaluation and solely dedicated to learning.

Change the focus from good/bad to more/less

Feedback should *not* focus on what your team members are doing well in and how they need to improve. It's useful to remember the original meaning of positive and negative feedback: it does not connote evaluation of good and bad but rather stability or change. In systemic psychology as well as systems theory, negative feedback loops maintain stability while minimizing change. Giving negative feedback means encouraging them to do less of something to reduce the fluctuations in the output. Positive-feedback loops, in contrast, enhance or amplify changes. When you provide positive feedback as a manager, it means you are encouraging your team to do more of something to bring about a change. These efforts must be balanced, because bringing about change and maintaining stability are both important to balance between chaos and rigidity, between change and stability.

To illustrate this point, let's return to our previous example of the vice president of software development of the logistics software company. On learning of the new competitive threat, you decide to expedite the launch of the next version of the software, which addresses some of the issues customers have cited as to why they are considering an alternative. Your feedback to the software engineers on your team should include asking them to develop more of what users need. In response, your team comes up with an idea to track client keystrokes and use that data to test algorithms. This creates a positive-feedback loop that can iteratively amplify the necessary changes with increasing speed. At the same time, you want to maintain stability of the overall program, so negative feedback would mean implementing fewer ad hoc change requests from customers, reducing fluctuations of outcome, and maintaining stability of the process. Using this approach to feedback, there is no evaluation of good or bad behaviors, only effective learning that leads to amplification or attenuation of change. You can implement this approach by asking your team members to start doing something, stop doing something, or do more or less of something.

Understand and provide context

Effective questioning that broadens the spectrum of possibilities asks not only about the content but also the context. Data without context is meaningless. Understanding the context improves the effectiveness of learning and helps us attribute correct meaning to incoming data.

Let's take an example. You have a daily check-in meeting with your staff every morning. You're perturbed that one of your team members is late to work very frequently. During your weekly one-on-one, you ask about what's going on with him. He tells you he lives thirty miles away from work. You immediately think, *That takes forty minutes maximum. You can definitely plan for that and come on time.* How would your response change if he tells you he can't leave any earlier because he can't drop off his child at daycare before 7:30 AM and the thirty-mile distance includes the six-mile stretch of I-5 between the I-710 and I-605 in Southern California? During the rush hour, these six miles take thirty-five minutes to traverse, and how long it takes to get through the six miles varies wildly depending on the traffic situation—sometimes hours, if there is an accident.

This is why we need context to make sense of data. With the deluge of content and big data, it becomes much more important for you as a leader to provide context to help your team members assign the correct and most incisive meaning to what they are observing, and understand how it fits into the whole. In this sense, leaders have to be meaning-makers in today's complex world. So, if you want your team to increase transparency in communication, provide an explanatory context. For example, distribute a section on transparent communication from Stephen R. Covey's *The Speed of Trust* or a study showing the effects of transparent communication on workforce engagement and performance by Vogelgesang, Leroy, and Avolio.[21]

> **Leaders have to be meaning-makers in today's complex world.**

APPLICATION

Because learning and facilitating learning in others is such an important leadership competency, I would like to spend some time challenging you to think about how you will apply these points in your own organization. Here is a summary of some practical recommendations from this chapter to turn your team into a learning organization:

1. Institute a mechanism to unlearn effectively, using a Bayesian measure. Use the following tools to constantly update prior beliefs in response to feedback from the environment. Learn to use questions effectively.

    a. Frame a question in a new light that expands the horizon of thinking by asking, "What evidence supports the opposite conclusion?" and "How else can we interpret what we are seeing?" Remember, having answers is *not* one of the Quantum Leadership competencies.

    b.   Ask about the context: *What would have to be true for this idea to be true? How complete is our set of prior beliefs?*

    c.   Don't be judgmental; be curious, and always err on the side of being positive rather than negative. Remember the Pygmalion effect—people rise to your expectations.

2. Implement simple rules for rapid processing of information.

    a.   Develop a strategy based on simple rules to increase processing speed of innovation (remember the simple rule example in new product development).

    b.   Change these simple rules when situations call for it.

3. Create new knowledge from profuse experimentation.

    a.   Set the expectation that experimenting and failing is absolutely okay—emphasize that failure is a necessary input to radical innovation.

    b.   Provide moderate (not too hard or too easy) challenges for your team to work through. Ask your team members how often they feel scared or overwhelmed because they don't know how to, or can't, do their job. If the answer is never, they need more challenges. If the answer is more than 40 percent, provide more resources to help them.

    c.   Provide a safe, fast way to fail, such as A/B testing, quickly iterating products with a "ship and iterate" approach. Using consumer panels in smaller, concentrated markets can provide rapid feedback necessary for successful diffusion of innovation.

4. Facilitate rapid adaptation through effective feedback, and empower others to do the same.

    a.   Make feedback safe. Separate evaluation from feedback. Explicitly state the purpose of feedback: for learning.

    b.   Separate the idea from the person giving the idea. Ideas need to be attacked, tested, and improved, separating the giver of the idea so it doesn't feel personal. In addition, once someone's ego is invested in the idea, it's no longer about the best idea; it's more about getting credit and politics. The team's commitment must be on constant learning that leads to the best decision.

c. Provide frequent, timely feedback.

d. Change the focus of feedback from "good or bad" to "more or less," adhering to the true meaning of positive and negative feedback—that of amplification or attenuation of change.

e. Eliminate or drastically simplify the annual review process from a bureaucratic procedure to a practical vehicle to provide timely feedback and learning.

5. Measure learnings instead of earnings. In the rapidly changing, highly complex VUCA world, organizations will benefit much more from measuring learning and tracking pattern recognition skills and false positive and false negative rates in the decisions they make than from measuring quarterly earnings, if they want to win in the long term.

CONCLUSION

Learning is correcting errors in reading signals from the environment and adapting accordingly. It is our main vehicle to defy the physical law of entropy, the natural trend for decay and disorder. It is also the most important vehicle to generate radical innovation, because when people challenge and learn from each other with openness and flexibility to correct prior beliefs, they make the best possible decision. This type of learning is possible only when there is already a foundation of safety, trust, and connection as a team. To unleash the constant learning that can help organizations reach a higher level of complexity and order, Quantum Leaders constantly update their prior knowledge using the Bayesian discipline as they get more information from the environment, and provide effective feedback to their teams to facilitate learning. They facilitate the use of heuristics for rapid processing of information, and they create new knowledge by instituting profuse experimentation of trial and error.

We've worked our way through five of the six core leadership competencies. Now it's time to address the ultimate goal of leadership: producing radical innovation.

Chapter 9

HIGHER COMPLEXITY AND RADICAL INNOVATION

L et's revisit the definition of radical innovation as we discussed in chapter 1: Radical innovation is a holistic, serendipitous result of many self-organizing, interdependent employees learning from profuse experiments using simple rules often to produce a minimum of 10x improvements, dramatically changing the existing industry dynamics and providing a new platform for other innovations to build on. Hopefully each word in this definition now makes more sense to you than it did in chapter 1. Radical innovation is the result of implementing the five preceding competencies. Effective self-management enables safety for team members, which frees them to pursue self-organization and differentiation, which provides a solid foundation for connection, which creates cohesive teams.

On the foundation of safety and connection, team members can freely explore and challenge each other, using iterative learning from profuse experiments. All these building blocks create the primordial soup in which positive complexity, such as a runaway international best seller, a new species that is fitter for natural selection, or a radical innovation that can be intentionally *stimulated* and serendipitously sparked. These competencies enable leaders to harness the same dynamics seen in negative complexity, such as a stock market crash, an uncontrollable epidemic, a subprime mortgage crisis, or a competitor starting a garage business that wipes out the existing business model. Radical innovation leads to improvements in costs or benefits to customers, and provides a new platform, a new paradigm, for others to build on. Let's look at how radical innovation is formed and what it looks like for a Quantum Leader to operate at the edge of chaos—the ideal condition for radical innovation.

THE EDGE OF CHAOS

The edge of chaos is where "the opportunity for information processing is maximized and most favorable to life."[1] Maximum complexity and order is reached at the edge of chaos. This is where you test the limits of your capabilities, adapting to unpredictable perturbations and constantly making iterative changes. This is where a living organism can thrive with life and creativity. In the words of Mitchell Waldrop, a physicist turned science writer, this is where "new ideas and innovative genotypes are forever nibbling away at the edges of the status quo, where eons of evolutionary stability suddenly give way to wholesale species transformation ... the one place where a complex system can be spontaneous, adaptive, and alive."[2] This is where major innovations have redefined history. The cumulative butterfly effect from each iteration gives rise to a spontaneous order: a new frontier of personal and organizational transformation. This is where organizations either "make it or break it" with constant trial and error in a safe environment, playfulness, humor, and autonomy grounded by loose, simple operating rules. Sure, it's more comfortable in the middle of the stasis, but oh, what a ride it is for those at the edge of chaos. The edge of chaos is about balance, emergence, higher complexity, order, and coevolution.

Balance

The edge of chaos is where the self-organization of individuals is balanced with connection as a unit (whether it be a couple, team, family, organization, society, or nation). Agents with maximum differentiation are linked with an optimal level of connection, forming the sweet spot between structure and chaos. It is characterized by a delicate balance and trade-off decisions between local incentives and self-interest against global organizational goals and values. It is also balanced between rapid knowledge dissemination against creating and storing of information.

At the edge of chaos, global cohesion is balanced with local self-organization, and robustness from diversity of input is balanced with depth of expertise from specialized focus. Here, there is enough stability to enable organizations and individuals to store information, but enough flexibility and variety to allow new ideas to flow with communication and adaptation. If you are not living at the edge of chaos, chances are you are too rigid and stable (soon to become irrelevant or leapfrogged), or too chaotic (soon to disintegrate into disorder). Firms become irrelevant if they stay in homeostasis for too long, or become overdictated by detailed rules. At the same time, they disintegrate into chaos if they lack the structure to organize and coordinate their efforts.

Emergence and higher complexity

The result of this delicate balance is not predictable. It is not deducible from or reducible to its component parts. The iterative, evolving adaptation and the resulting form of higher emergent complexity comes from a fragile balance between structure, which allows for planning and execution, and chaos, which allows for rapid change and innovation.

Higher internal complexity generates more options when faced with a choice. We have a very friendly chocolate lab named Brownie. She knows that she goes into her kennel at 10:00 PM, but she stands in front of the metal wire door that is ajar instead of pushing the door open. With less complexity than a human, Brownie has fewer options for action. Creating higher complexity in organizations provides more options and broader strategic maneuverability. Indeed, increasing internal complexity is the ultimate goal of leadership.

The best way to achieve the highest level of complexity as a leader and as an individual is to excel at what makes us uniquely human—the abilities that are exclusively well-developed among humans. Recall the different regions of the brain and how it has evolved over time (discussed in chapter 3): the lowest, most primitive part of our reptilian brain, the brain stem, governs our safety and survival needs. The next level up in brain anatomy, the limbic system, which we share with other mammals, governs our attachment needs. The most evolved part of our brains is the cortex, shared with primates, which implements logic and decision-making. Of the cortex, what is uniquely well-developed among humans is the medial prefrontal cortex, which governs self-awareness, self-referential processing to correct our mental model based on new information, fear modulation, empathy, moral reasoning, and emotion regulation, which are all bases for effective leadership. Now we know these are the foundational principles to establish safety with others and create connection, which unleashes people and organizations to create radical innovation.

Once again, we see how both the evolutionary structure of our brains and the steps to Quantum Leadership allow us to reach the highest level of complexity.

Higher order

Entropy, which we covered in the previous chapter, is also known as disorder. As Richard Feynman, American theoretical physicist and pioneer in quantum mechanics, explains:

> *Suppose we divide the space into little volume elements. If we have black and white molecules, how many ways could we distribute them among the volume elements so that white is on one side and black is on the other? On the other hand, how many ways could we distribute them with no restriction on which goes where? Clearly, there are many more ways to arrange them in the latter case. We measure "disorder" by the number of ways that the insides can be arranged, so that from the outside it looks the same. The logarithm of that number of ways is the entropy. The number of ways in the separated case is less, so the entropy is less, or the "disorder" is less (or order is higher).*[3]

From this perspective, it should now make more sense why individual and organizational differentiation with strong boundaries is a prerequisite to building higher order and higher complexity. This is also consistent with the principle that we need to be a coherent light source with single frequency with no internal interferences so that we can combine with others' coherent light sources to a much higher positive amplitude than we can produce alone. When we are highly differentiated as individuals, not enmeshed with other people's identity and boundaries, we can create higher order and complexity, which increases our chances of survival as a species and creates more options for happiness. Higher order also increases our chances to thrive as an individual and create radical innovation as an organization. The type of boundaries that define healthy relationships among people and effective teams optimized for innovation and higher order are porous—not rigid like a brick wall or enmeshed like a chicken wire frame, but porous like Swiss cheese, allowing a free flow of information and closeness but still holding the integrity of the differentiated structure of identity and ideas. Differentiation that creates higher order also applies to teams and organizations. Quantum Leaders facilitate differentiation of teams and individuals within them in order to prepare them to produce higher order and complexity.

Coevolution

We operate at the edge of chaos when we coevolve with the environment through loose structure, simple rules, and flexibility that allow for innovation and adaptability from rapid iterations of feedback. Because we are all part of nested systems, when one component of the system changes, the rest of the system is affected by the change, and responds by changing itself. Coevolution is what makes it possible to create a platform of radical innovation upon which others can build their incremental innovation, which is the source of the new sustainable competitive advantage. When we evolve together with the environment as a system, whether it be a couple in a family, a team in an organization, an organization in society, or a nation in the world, we reach a higher level of complexity. Incidentally, evolution and creation are not mutually exclusive, as discussed in this book.

A PUNCTUATED EQUILIBRIUM VERSUS THE ADJACENT POSSIBLE

Networks near the edge of chaos adjust to the environment at an accelerated rate and trigger a cascade of changes that result in a huge spontaneous transformation of self-organized criticality. In the late 1960s, biologist and paleontologist Niles Eldredge was working with Stephen Jay Gould at the American Museum of Natural History in New York. While studying the evolutionary history of dinosaurs, they became curious about the significant gaps in the fossil record of dinosaurs. Instead of gradual evolution of one species into another, they saw sudden jumps into new species. Up to that point, the predominant theory of evolution had been *phyletic gradualism*: the slow and steady operation of gradual natural selection. But dinosaur fossil records indicated that the history of most dinosaur species is dominated by sudden stasis, rather than Darwin's model of gradual fine-tuning for a better fit with the environment.

The radical evolution of the dinosaurs was brought about by major environmental perturbations, such as asteroids, or big shifts in weather. When you are safely in the center of a stasis, you make small, incremental changes because you are not challenged by environmental perturbations that push your limits and require radical behavior change. Most of these radical adaptations occurred in rare, isolated episodes, when a single species split into two distinct species (bifurcation), rather than one species gradually transforming into another, which was then followed by a long period of stasis. Eldredge and Gould named this process "punctuated equilibrium." Their landmark paper was published in the prestigious journal *Nature* and presented convincing evidence that the traditional Darwinian view of evolutionary history missed an important building block (at the publication of this book, their paper has been cited more than five thousand times).[4]

Eldredge and Gould discovered a foundational principle of radical innovation. At some point, the trial-and-error results from many self-organizing employees bounded by simple rules reach a critical inflection point, beyond which lies spontaneous order, a phase transition, game-changing radical innovation, breakthrough learning, and runaway social phenomenon, because the rapid feedback and adaptation follows a power-law distribution and autocatalysis. This is how stock market crashes[5] and infectious diseases happen on the negative complexity side, and innovation[6] and the step-function history of evolution[7] happen on the positive complexity side. The result is unpredictable, sudden, sweeping consequences that redefine industry dynamics, a new paradigm or framework upon many subsequent innovations are built, which then stabilize until the next radical innovation comes along.

One might get confused about the conflict between the concepts of *punctuated equilibrium* and the *adjacent possible*, a term coined by Stuart Kauffman, which refers to the area of possibility for innovation.[8] Organisms keep expanding into the next sphere of possibilities. The adjacent possible opens doors for the next iteration of innovation to expand the platform and foundation for diffusion—innovations build on top of other innovations. In the late 1990s, when I was working for Accenture as a strategy consultant, it built a retail industry lab with prototypes of a smart fridge that detected the level of milk and automatically ordered a new carton delivered by Peapod, complete with smart home automation and remote control. Sounds familiar? Yes, these services are being accepted by the early majority now, a full twenty years later. Although brilliant, these concepts were too early for their time, and weren't successfully implemented because the intermediate adjacent possible was not present back then. Technology platforms such as RFID (radio-frequency identification), which makes it possible to identify individual members from the key fob they carry, networking software and hardware, and wireless protocols that enable networked control of computer-controlled power boxes, LED lights that power the internet of things (the connection via the Internet of computing devices embedded in everyday objects, enabling them to send and receive data), cloud computing, and the like had not yet been introduced, so Accenture's retail lab concept didn't have enough to build on. In other words, it didn't have an adjacent possible.

To clarify the potential conflict between these two concepts, it is helpful to look at punctuated equilibrium as the *result* of radical innovation, and the adjacent possible as the *ecosystem and process that enable* radical innovation. Once radical innovation surfaces, the impact is punctuated equilibrium: a radical, unpredictable, nonlinear departure from how things have been done.

INTEGRATION

In individuals, operating at the edge of chaos produces a state of integration where uniquely differentiated parts of a complex system are connected within the individual and balanced within the system. This state of integration creates a whole greater than the sum of its parts, and is characterized by harmony, congruence, and well-being. In the words of the late Béla Bánáthy, a Hungarian American linguist and professor at San Jose State University and UC Berkeley, integration refers to "the state in which the different markers communicate, coevolve, interact, interpenetrate, and enhance one another. An evolved entity, which is more differentiated and integrated than another, is more complex than an entity that is less differentiated and integrated."[9] Pursuing a higher level of integration is a worthy goal for organizations and leaders within them because it produces a higher level of complexity. The more complex an organism, the more options it has. Some of the important elements of integration are intuition, harmony, authenticity, and play.

Intuition

When you're integrated, you see how you are influencing, and are influenced by, others in the system. When you're integrated, you are not rigid or chaotic but open and flexible to new thoughts. Such a leader understands how past experience contributes to one's experience of the present, which shapes how one views the future. As a parent, you are aware of how your own experience of growing up shapes how you parent. You allow your children to learn from their own failures and mistakes, and yet are available to guide them.

Harmony

As a leader, when you are integrated, you are balanced between holding someone accountable and providing safety and connection for the team. You are strongly grounded in your own self-respect and strong boundaries, yet you negotiate the delicate balance with compassion and kindness for others. You can balance the needs of individuals to self-organize with the needs of the organization for coherence. You are able to weigh your individual needs against those of your team. Another form of integration—the balance between the left and right hemispheres of the brain—manifests itself in a symmetrical brain-wave pattern between the two brain hemispheres, the whole-brain state.[10] People in a whole-brain state experience harmony and balance between right- and left-brain functions. Striving for harmony and balance in all major aspects of life should be an important goal of any leader; finding balance with others in the same ecosystem must be one as well.

Authenticity: Bringing your whole self to work

The behavior of an individual operating at the edge of chaos is congruent and integrated across bodily sensations, thoughts, feelings, and actions. You are authentic when there is no discrepancy among these aspects of you: you feel what you see, express what you feel, think what you feel, and say what you think and feel. Integration also means you are congruent across all roles you play, whether as a spouse, parent, sibling, churchgoer, leader, employee, or citizen.

Stewart Butterfield, the CEO and cofounder of Slack, a collaboration messaging software, describes this action as bringing your whole self to work, not just parts of you. Authenticity builds safety, trust, and connection, and it speeds up team communication. The jerk boss (like one of my former bosses who told me she had more knowledge under her big toenail than I did in my brain) we see every day at work who saps the last drop of life out of us is actually, most likely, acting out of fear. When we present a facade that might be more appealing and acceptable to others, we (and those trying to connect with us) only feel empty because we cannot connect with a facade. When we are authentic, showing our authentic and even scared and insecure selves, we can bring our whole selves to work, and tap into the maximum potential of our wholes (not just a professional self) on a foundation of secure attachment and acceptance by our work families.

In corporate America, where professionalism counts more than authenticity, we have developed an overreliance and preference for the left brain. In the process, we have justified the thoughts, such as work-life balance, as if it's a zero-sum game where if we spend one more unit of energy at work then we become one less unit available for our families, and "professionalism is not emotional." We need to introduce *more* authentic emotions at work, not less. Bringing your whole self, including the messy emotions, makes you authentic, facilitates trust, and speeds up communication and decision-making processes (recall the Navy SEALs rescuing Captain Phillips from the Somali pirates and Sully and his first officer's quick decision-making in the Miracle on the Hudson). Individually, when you are integrated as a whole person, it allows more efficient and accurate information processing across the brain's corpus callosum, which integrates the left and right hemispheres. Being authentic requires courage and vulnerability, which requires the foundation of safety and trust. In other words, safety and authenticity are mutually reinforcing, and it takes time to build authentic relationships.

Companies that recognize the benefit of "bringing your whole self to work" must, in return, provide more flexibility and help to increase the quality of life with their employees' families. For example, GE rolled out in 2015 a permissive approach to paid time off for exempt employees, where they can coordinate with their managers to take the time off and receive enhanced parental leave benefits. GE employees can now take up to ten weeks of parental leave (six paid and four unpaid) after the birth or adoption of a baby. Through the "Moms on the Move" program, GE moms in the United States who are nursing and traveling for business can ship their milk back home for their babies.

As you can see, becoming an integrated boss who provides safety and connection for others does not only make good business sense (because it provides a foundation for radical innovation); it also improves our quality of life and overall happiness.

Play

Developing more of the right-brain elements of fun and spontaneity can spark radical innovation. In the words of the late psychologist and professor J. Nina Lieberman, "Play and its quintessence, playfulness, arises in familiar physical settings or when the individual has the pertinent facts; . . . [then] imagination enters by twisting those facts into different combinations, not unlike the operation of a kaleidoscope."[11] Playfulness is about joy, humor, and spontaneity. The end product is imagination and creativity. In other words, playfulness is an essential ingredient for the primordial soup that gives way to radical innovation. This type of playfulness can be unleashed only when the amygdala is at bay, feeling safe. This sense of safety enables people to imagine and explore, instead of waste energy watching their backs. That's why having fun at work, feeling safe, and innovation cannot be separated. As leaders, setting the tone for safety and play is an important part of your job. Bring more humor (the safe kind, not the sarcastic kind), fun, and laughter into work. Nobody, not even a working stiff, wants to work for a stiff.

How to increase integration

Daniel Siegel indicates that strengthening the medial prefrontal cortex region in your brain helps improve your capacity for integration. Two major conduits are available to do this.

The first is secure attachment based on communication using both right- and left-brain signals. A secure attachment to another allows the activity of your mind to sense and respond to the activity of another. When you feel safe, seen, understood, and cared about, the resulting secure attachment stimulates the growth of the integrative fibers in your brain,[12] which also increases resilience, as we reviewed in chapter 7. Quantum Leaders develop their capacity for integration, and thus for higher complexity, by building healthy relationships. As you can see, being a great leader requires integration across all aspects of life, meaning you are unlikely to become an effective leader if your personal life is not in order, since the quality of your personal relationships greatly affects your ability to be an effective leader.

Second, a Harvard study, and many more like it, have found that regular mindfulness meditation actually changes the structure of our brains in as few as eight weeks.[13] Mindfulness meditation significantly increases the gray matter concentration in brain regions involved in integration, learning, and self-management in the brain. Mindful meditation also improves memory processes, emotion regulation, self-referential processing, and perspective taking—all important abilities to unlearn past programs and learn new ones in order to make sense of what is happening now. Being mindful means you consciously embrace your present experiences with judgment-free openness, curiosity, and acceptance. With self-reflective insight (the ability to map your thoughts and emotions), you are able to use the same map to see other people and phenomena in the world, which enables empathy and compassion.[14] You can see the patterns and systemic processes behind what is currently happening, rather than becoming bogged down by the content. Simply taking ten minutes every day for eight weeks for mindfulness meditation can actually reshape your brain to become more integrated and increase your sense of well-being.

Third, carefully managing your thoughts and redirecting negative ones to positive ones can increase integration. According to attachment research, what predicts the quality of attachment parents provide their children is not whether the parents received good or bad parenting themselves during childhood but how they make sense of the parenting they received.[15] If your thought is that you were mistreated because you were not good enough to get your parents' attention, chances are you will end up mistreating your children because your belief that you are not good enough will draw your children into your subconscious efforts to make you feel better about yourself. But if your thought is that your parents did the very best they could to love you, given how they grew up, your sense of self is preserved and you are likely to raise emotionally well-balanced children who are securely attached to you. I have covered many aspects of how to manage your thoughts throughout this book, such as positive mental frames, and internal locus of control.

The result of integration

Integration is not easy to achieve because it requires a delicate balance between conflicting goals and trade-offs among priorities with equal merits. What is the reward of being integrated? Dr. Daniel Siegel describes it as kindness, resilience, and physical, mental, and emotional health; an overall sense of well-being and equanimity.[16] In addition to improved quality of life, integration can help you live longer: increasing the integrative fibers in the prefrontal region boosts the production of telomerase. Telomeres are like caps that protect the ends of chromosomes from fraying. As the cells divide, telomeres shorten until they run out. Then, the cells can't divide anymore, which means we die. It turns out that practicing mindful meditation, and the resulting increased integration, can reverse telomere shortening by expressing more telomerase, an enzyme that rebuilds the telomeres of chromosomes.[17] Mindful meditation involves consciously redirecting your thoughts to perceive a situation as exciting or horizon-expanding instead of threatening.

Integration in and of itself has value as a result of secure attachment and self-reflection, but it also produces a higher level of complexity: more options for action and a better ability to adapt to the environment, rendering one fitter for survival.

CONCLUSION

Integration is the pinnacle of evolution of all species. High integration implies more complex, evolved, well-adjusted beings who are more capable of producing radical innovation. The preceding competencies of effective self-management, providing safety, creating differentiation, strengthening connection, and facilitating learning culminate in an environment ideal to produce radical innovation. This environment is called the edge of chaos, a condition where stability is balanced with change, self-organization with simple rules, differentiation with connection, and exploration with exploitation. When organizations and individuals coevolve with the environment while balancing multiple equally meritorious priorities, they maximize their chances of growth and radical innovation, and increase complexity, the ultimate goal of Quantum Leadership. A higher level of complexity generates not only a greater state of well-being—a worthy goal in and of itself—but also generates more options for action and a better fit with the environment, which improves the odds of survival.

Chapter 10

QUANTUM
LEADERSHIP
IMPLEMENTATION

B eing a Quantum Leader requires many skills that are hard to master. Many of those skills don't come naturally to most of us, and call for balancing and trading off between good things with equal merit. To prioritize how to reap the highest benefit for your efforts, it's important to get a clear view of where you are. As I mentioned in chapter 1, you can visit my website (www.sunniegiles.com) to get a complimentary assessment of your leadership strengths and weaknesses for radical innovation compared to other leaders around the globe. Ideally, you would have taken this assessment before you started reading this book to avoid the bias from reading this book. But if you haven't gotten it yet, go ahead and get it done now.

This chapter focuses on implementing the six leadership competencies required for radical innovation. We'll cover some of the leadership competencies that cut across multiple competency groups, and concentrate on the role of a leader as a whole, rather than the individual competencies we've already covered.

QUANTUM LEADERSHIP ASSESSMENT

Six competency groups

This section reveals where you rank in each of the six competency groups: self-management, safety, differentiation, connection, learning, and radical innovation. This is based on your self-report, and so is only as accurate as your assessment is honest.

Often, leaders find it helpful to get a view of their competencies from their direct reports; this information can be generated in a more in-depth customized program we provide at Quantum Leadership Group. These multiangle reports can be compared with those of other teams in the same organization, and the CEO can quickly assess the leadership competency gaps in the organization and start a program to strengthen them.

Here we will focus on the individual report:

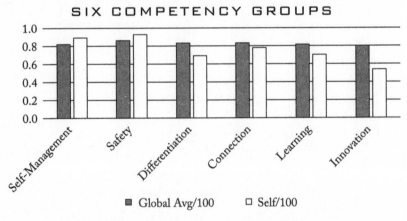

Figure 10.1 Individual report of Quantum Leadership competencies

Our first step is to focus on the categories with the greatest differences between the global average and your self-assessment. In figure 10.2, we see this leader's strongest competency vis-à-vis other global leaders is effective self-management. Even if her absolute score is high for safety, her score for self-management exceeds the global average by more than her score for safety. Her weakest skill is stimulating innovation. Although each competency builds on the previous one (i.e., self-management is the foundation), leaders may excel in higher-level skills when they are lacking in lower-level competencies. In this situation, that is not the case.

	Global Avg/100	Self/100
Self-Management	0.84	0.92
Safety	0.88	0.95
Differentiation	0.86	0.71
Connection	0.86	0.80
Learning	0.84	0.72
Innovation	0.82	0.55

Figure 10.2 *Individual results, vis-à-vis global average*

Another point worthy to note is how each competency group compares with the rest. Here, this leader scored very highly on safety at .95 but innovation is only at .55, suggesting that more awareness and efforts at innovation—perhaps reallocating some effort and attention from safety to innovation-related activities—would be useful.

You might feel discouraged if your score is lower than the global average. I would strongly encourage you not to let that happen. Rather, start with something that can make a big difference. Pick one competency that shows the greatest gap from the global average. Understand what specific actions constitute that competency. Start with two or three actions you can take (never more than three), and implement them consistently over three or more months. Examine yourself if you experience any resistance during the process. Be curious rather than judgmental about the source of the resistance and work through it. From my experience coaching hundreds of leaders, this is how breakthrough personal growth starts.

And this is how permanent change happens: when you work through this resistance, you discover hidden implicit mental filters that no longer serve you. Then you can replace the mental filter and rewrite the program. The subconscious resists change. Instead of *telling* your cortex brain the reasons why you need to change, which keeps the core reason why you can't change still intact, you actually need to rewrite the subconscious program.

Most of the time, this kind of deep self-discovery is hard to achieve by yourself. That's why you need a coach, a mentor, or a growth partner you feel safe with, who can guide you through this journey with objectivity. Your coach can shed light on the patterns of which you are unaware. If you can't or don't want to hire a coach, find someone who shares the same commitment for growth, and form a buddy arrangement to coach each other. If you don't have a buddy, come to my website (www.sunniegiles.com/contact) and request a buddy. We will match you with someone who could be a good fit for you.

Radical innovation cannot be planned—only facilitated and stimulated. So what can you do as leaders to create an organization that produces radical innovation, other than just hope that the accidental radical innovation will fly into your mouth as you have it open toward heaven? This chapter is about taking tangible action steps that cut across multiple competencies.

CEO AS CHIEF MEANING-MAKER

One of the most important jobs of a leader is to correct errors in how your team interprets incoming signals from other people or the environment (as you may recall, this is my definition of learning) and assign correct meaning so they can unleash the power of beliefs, make effective decisions, and execute for results.

In a study of eighty-four hotel housekeepers, professors Alia Crum from Stanford University and Ellen Langer from Harvard University told a group of housekeepers that the work they do is good exercise and satisfies the surgeon general's daily recommendations for exercise. Another group of housekeepers wasn't given this information. At the end of a four-week experiment, the two groups were compared. The treatment group showed significantly decreased weight, blood pressures, body fat, waist-to-hip ratio, and body mass index, whereas the control group showed no difference.[1]

Simply being told that their work was good exercise was enough to produce a significant physical change. Both the treatment group and control group did the exact same thing as before; the only thing that changed is the belief that cleaning hotel rooms is good exercise rather than drudgery.

On an organizational level, Quantum Leaders can tap into this extraordinary power of belief not only for themselves but also for the teams they lead. This leadership role cuts across many competency groups, as you will see in the following pages.

Consciously choosing your beliefs

When incoming sensory signals are collected in the thalamus, in the limbic system the signal is sent over two paths: a long one and a short one. As we discussed in chapter 3, the short path enables the amygdala to take fast action, based on the associative conditioned memory from previous experiences, before the cortex fully processes it along the long path. If a meaning of threat is assigned, the fear emotion gets activated to take fight, flight, or freeze. Perceptions collected in the thalamus are sent through the cortex on a long path, which assesses the situation according to logic and reason (meaning is assigned), decides if the amygdala response needs to be modified, and elicits emotions accordingly. It's important to remember that our emotions follow the meaning our brains assign.

Let's say your team has just closed on an important deal you've been working on for months. Although you had a minor role in the deal, your team was recognized in a company-wide email on the win. A colleague, whom you sort of know but are not close to, comes up to you and gives you a fist bump and says, "You're the bomb!"

How would you respond? That depends. If you grew up in America, you might smile big and say, "Thanks!" What went on between the combined signals of "You're the bomb!," the fist bump, your colleague's smile, and your response? Your thalamus sent the incoming perception of the fist you saw and the words you heard through both paths. In a split-second process, the short path through the amygdala determined it was not a threat, so it relaxed. The long path through the cortex reached the same conclusion, and in fact determined the incoming signal to be warm and safe. Happy and relaxing neurotransmitters, such as oxytocin and dopamine, were stimulated, and you responded appropriately with "Thanks!" and a big reciprocal smile.

But what if you're a Rohingya Muslim refugee, recently immigrated from Myanmar to escape ethnic cleansing? You got a professional job because of your college degree and professional work experience, but a fist flying at you with the word "bomb" would be enough to trigger an amygdala's fear response from a threat (meaning-making), which would elicit the initial emotion of "fear and shrink" or "get angry" on the short path. Then the cortex information processing on the long path would kick in and determine you're safe, and you (hopefully) modify your initial amygdala reaction of fear. GABA (gamma-aminobutyric acid) released in cortex neurons have a calming effect, soothing the hyperactive limbic system. You manage not to flinch or raise your fist in defense. This scenario is a microcosm in slow motion of what happens to all of us many times every day, and illustrates the point that the emotions we feel depend on the meaning we assign to what we perceive. An important part of a leader's job is to remove obstacles to speedy communication by ensuring accuracy of communication and help others assign correct meaning to what they see.

Correcting errors in meaning-making: The case of Ryan

To consciously choose more adaptive mental frames, it is important to become aware of our maladaptive mental frames first, which is hard to do because they are mostly under the surface of our conscious brain. Let's see how we can discover our subconscious mental filter using the case study of Ryan.

Ryan, with his 6'2" toned body that earned him a Division I football scholarship for an engineering degree in college, stood in front of me tentatively. His eyes darted subtly across my face as if he were taking my measure, and pleasantly narrowed when he gave me a magnetic smile. Between the smile and his warm handshake, I could sense why he was known for his charming personality in the firm and his circle of clients.

"I should be at the peak of my career," Ryan said slowly. It had been a grueling journey through Yale Law School, as an associate, and now, at age forty-three, as an equity partner in one of the top international business law firms in the United States. His firm's compensation curve was uniquely designed: his bonus increased at an accelerating rate once it cleared the minimum. He could increase his compensation by generating more client deals or carefully managing salary expenses and other costs of the intellectual property practice he was leading. He had to clear the minimum requirement allocated to him to keep his status with the firm. The issue was that he would start disengaging from work as soon as he hit the minimum mark and met his numbers for the year.

"I guess what really bothers me is not just about the money," he continued. "I know it's not hard to bring in more revenue and double my income, which will be nice, but I feel like I am going up against an invisible wall." He had always excelled: top of his class, top law school, and a top law firm. But he is now barely average in his job performance. "I think something is keeping me from reaching more. It's like an invisible barrier I can't get through." He looked away with a sigh.

We started working together in biweekly coaching sessions, as part of the firm-wide leadership development program. I learned that Ryan had a very happy childhood; he had a lot of loving memories of playing with his dad (fishing, playing football, camping) and his mom (baking cookies, singing him to sleep, making his favorite broccoli cheese casserole). When he was ten years old, his parents divorced. When his father married a woman from out of town, he moved, and Ryan hardly saw him anymore. Shortly after that, his mother married a millionaire. Ryan quickly learned he had to get a paper route to earn money, because every time a phone bill came his stepfather would take a yellow highlighter and mark all the calls Ryan made to his father, expecting reimbursement. From these experiences, deep in the subcortical structure of his brain, Ryan's amygdala made the meaning that money jeopardizes family relationships.

As a result, regardless of how many times his logical cortex brain told Ryan he could bring in significantly more money (and all the benefits associated with it), Ryan's reptilian brain, working with the amygdala to keep him safe from what it remembered as a threat to his safety (the risk of not seeing his father), produced a powerful and automatic response that overrode the cortex brain's message. Reptilian messages about safety always trump the cortex brain's appeal to logic and reason. Making more client calls and generating more business for the firm meant he was jeopardizing his attachment relationship with his father, which was critical to his survival as a child.

After working through this subconscious defense, Ryan was able to replace this fear-based program with a new, more adaptive program: financial success enriches his family relationships. As a result, Ryan achieved the third-highest profit in his firm the following year. More important, he felt a sense of freedom and balance in his life.

"I feel free. Nothing is keeping me suppressed anymore," he said in a later session, with his face beaming with quiet self-assurance. He even walked differently—he carried himself with more confidence.

This type of unlearning old meaning and assigning new meaning as new evidence presents itself, adapting to new information, is critical both in individual and organizational transformation. *Any organizational change is implemented at the individual level.* Any organizational capacity for change starts with individual unlearning of the fear-based messages that might prevent change and learning. Even though Ryan's paper route days are long gone, the same limiting belief was still shaping his view of others and himself, creating a distorted view of the world.

Without addressing this point, any learning that appeals to the cortex with new information is only temporary. He could cite to himself all the benefits of more money until blue in the face—"More money means better lifestyle," or "More money means more acceptance," or "Money means more golf"—but the subconscious fear is more powerful than any message his cortex could generate. This is part of the reason why, as the *Wall Street Journal* reported, US firms spent about $156 billion on employee learning in 2011, but some 90 percent of new skills were lost within a year.[2]

Ryan's newfound freedom and achievement started with his awareness about a limiting belief. How do you know if you are running into a limiting belief?

1 . Your limiting belief is applied to other general situations (from the specific situation of the phone bill to other life situations such as work performance).
2 . The belief presents a distorted picture of current reality.
3 . The view is held rigidly.

These are not easy to detect—hence the need for self-awareness and self-management as a foundational competency and help from a safe third party in the process. Correct meaning-making involves unlearning old messages, and consciously choosing more effective mental models.

Clarifying

My sixteen-year-old daughter is/was a classically trained pianist (I don't blame her for moving on to percussion, away from the grueling two and a half hours of daily piano practice). When she first received a repertoire piece from her teacher, she started by listening and watching the whole piece played by a great pianist on YouTube. Then she learned to play the piece herself, one section at a time. Most people would think—I certainly did before I witnessed her training—that learning the piece and playing it all the way through would be the end of her training. But I quickly learned that this is only 25 percent of the work. Her real work began at this point, constantly shaping the dynamics, refining her phrasing and fingerings, balancing and shifting the left and right hand dynamics as necessary, practicing arpeggio techniques countless times to indelibly carve them into her muscle memory, coordinating her pedal and hands in perfect timing, infusing her showmanship and emotions to accentuate musicality, and so on. When she put all those pieces together, the final output was an extraordinary performance that deeply touched people's hearts, adding to the original composer's intent in both musical and technical representation.

Ideas work much the same way. When an idea is first introduced, we tend to want to implement or reject the idea right then. But the introduction of the idea is only 25 percent of the work. We need to clarify it for more precise meaning, poke holes, toss it around, refine it, add to or delete from it, and then debate it to make it a masterpiece. It doesn't have to take long, but it is critical for every idea to go through this refining process before you decide on it. Even if we decide to vote it down, the refining-and-clarification process makes the decision much more accurate.

To implement this skill, you need to help others clarify their own thinking when they first assign a meaning to what they hear or see. Here is a case in point with a summarized dialogue between Anne, a sales executive working for a device company on a sales call, and John, one of her customers who oversees a region of retail stores.

> JOHN: I wish your customer service was better.
> ANNE, *BEING CURIOUS*: Oh? Can you tell me more
> about what you mean? In what aspect?

If Anne were defensive here, instead of curious, she might have said, "We have excellent customer service records. Over 80 percent of calls to the call center are answered within sixty seconds and our Net Promoter Score is 68 percent, the highest in our industry, and blah blah blah." The customer would have stopped talking about his issue, which would have shut off a valuable avenue for discovery. If she was overeager to solve the problem, she might have said, "We are committed to excellent customer service. What issues do you have with our customer service?" This approach is slightly better, but only slightly, because she is jumping to the solution without fully understanding what the real issue is.

> JOHN: They take forever to respond back to me when we call for replacement.
> ANNE: So is it the speed of response that bothers you, or is it the fact that you are having to call in the first place?

Here Anne is making a conjecture based on what he says. The first part of the question is repeating back his words, and the second part is conjecture, taking what she heard one step further. She imagines how she would feel if she had to make such a call.

> JOHN: Well, I wish I didn't have to call in the first place. Even though your quality is one of the highest in the industry, your DOA rate is still too high. And a lot of the devices get broken about six months into service.
> ANNE: Hmm, I can sense your concern about the quality of our products. What is the impact on your organization when our device malfunctions?

DOA refers to "dead on arrival"—that is, the device is not working when the customer first receives it. Here Anne helps John recognize that the product malfunction in and of itself is not an issue; rather, the impact of the malfunction is the issue.

> JOHN: I'm just afraid it's going to drive down our customer satisfaction numbers when they get frustrated with your defective devices.
> ANNE: Ah, what happens for you with lower customer satisfaction?
> JOHN: I actually lose part of my budget next year, because their philosophy is to feed the winners and starve the losers. And part of the metrics they track to identify losers and winners is customer satisfaction. So if my customer sat numbers are low, I lose my budget and customers to another region with higher customer sat.

ANNE: Ah, now I see why this is such a big concern for you. So, which would be the real issue you would like to see resolved, our product quality, or your customer satisfaction? How would you respond if I told you your customer sat could actually improve while our DOA rate is being worked on?

Here Anne is again clarifying and identifying the most pressing, real issue at the heart of the customer's concern.

JOHN: Well, if you put it like that, I guess getting higher customer sat would be what I am really concerned about.

ANNE: I see. What data do you have about what drives your customer satisfaction? I am trying to understand how we can make the biggest impact in improving your customer satisfaction.

Again, Anne is helping him clarify his thinking.

JOHN: We just track customer sat trends, not really drivers. We know which questions contribute the most to the overall customer sat number, but I am not sure if they are drivers per se.

ANNE: Would it be helpful for you if we surveyed your customers to identify the real drivers of their satisfaction with your company? We have a platform to track our customer satisfaction, and we can just charge you our cost to run a survey with your customers.

Here she is solving John's most pressing issue, of which Anne's company's product quality is only a part. She is sitting on the same side of the table as a team with John, tackling the issue of customer satisfaction.

JOHN, PERKING UP: Yes, that would be great.

ANNE: I am not suggesting that we look into the drivers of your customer sat to evade your concern about our product [*clearing the air, proactively detecting, and addressing his concern*]. We take your concern about our product quality seriously. May I suggest a fifteen-minute call with our product engineering team, so we can capture your concern about the quality more in depth? If it's the RFID issue, we are working on it feverishly, and we are very close to resolving the issue, but I want to make sure we understand your concern accurately. At the same time, now that we understand what your most pressing concern is, we want to help you resolve that right away while we're working on our quality issue.

Now Anne is a solid partner with the customer instead of a vendor trying to sell devices. She helped him clarify his thinking, and as a result identified a far better solution than she would have had she just focused on customer service, or even quality issues at her company, as John initially stated. It's also important to note that when John first brings up customer service as the issue, rather than product quality, he has no intention of trapping Anne with a red herring; he just blurted out what came to his mind first, because he hadn't rigorously clarified his thinking.

The same process can be applied at the team level. When clarifying ideas, first you confirm what you meant is what was received, and vice versa. Then keep asking questions, at times using conjecture to push the thinking beyond the literal words you have just heard. It's often helpful to listen for the emotion behind the words, rather than the words themselves, and listen for what is not said, rather than just what is said.*

Contextualization

When you contextualize what you ask your team to do more or less of, you provide the context through which you can assign correct meaning.

For example, in 2005 Delta Airlines (then the third largest airline in the United States) filed for bankruptcy, citing rising fuel costs and stiff competition from low-cost carriers. But how it pulled itself out of bankruptcy is really spectacular, as told by Jim Whitehurst, now CEO of Red Hat, in his book *The Open Organization*.[3] Delta identified the most

---

* This type of skill takes focused efforts and practice to solidify, which my company offers in a two-day transformational communication training program.

critical measures for each major area of operation. In order to galvanize the employees, Delta's new management team told its employees that on-time performance was the single most important thing they could do to pull the company out of bankruptcy. Deep pay cuts and layoffs had made the effect of bankruptcy real to them. Now on-time performance and how it contributed to the big picture had a personal meaning to them; they knew the context within which they were being asked to produce on-time performance.

Delta's on-time performance went from the worst among major carriers to the best in just two years. The clarified meaning that energized the workforce produced significant improvements in other areas as well: the RASM (revenue per available seat mile), an industry standard measure of profitability, was ranked at 95 percent of the industry in Q1 of 2007, the highest in years. Delta generated top-tier employee productivity, and paid sick leave was reduced by 11 percent in 2006. It also opened more profitable international routes. With the management and unionized workforce united on the same goal, they fought off a hostile takeover bid from US Airways and a hedge fund's attempt to sell or break up the company, leading the company out of bankruptcy in April/May of 2007. When Delta's employee efforts for on-time departure was contextualized as the most important thing *they* could do to save the company from bankruptcy and a hostile takeover, it unleashed their passion, and they achieved extraordinary results. Goals thus developed have a much deeper meaning than simply fulfilling the request of a boss.

Contextualization can also accelerate the speed of change in an organization. Let's say you're the CEO of a traditional company who has encouraged employees to work at home for many years, partly so you can save real-estate and other fixed costs related to maintaining a physical location, and partly in response to employee feedback that they wanted more freedom. But then you increasingly realize the need for actual employee interactions as a vehicle for encouraging serendipitous encounters, satisfying the need for dense (frequent) interactions that can spawn radical innovation. So you involve your team to evaluate, debate, poke holes, and decide the issue of employees working from their homes.

In addition to providing "whys" that create meaning for what they are being asked to do, context primes our neurons and provides directional guidance to help us interpret incoming data, creating a primordial soup in which innovative ideas can germinate. When you tell your software development team that a potential competitor is launching a product addressing one of your product's major weaknesses, which could quickly take market share away from your company, your software engineers can research the pros and cons of your competitive product, accompany sales reps on their calls to capture customer feedback directly, and attend industry conferences. There they can process new information from the conference talks, as well as informal conversations with people they meet, within this context. Then brilliant chance genius can strike with inspiration that can develop into breakthrough innovation. We cannot control when and how genius will strike, but we can stimulate the primordial soup of the mind within which it can happen.

This is why it's important to frame your mission in a way that ignites your team's passion. What they do then becomes a contribution to advance the cause they are passionate about, instead of a means to bring in a paycheck—drudgery indeed.

CEO AS SYSTEMS THINKER AND CHAMPION OF SIMPLE RULES

In a 2013 study of sixty thousand leaders from 140 countries, the Management Research Group found that what differentiates highly effective leaders most from others was strategic thinking, which it defines as identifying the impact of decisions on various internal departments, suppliers, and customers and thinking in multiple time frames, short-term and long-term.[4] I call this leadership competency *systems thinking*. You can greatly improve your systems thinking–skills by practicing pattern recognition, thinking in frameworks, and managing with simple rules.

Systems Thinking

Mehmood Khan, PepsiCo vice chairman and chief scientific officer of its global R&D center, encapsulated systems thinking when he stated:

> *Many of the biggest challenges the world faces today are interconnected. For example, global health issues related to diet and nutrition require*

changes to our global food system. These changes, in turn, have impli-
cations for our environment and the availability of natural resources.
At the same time, changes in food production and the environment will
affect the livelihoods and working conditions of a large portion of the
global workforce. Viewing these issues in isolation risks uneven out-
comes that could undermine progress as a whole.[5]

Systems thinking requires one to view things as systems, synthesizing all the aspects of complex systems I have shared with you so far. I will briefly reiterate them:

- View organizations and individuals as parts of a system, constantly shaping and being shaped by the environment. For example, you are curious about what could be driving the low performance of a team member, other than an immediate attribution that he is not capable or motivated. You ask yourself if you have a bias against someone with a southern accent, since you have always found it a bit unprofessional. Then you realize you had a coworker with a southern accent who was really slow and dragged down your team performance. Sensing your low assessment of his performance, he gets depressed, which exacerbates his poor performance. You need to realize that your preconditioned bias actually *shapes* his low performance in an autocatalytic, recursive cycle in a system. You need to realize that your team member could be living up to your bias—you are seeing what you have been primed to see in him— and take steps to communicate your bias to him and express your confidence in him.

- When a part of a system fails, do not blame what is immediately visible, but trace the sources that caused the failure and how different components interact with each other. For example, when an important product launch deadline is missed, resist the urge to blame the obvious target: the product development team. When you investigate the big picture, you might discover engineering didn't deliver the prototype to test in time. Marketing didn't deliver the customer requirements to incorporate in the prototype to engineering in time because of a breach in the customer database. In this case, punishing the product development team for missing the deadline does little to fix the problem if the security vulnerability remains; you must address the IT security issue first.

- Look for oscillation patterns and identify sources of leverage behind a power-law distribution. Here is an example. Since you're a savvy systems thinker from all the knowledge you have obtained from this book, you realize 10 percent of your customers drive 80 percent of your sales. You track the customer conversion cycle, and realize your customers buy after being exposed to your message a minimum of three times. You also test and confirm that the more communication channels they are exposed to, the higher the conversion (e.g., email marketing, Facebook advertising, and magazine advertising). Then you develop an optimization model based on frequency, cost of marketing channel, and conversion effectiveness, and keep refining the model on various platforms and times using A/B testing. According to early test results, you need to feed more successful initiatives with more resources, and starve less successful ones. You use feedback as a mechanism to build the momentum generated by the repeating patterns (see chapter 8 on learning).

Pattern Recognition

Radical innovation is a spontaneous result of self-organizing agents' profuse experimentation following simple rules. In chapter 6 we explored the importance of detecting the drivers and processes of patterns. Some repeated patterns give rise to self-organized criticality, which is evident in all living organisms, including neurons, people, and organizations. These patterns are called oscillations, meaning repeating patterns in complex systems. To bring about radical innovation, you need to get your fingernails dirty and execute on the *content* (so you can stay current with the realities of the front lines), but at the same time you need to keep your head above the fray and see the *process* of how things happen and what the structure of interactions is. Sure, it's hard to predict precisely when self-organized efforts will cross over the critical point and show criticality, but when you can recognize oscillation patterns and test your hypothesis of what you're seeing as a trend, you can see around the corner and stay ahead of the curve. Investigation for patterns often leads to identifying opportunities for radical innovation. To help you improve this skill, try the following:

1. **Pay attention** to what you see and what is driving the process. For example, you hear one of your teenage daughters arranging a party to watch a Netflix original show premiere in your home. Before you go into lecture mode about no booze during the party or grilling her about who will be there, ask her why she would prefer watching a Netflix show at home versus watching a new release in a theater. You notice her enthusiasm as she tells you she likes to watch things on a comfortable beanbag, laughing and chatting with her friends. Then you think about what Netflix is doing: bypassing the production and distribution companies and going direct to consumers, while solving their pain points (wanting to talk with friends and sit or lie in a relaxing seat while watching a new-release movie). You take a mental note: channel disintermediation. A few days later, you are talking to your buddy at work, and he tells you he is going to Australia and will save 30 percent on transportation costs while he is there by taking Uber instead of a cab. You ask him what else he likes about using Uber, and he says not having to deal with cash and foreign currency exchange. Then you think about what Uber is doing: bypassing the taxi company and connecting drivers and consumers directly, while solving their pain points (having to carry cash or handle payments when you're in a hurry and the inability to predict when you will get a taxi). You make a mental note: channel disintermediation. Then you remember the mental note about Netflix a few days ago.

2. **See if you can identify any trends** of two or more data points. Now you see a line from the two data points and see a pattern. Once you see a pattern, don't jump to a conclusion yet; what you're seeing is a trend.

   a. **Form a hypothesis.** Now you form a hypothesis that channel disintermediation is a megatrend. Set up a way to test the hypothesis, and ask yourself, "What conditions would have to be true for this hypothesis to be true?" You come up with a few conditions:

i. Consumers are getting more intelligent so they don't need the middleman's handholding.

ii. Technology improvements lower the search cost and enable transparent, fast information exchange between the consumer and the supplier.

iii. The product/service category has been around long enough and in the mature stage in the product-life-cycle curve so people are comfortable using it.

iv. The product/service category is in a regulated or oligopolistic industry, which stifles innovation.

v. There's a relatively high margin (>30 percent) of incumbent players.

b. **Test the hypothesis in your industry.** You then test to see if these conditions are satisfied in the industry of your interest. You research and discover that the eyeglass industry satisfies all the conditions, with Luxottica having 80 percent market share on design, manufacture, and distribution of eyeglasses. Diverse exposure to previous experiences, or having people with diverse viewpoints, is very helpful in the process to identify opportunities. This process can be the beginning of radical innovation, as in the case of eyeglass industry newcomer Warby Parker, whose founders dropped out of Wharton's MBA program to create $1.2 billion in market capitalization after five years.

As you can see, everything starts with an observation from a serendipitous experience. If you're working for a company where you have to constantly watch your back or otherwise feel unsafe, you will not be able to let your mind wander freely to notice the extraordinary patterns in the ordinary. This is why all the leadership competencies of self-management, providing safety, creating differentiation, strengthening connection, and facilitating learning are crucial building blocks for radical innovation.

Frameworks

When MBA students interview for consulting jobs, two types of interviews are conducted: a fit interview and a case interview. A fit interview assesses literally how well the candidate would fit into the culture of the company. A case interview, dreaded by most MBA students aspiring to enter management consulting, assesses how structured and analytical their thinking is. The interviewer presents a client's situation—for example, a client is trying to assess how to improve dwindling profits—and asks the candidate how one should approach the issue. To avoid boiling the ocean (trying to address all potential scenarios and drowning in the process) or suffocating in a rabbit hole (picking one irrelevant scenario and going into it deeply), you must use frameworks to organize and test your hypotheses in a mutually exclusive, completely exhaustive (MECE) fashion.

Barbara Minto's book *The Pyramid Principle* (Prentice Hall, 2010), shows how to organize your thoughts using this approach. One response might be "Profit is driven by increasing revenues and/or reducing costs. So, the first line of analysis would be categorized into these two buckets. Revenues and costs are MECE. Then you would drill down to the second line of analysis by expanding each box, revenue into existing products and new products, which are again MECE. Continue drilling down until you complete the entire chart."

In a similar way, making extensive use of frameworks is an easy way to execute on this concept. You can use simple frameworks that boil down the most germane thoughts in simple, often pictorial, representations to communicate to others in a powerful way. An example of a framework is a two-by-two matrix with four quadrants, with a horizontal axis representing one aspect and the other axis representing the other aspect. If these two axes are not correlated, it's better, but it works as long as they are not too similar. For example, in your Quantum Leadership assessment report, you will find soft skills and hard skills presented in a two-by-two box.

Continuing on with the example of eyeglasses, to show major customer segments, you could show a two-by-two framework with convenience on one axis and fashion on the other (cost is a given—very few people would choose high cost and low convenience, or high cost and low fashion), assuming these are the two most important factors people consider when they get eyeglasses:

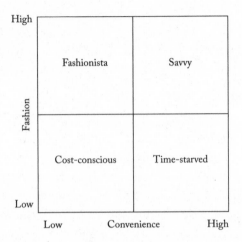

Figure 10.3 Customer segments of the eyeglasses market

Then you can develop your customer experience requirements, marketing messages, and product/service offerings based on the segments you choose to target. If you can boil down the two most important factors for something you're trying to portray, this two-by-two matrix is a powerful and simple way to organize your ideas. But there are many other frameworks, such as McKinsey's nine boxes for talent development.[6] There are also acronym-based frameworks such as SMART (specific, measurable, attainable, realistic, time-bound), which describes the requirements for setting goals, and AIDA (attention, interest, desire, action), which describes the buying stages of a customer.

Simple rules

Once you've created a framework, you can develop simple rules to communicate it. For example, allocate 75 percent of the marketing budget to the savvy segment and 25 percent to the time-starved, organizing your entire company's strategy, operations, and marketing communication around the convenience attribute. Quantum Leaders (after clarifying and debating with their teams) make and update simple rules for optimal results, encourage rapid iteration of profuse experimentation, and ensure team members fail fast and safely in the process. They tolerate and embrace failure as a necessary input for radical innovation. As a leader, you need to have one eye on executing the simple rules and the other on evaluating them. It's your job as a leader to identify when the rules need to be changed to reflect the changing factors in the environment. For more on simple rules, see chapter 8 on learning.

CEO AS SELF-REPLICATION ENABLER: STEWARD OF THE CULTURE

One of the hallmark attributes of systems is that they are self-similar, meaning they replicate themselves—which contributes to building the momentum behind self-organized criticality and increasing internal complexity. As a leader, you need to find a way to enable your organization to self-replicate. That's why setting the right tone with culture is so important. Consistently communicate through actions, words, and stories how you want your culture to be. Another of the best ways to communicate and foster culture is through a brand. As discussed in chapter 7, when leaders consistently communicate the constraints of the organization in terms of what is off- and on-brand, they provide clear direction and speed up decision-making; more important, though, this process enables replicating self-similar patterns that defy the odds and burst forth into radical innovation (recall the example of the alveolar structure of our lungs from chapter 8).

Develop next-generation leaders

Another scalable way to replicate success formulas is by developing next-generation leaders who can develop their own teams and replicate the same formulas. How do you develop next-generation leaders? Start with the context: why leadership competencies must change (to respond to increasing complexity in the environment). Share this book and the other resources referenced here. Leaders' roles are very different in the VUCA age, when decisions need to be made in uncertainty and knowledge workers are smarter than the leader, demanding independence for self-organization. Select a few people to mentor and share your wisdom and experiences of success and failure.

FACTORS SHAPING THE COMPLEX ENVIRONMENT

An understanding of complex systems and how they apply to business and leadership can give you powerful tools to understand, describe, and profoundly change how you view the world. It can also give you tools to see around the corner for future trends. Below are some factors shaping the VUCA business environment, based on the concepts I have shared in this book so far.

Increasing collective intelligence—democratization of information

Complex systems naturally pursue higher levels of complexity, organization, and intelligence. Over time, collective intelligence enables the mass to do what experts do. This is the basis of the observation of Clayton Christensen from Harvard Business School, who revolutionized the world in 1997 with his thoughts in *The Innovator's Dilemma*.[7] This dynamic has led to a clear trend for business models to draw on consumers' collective power and wisdom, such as the use of crowdsourcing by Wikipedia and Linux and crowdfunding platforms like GoFundMe.com. How can you use the power of collective intelligence in your business?

From purchase to subscription

As consumers' collective wisdom increases, and technology continues to drive the cost of accessing data down, consumers demand more flexibility, such as moving away from a purchase model to a subscription model and more unbundling of packaged services. They refuse to be tied down to bundles of services such as cable, phone, and internet. They are no longer willing to overpay for a product they use only once or twice, such as movies or games, or for purchasing technology with high initial capital outlay and upkeep costs for fast changes, such as IT storage. Instead, they want subscription-based services such as Netflix and Hulu for movies, and cloud-computing storage such as that offered by Amazon and IBM. How can you turn part or all your business into a subscription model?

Open environment and architecture

Because collective intelligence can be better implemented in an open architecture than in a proprietary one that could incur a switching cost for conversion or create artificial friction in the information flow, companies operating in an open environment gain more traction faster. Agents in an open system exchange information and resources to coevolve with the environment, creating a vibrant ecosystem. Red Hat in software development, the Linux operating system, the Android mobile operating system, the OpenStack cloud computing platform, and the R software environment for statistical analysis are all examples of this trend. How can you open up your proprietary platform (balanced with protecting your core trade secrets) to create a vibrant ecosystem of customers, suppliers, partners, and even competitors?

Channel disintermediation—death of the middleman (vertical integration)

As consumers gain more collective intelligence, power shifts from the producer to the consumer. Frictionless information exchange in the open environment reduces search and transaction costs, enabling consumers to directly transact with the supplier—channel disintermediation. This is the era of the death of the middleman—a phenomenon that explains the demise of the big box retailers slain by Amazon.

The rise of Qualtrics and SurveyMonkey, with their easy-to-use online survey software and analysis platforms, has displaced many traditional research companies. Working with traditional research companies is expensive and time-consuming. Ancestry.com, the world's largest online family history resource, boasts two million paying subscribers. It used Qualtrics to reduce costs to the tune of $10,000 per research project, which enabled them to conduct more research with a faster turnaround time. No longer do consumers in need of market research need to go to experts; Qualtrics has enabled them to do what the experts do.

The same dynamics are observed in several different industries:

- In the taxi industry, Uber and Lyft connect consumers directly, as AirBnB has done for lodging.
- In the lighting industry—which has traditionally relied on large distributors such as Wesco and Rexel—lighting manufacturer Cree sells directly to the consumer through the internet.
- In the auto industry, Tesla sells directly to the consumer, bypassing dealerships.
- As movie production is digitized and consumers get more direct access to movie production companies, the value chain of film manufacturing, processing, and distribution has been disintermediated, so there is no longer need for intermediaries between producers and consumers.
- Video rental stores are long gone, and big movie studios are feeling the threat of Netflix and Amazon, who are developing content themselves and distributing to customers directly.

Where is your company in the value chain, and how vulnerable are you to disintermediation? What can you do to disintermediate others in the value chain? If you are AC Nielsen, a traditional incumbent in the market research industry disrupted by Qualtrics, how do you need to reinvent your business model and create value? Perhaps by educating customers on how to use the Qualtrics tool, help interpret the results, and present the results in a user-friendly presentation package? To identify opportunities for disintermediation, use the simple rules in the pattern recognition section earlier in this chapter.

Convergence (horizontal integration)

If channel disintermediation is vertical integration, convergence is horizontal integration. As companies at the supplier end of the value chain vertically integrate to connect directly with the end consumer, and a trend for an open environment grows in society, the faster speed of processing information and feedback responding to that information enables higher interdependence among all subsystems in an environment. This interdependence leads to blurring of the business scopes of the companies sharing an ecosystem, which makes it difficult to clearly define what business one is in.

This dynamic creates what some are calling the "big blur," in which everyone is getting into everyone else's business, creating a huge push for convergence of various technologies and platforms. To make smarter products, companies incorporate more functions that cut across many business scopes. In addition, this trend makes it harder to clearly delineate competitors from suppliers or customers. Who would have thought Google would be competing with Ford or BMW? But it is, with its self-driving car, Waymo. In the internet of things space, AT&T is competing with Amazon (which started out as a bookseller) and Cisco (AT&T's supplier turned competitor). Microsoft is a supplier for Samsung, but competes with it in a pursuit to turn a phone into a PC.

Connectivity & interdependence

As complex systems attain higher levels of complexity, they seek more connection with other subsystems. For example, the tsunami of the internet of things (IoT) will redefine how connected everything will be. Gartner predicts that 212 billion devices will be connected through the IoT by 2020. In 2016 Japanese internet and telecommunications conglomerate SoftBank bought the UK-based microprocessor company ARM for $32 billion. ARM commands a 90 percent market share, which will fuel the growth of the IoT market. Here is the annual revenue history of ARM before the acquisition:

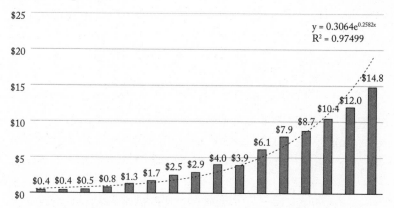

Figure 10.4 *Chips containing ARM processors shipped, $billion/year*

The trend line shows a clear exponential growth trajectory. Whenever you see a trend line like this, be on the alert; this could be the beginning of a radical phenomenon that has cleared the initial germination period and is about to cross over the inflection point.

Most current management tools and training are based on Gaussian distribution, using the assumption of normal distribution of errors, which does not reflect today's VUCA reality. We need to provide leadership training informed by complex systems framework and tools such as the power-law distribution.*

Systems-based solutions

Many of the world's intractable problems are systemic in nature, and hence must be solved from a systems perspective if we don't want to settle for temporary solutions. As discussed in chapter 7, to solve global warming, we must first understand the systemic dynamics of this issue.

Another example is our approach to health care that only treats symptoms, fixing what is most visible instead of looking at the human body as a system with interdependent parts. For example, when someone gets a bacterial infection, instead of searching for the root cause of the infection, such as compromised liver function, doctors are likely to prescribe antibiotics, which kill the bacteria as well as healthy gut flora and at the same time further toxify the liver. When the treatment is over, the immune system no longer has the gut flora it needs to fight off new pathogens. Then your doctor calls in another round of antibiotics, and the vicious cycle starts all over again.

EXAMPLES OF THE
QUANTUM COMPANY

Case Study: Netflix

In the beginning of 2017 Netflix was valued at $62 billion, which it built in only twenty years. It started renting DVDs by mail in 1997,

---

* My company provides a three-day training course for radical innovation encompassing many concepts from this book.

competing with Blockbuster and Hollywood Video. In 2000 Netflix offered itself to Blockbuster for $50 million, which then-CEO of Blockbuster John Antioco rejected (I am sure Antioco gets an ulcer every time he thinks about that). Netflix's subsequent success in the DVD-by-mail business contributed to the demise of Blockbuster. Then Netflix changed its business model to subscription-based video streaming, competing with streaming companies such as Hulu and Amazon, as well as companies like Comcast and Time Warner that provide access to the content. Netflix then vertically integrated by entering the content business itself, producing in-house shows such as *House of Cards* and *Orange is the New Black*. Thus, it became a competitor to traditional studios and networks such as NBC and HBO.

In 2016 Netflix landed fifty-four Emmy nominations, which represents a serious threat to networks. Netflix spent over $5 billion that year to release 126 original series, comprising six hundred hours of programming—more than any other network. Networks are experiencing increasingly tight margins because (1) the move by Netflix to produce original content forces them to produce more original content, which costs more than relying on reruns, and (2) people are turning to Netflix to binge-watch a whole series, instead of watching reruns on the network or cable, which lowers their ratings and income from advertising on those reruns. Netflix is now competing successfully in the distribution (Hulu, Amazon Video), content (TV networks), and access (cable companies) businesses.

Netflix clearly understands the power of the wisdom of the crowd. In October 2006 Netflix wanted to develop recommendations at least 10 percent closer to the actual preferences of its customers, as measured by their own ratings after watching a show. Netflix issued a challenge with a prize of $1 million for anyone who could improve Netflix's show recommendation algorithm by 10 percent. More than forty thousand teams participated. The contest was an extraordinarily difficult challenge, since participants had to comb through over a hundred million movie ratings to find a pattern. After three years, a winner finally emerged: a team made up of seven people, including statisticians, machine-learning experts, and computer programmers in four countries, who entered the contest as three separate teams but later merged into one. Netflix tapped into the power of collective intelligence on more than one dimension. But there are other principles that have helped catapult Netflix to stratospheric growth and market capitalization.

Reed Hastings, CEO of Netflix, has talked about how Netflix lets its employees self-organize, one of the essential tenets of Quantum Companies that we've thoroughly discussed. Netflix management thought, "There's no clothing policy at Netflix, but nobody comes to work naked, because employees know the right thing to do. Salaried employees don't track overtime when they work nights and weekends, so why should the company track their vacation days?"[8] So their vacation policy is *not* to have a vacation policy. Same goes with the expense policy—there is no expense policy, nor a department to ensure compliance to expense policy. Netflix employees decide for themselves how many vacation days they take and what expenses they get reimbursed.

Netflix's simple rule to guide the absence of vacation and expense policies is just five words: *act in Netflix's best interest.* Their simple rule to guide what kind of culture it wants to foster? "We're a team, not a family. We're like a pro sports team, not a kid's recreational team." They also use the simple rule that "adequate performance gets a generous severance package" and use the Keeper Test to identify those whom they should try hard to keep in and out of the company: "Which of my people, if they told me they were leaving for a similar job at a peer company, would I fight hard to keep at Netflix?"

As a result of implementing self-organization, simple rules, and other principles of radical innovation, as of 2017, Netflix was the number one performing stock in two out of the previous four years among the S&P 500 companies.[9]

What's next for Netflix? Maybe they will tap into the collective intelligence of their massive subscriber base and use artificial intelligence to formulate their feedback on what they want to see for developing Netflix's programs. The greatest obstacle for Netflix customers, most of whom want the option of consuming content over their mobile phone, is the cost of mobile data. If Netflix again vertically integrates by providing cellular data, it will dramatically shift industry dynamics, expanding its scope into the pipe business and competing with the likes of AT&T and Verizon. Or maybe it will launch into the TV hardware business, fully equipped with technologies for a global internet TV network. Nobody outside the company knows, but Netflix has become a radical innovator in all the new business scopes it has entered, and has earned consumers' permission to expand its brand into new areas.

TRANSFORMING FROM A TRADITIONAL COMPANY TO A QUANTUM COMPANY

Case Study: GE

Since it started with a lightbulb Thomas Edison invented 125 years ago, GE has become one of the largest manufacturing companies in the world, with US$12.4 billion in revenues. Studying its journey to transform itself from a stodgy manufacturing company of the Industrial Revolution era to one fit for today's VUCA environment sheds light on how other traditional companies can transform themselves into Quantum Companies.

In the Jack Welch era, the prevailing management tool was Six Sigma and quality control as their mantra, as he said in his 1997 letter to the shareholders: "The centerpiece of our dreams and aspirations for this great Company—the drive for Six Sigma quality . . . We are feverish on the subject of Six Sigma quality . . . because we see it as the ultimate way to make real our dreams of what this great company could become."[10]

GE required all exempt employees to undertake a thirteen-day, one-hundred-hour training program in Six Sigma methodologies and complete a Six Sigma project by the end of 1998. Welch famously said in a 2009 Society of Human Resources Managers conference that "there is no such thing as work-life balance" and "there are work-life choices, and you make them, and they have consequences,"[11] emphasizing the importance of sacrificing personal life for advancements at work. GE used the 2:7:1 rule where they reward the top 20 percent and push out the bottom 10 percent and promoted internal competition—hardly an environment that promotes safety. GE also used the sequential product development process that took more than five years to develop new products for big products, which started with a sales team giving design requirements and leaving the development process.

But recognizing the tidal shift in the VUCA business environment, it has instituted major change initiatives and introduced cultural transformation. GE is embracing the Silicon Valley culture with smart machines that integrate sensors and big data. In January 2013 GE launched FastWorks, combining the Lean and Agile software development approaches, a startling move for an industrial manufacturing company. FastWorks focuses on quick deliverables and fast learning, involving customers from the very beginning. GE's new approach is to capitalize on experimentation and adaptability, building and iterating products, instead of perfecting the product to be almost defect free (3.4 defects in one million opportunities). It provides broad frameworks to follow and passes on ownership and autonomy to local product teams. As part of this program, GE trained five thousand senior leaders on the new FastWorks methodology on a road show.

In August 2015 GE also abolished the 2:7:1 comparative annual performance rating system, and introduced an app called PD@GE (performance development at GE) to enable real-time frequent feedback. They used to "evaluate" employee performance and boot out the bottom 10 percent who didn't perform well, but in this new system, the role of a boss is to advise and support, not evaluate and command. Their annual performance meetings are more for providing coaching, guiding their employees on how best to achieve their goals, instead of evaluating their performance. It's not performance evaluation but performance development. Managers are expected to have frequent conversations with their employees on how they are doing on their goals. The app provides summaries of these conversations with the main aim of constant improvement. The app can help them set and share objectives without sitting down face-to-face, summarize and concisely show work progress in one place, and can even send and take care of small requests that hinder their productivity, such as computer repairs. Through this process, they can speed up communication using shorthand, attaching files, and even writing messages by hand. They increased the average number of direct reports for a manager from four to seven, flattening the hierarchy. The new leadership mantra is to inspire connection, develop people, and allow self-organization instead of the "command and control" system of the Jack Welch days.

This change in GE's corporate culture for more flexibility even extends to how employees schedule their work. In 2015 GE rolled out a permissive approach to paid time off for exempt employees, where they can coordinate with their manager to take the time off.

In a blog post for GE employees, Dylan Law, a project engineering manager with GE Power in Sydney, Australia, shares his day:[12]

7:00 AM Arrival at work

2:30 PM Leave work to take care of children and cook dinner before mum arrives
5:00 PM Mum arrives and we have dinner together
6–7:00 PM Toddler bed time rituals
7:00 PM I log in and am back into work for 3 hours

Law reports that he is more productive and enjoys more family time, and working early and late connects him with the workday in the rest of the world's time zones.

Raghu Krishnamoorthy, vice president of executive development and chief learning officer at GE, spoke on the new model leader:

The leader of old used to compete to win, the leader of the new collaborates to win. The leader of old fitted in; the leader of new values diversity. The leader of old used command and control; the leader of new connects and inspires. Learning is not just a classroom experience—it's available to you all the time, anywhere. We are continuing to focus on skill building but also have to factor in things like how do you teach people courage, trust, and empowerment.[13]

All these change initiatives are transforming GE into a start-up with 350,000 agile, smart, flexible, and self-organizing employees. Jeffrey Immelt, who retired in August 2017 after seventeen years as CEO at GE, said the following to encapsulate GE's new approach in his commencement speech to the graduates at New York University's Stern School of Business:

We are entering a volatile global economy, the most uncertain I have ever seen . . . And as a response, we will localize . . . We can accelerate growth by solving local problems. Complex and centralized bureaucracies are obsolete. The days of cycling global ideas through a central headquarters is over. Globalization requires pushing capability to local teams who are empowered to take risks without second guessing. Change requires new business models . . . leaner, faster, more decentralized. So be flexible, be bold, don't fear criticism.[14]

To facilitate collective intelligence, GE launched several new digital learning platforms such as BrilliantYou, an initiative to disseminate learning from its famous Crotonville learning center programs into the hands of all employees. It provides a platform to build and use collective intelligence at GE. It facilitates learning not only by taking structured classes but also using social, personal experience, getting feedback from others, and finding what's working and what's not working from its employees. On the BrilliantYou app, the content you see is customized for your needs and your content consumption habits. The AI behind the app presents courses, videos, and other materials that might be important for your role or of interest to you. Based on your meeting schedule it has access to, it could pull up content that might be relevant to you to prepare for the meeting. Now GE measures learning effectiveness, not performance.

Paul Fama, GE's learning leader, said of this new learning platform:

> *Learning used to be an event. Now we have to create learning everywhere we go. It has to be frictionless, omnipresent, behavior shaping, individualized, based on myriads of experiences, continual, and a daily digital habit. Leaders learn from each other and the communities they develop. Learning has to be customer-centric—we need to go to the learner, real time, when they need us, how they need us, instead of the other way around. To measure the quality of learning, we use rating systems. We use habit metrics on what they are looking at and how often, and adjust the user experience and content based on the data.*[15]

Immelt also said in a 2016 LinkedIn post:

> *[We are in the midst of] our transformation into the world's largest digital industrial company to our company's evolving culture that's focused on decentralized decision-making, speed, and startup-like mentality . . .*
>
> *If you are joining the company in your 20s, unlike when I joined, you're going to learn to code. We are also changing the plumbing inside the company to connect everyone and make the culture change possible. This is existential . . .*
>
> *Culture and attracting the right talent are also why we are moving from suburban Connecticut to downtown Boston. It's an ecosystem*

made by and for innovation. In Boston, we can be challenged by a doc-tor from Massachusetts General or by a student from MIT. We need to be in this environment.

We are also changing the way we evaluate our people. We're trying to end anything that was annual or quarterly and make everything more real-time.[16]

GE's new culture is also evident in its messages to recruits: "GE today is a digital industrial company. Our goal is simplification. Fewer layers, fewer decision points, democratization of information, flexibility of work environment."[17]

In a LinkedIn post from May 2017, Susan Peters, GE's head of HR, summarizes GE's culture change:

There's no room for the old "command and control" style of leadership; coaching and empowerment are in. Dusty org charts are giving way to dynamic, data-driven, self-organizing teams. Transparency and candor are producing better outcomes, faster.

The most effective leaders in The Emergent Era will be the ones who can operate across multiple contexts and turn apparent chaos into simple opportunity . . .

You don't need to have all the answers. But you do need to ask better questions . . .

Execution is everything. And it's also not enough . . . Engaged employees will astonish you with their achievements.

What feedback loops exist? Can you create more? . . . [This is how we] identify new opportunities for improvement. And it's accelerating our progress . . . Stay focused on what you can learn from one moment to the next, and how you'll apply what you learn—it will help you turn self-awareness into self-confidence.[18]

Albeit still early in the process, all these transformational efforts are paying off. GE developed the first refrigerator using the FastWorks method at half the cost and time typically spent on a new product. It used to take them five years to develop a new gas turbine but now it takes them thirty months. It has reduced the product development cycle by more than 30 percent and the speed it takes to respond to customer feedback has accelerated fourfold. I believe GE's transformation into digital industrial will be recorded as one of the most revolutionary corporate change initiatives in history.

FUTURE LEADERSHIP MANDATES

As mentioned, the digital revolution of the twenty-first century changed the basis of competition in a massive way, turning the business environment into one dominated by complexity. What follows is my summary of desired leadership competencies from a traditional lens and how businesses must change to win in the complex era.

Decision-making

In this VUCA age, trying to predict, control, and eliminate variances is a losing game. Too many things are happening too fast, and the interactions are too interdependent and dense. The resulting decoupling of information from power and responsibility, as mentioned in chapter 1—that is, where information resides with front-line employees, but power and responsibility resides with top managers—is deadly in today's fast-moving business environment. Given the nature of increasing complexity, leaders' roles must change from command and control to decentralization and empowerment of others. Decisions must be made at the boundaries of the organization, where it interacts with others in the environment because that's where information is most current and relevant. Employees will demand more autonomy and self-organization.

Control and accountability

In organizations with self-organizing employees, control moves from the center to the masses. In an article for *Harvard Business Review,* Jim Whitehurst says that control comes from shared norms of self-policing communities, not from position titles or policies.[19] Similarly, accountability comes more from peers and other interdependent parts of a system you share. Therefore, leaders must build a team that heals itself by curating peer policing. To institute this type of self-policing, leaders must clear all hurdles in communication by maximizing transparency (e.g., share everything in an all-hands meeting, except things that will put you in jail or devastate your company).

Performance review and feedback

Instead of annual performance reviews, leaders must provide real-time feedback, focusing on what they want to see more and less of, instead of good or bad performance. Performance evaluation must be separated from feedback to facilitate safety and maximize learning.

Risk management

With increasing complexity in the environment, too many things are happening too fast. Managing risks needs to change from turning to manuals or policy and procedures to fast failures on a small scale, such as the "ship and iterate" approach to a product launch. Leadership competencies must include flexibility in thinking, tolerance for ambiguity, and resilience to failures.

Results

In addition to quarterly short-term results or annual medium-term results, leaders must also be evaluated on less visible but critical elements that have an impact on the organization's long-term survival, such as building an ecosystem, creating open architecture, or facilitating coevolution. These long-term initiatives can take a back burner if companies are just focused on quarterly results. While attending only to the short term, they run the risk of someone else's radical innovation making them irrelevant. Therefore, structuring an incentive plan that incorporates long-term results are encouraged, such as implementing a five-year rolling average.

CONCLUSION

This book is a culmination of over twenty thousand hours of organizational consulting, training, coaching, teaching, strategy development, my own research, and thoughts from other researchers and practitioners in many disciplines—such as quantum mechanics, complexity science, systems studies, neuroscience, psychology, and business. I hope you can benefit from this book as I have benefited from all the raw materials and experiences I used in this book.

I encourage you to go to www.sunniegiles.com and take the Quantum Leadership assessment, if you haven't already. Download the worksheet to help you start implementing the competencies you want to focus on. View the videos available in the Resources section to get a better understanding. Request a buddy for an accountability partner. I had to intentionally limit the scope of this book to what and why, and exclude much of how to implement the change because of the sheer volume of the content I wanted to cover. You can take the training courses (three-day Quantum Leadership for Radical Innovation course, two-day Transformational Communication course, both in-classroom or online) available from my company or other Quantum Leadership–certified training providers if you want to accelerate your change efforts. As you transform your leadership skills, an amazingly rewarding journey opens ahead of you, both personally and professionally. You can also get certified as a Quantum Leader for Radical Innovation, CQL (Certified Quantum Leader), which sets you apart from many other managers as a good boss whom others enjoy working for and a vetted leader trained in the principles of radical innovation. As you expand the circle of your influence by implementing the concepts in this book to your family and work, you contribute to creating higher complexity and evolution of our human species. And I dare say that you become happier in life, because the higher complexity you achieve, the more fulfilled you feel as human beings.

NOTES

INTRODUCTION

1. Demis Hassabis, Twitter post, March 21, 2016, 4:00 AM, https://twitter.com/demishassabis/status/711870170067836929.
2. David Silver et al., "Mastering the Game of Go with Deep Neural Networks and Tree Search," *Nature* 529 (2016): 484–89, doi:10.1038/nature16961.
3. Eric Schmidt and Jonathan Rosenberg, *How Google Works* (New York: Grand Central Publishing, 2014).
4. Laszlo Bock, *Work Rules!: Insights from Inside Google That Will Transform How You Live and Lead* (New York: Twelve, 2015).
5. Larry Page and Sergey Brin, "'An Owner's Manual' for Google Shareholders" (Founders' IPO Letter, S-1 Registration Statement, Investor Relations, Alphabet Investor Relations, 2004), https://abc.xyz/investor/founders-letters/2004/ipo-letter.html.
6. Silver et al., "Game of Go."
7. Schmidt and Rosenberg, *How Google Works*.
8. Jim Giles, "Internet Encyclopaedias Go Head to Head," *Nature* 438 (2005): 900–901, doi:10.1038/438900a.
9. Schmidt and Rosenberg, *How Google Works*.
10. Schmidt and Rosenberg, *How Google Works*.
11. Boston Consulting Group, "The Most Innovative Companies: An Interactive Guide," *bcg.perspectives*, January 12, 2017, https://www.bcgperspectives.com/content/interactive/innovation_growth_most_innovative_companies_interactive_guide.
12. Peter A. Thiel and Blake Masters, *Zero to One: Notes on Startups, or How to Build the Future* (New York: Crown Business, 2014).

CHAPTER 1: A NEW PARADIGM OF LEADERSHIP

1. Graeme Wearden and Nick Fletcher, "Brexit Panic Wipes $2 Trillion Off World Markets—As It Happened," *Guardian*, June 24, 2016, https://www.theguardian.com/business/live/2016/jun/24/global-markets-ftse-pound-uk-leave-eu-brexit-live-updates.

2. CNN Arabic Staff, "How a Fruit Seller Caused Revolution in Tunisia," CNN, January 16, 2011, http://www.cnn.com/2011/WORLD/africa/01/16/tunisia.fruit.seller.bouazizi/index.html

3. Pablo Tovar, "Leadership Challenges in the V.U.C.A World," *Leadership Thoughts* (blog), September 14, 2016, http://www.oxfordleadership.com/leadership-challenges-v-u-c-world.

4. "Ebola Situation Report," World Health Organization, March 30, 2016, http://apps.who.int/ebola/current-situation/ebola-situation-report-30-march-2016; "Previous Outbreak Updates," Ebola (Ebola Virus Disease), 2014–2016 West Africa Outbreak, Centers for Disease Control and Prevention, March 24, 2016, https://www.cdc.gov/vhf/ebola/outbreaks/2014-west-africa/previous-updates.html.

5. "Outbreaks Chronology," Ebola (Ebola Virus Disease), Outbreaks, Centers for Disease Control and Prevention, July 28, 2017, https://www.cdc.gov/vhf/ebola/outbreaks/history/chronology.html.

6. See "Western Africa Population (Live)," Worldometers, http://www.worldometers.info/world-population/western-africa-population.

7. "The Economic Impact of the 2014 Ebola Epidemic: Short and Medium Term Estimates for West Africa," World Bank, October 8, 2014, http://www.worldbank.org/en/region/afr/publication/the-economic-impact-of-the-2014-ebola-epidemic-short-and-medium-term-estimates-for-west-africa.

8. "Cost of the Ebola Epidemic," Ebola (Ebola Virus Disease), 2014–2016 West Africa Outbreak, Centers for Disease Control and Prevention, August 8, 2016, https://www.cdc.gov/vhf/ebola/outbreaks/2014-west-africa/cost-of-ebola.html.

9. George A. Miller, "The Magical Number Seven, Plus or Minus Two: Some Limits on Our Capacity for Processing Information," *Psychological Review* 63, no. 2 (1956): 81.

10. Nelson Cowan, *Attention and Memory: An Integrated Framework* (New York: Oxford University Press, 1997).

11. W. Michael Cox and Richard Alm, "You Are What You Spend," *New York Times*, February 10, 2008, http://www.nytimes.com/2008/02/10/opinion/10cox.html; "TUNING IN: Communications technologies historically have had broad appeal for consumers," *Wall Street Journal*, Classroom Edition, 1998, http://www.karlhartig.com/chart/techhouse.pdf.

12. Sunnie Giles, "The Most Important Leadership Competencies, According to Leaders Around the World," *Harvard Business Review*, March 15, 2016,

https://hbr.org/2016/03/the-most-important-leadership-competencies-according
-to-leaders-around-the-world.

13. Stephen W. Porges, "Orienting in a Defensive World: Mammalian Modifications
of Our Evolutionary Heritage. A Polyvagal Theory," *Psychophysiology* 32, no. 4
(1995): 301–18.

14. Christoph H. Loch and Bernardo A. Huberman, "A Punctuated-Equilibrium
Model of Technology Diffusion," *Management Science* 45, no. 2 (1999): 160–77.

CHAPTER 2: COMPLEX ADAPTIVE SYSTEMS: HOW ALL LIVING THINGS WORK

1. Edward N. Lorenz, "Deterministic Nonperiodic Flow," *Journal of the Atmospheric
Sciences* 20, no. 2 (1963): 130–41.

2. Christopher M. Danforth, "Chaos in an atmosphere hanging on a wall,"
Mathematics of Planet Earth (2013).

3. Malcolm Gladwell, *The Tipping Point: How Little Things Can Make a Big Difference*
(New York: Little, Brown, 2006).

4. Geoffrey A. Moore, *Crossing the Chasm: Marketing and Selling High-Tech Products
to Mainstream Customers* (New York: HarperCollins, 2002).

5. Tom Byers, "Ten Enduring Success Factors for High Technology
Entrepreneurship," eCorner, Stanford, January 18, 2006, http://ecorner.stanford
.edu/podcasts/1563/Ten-Enduring-Success-Factors-for-High-Technology
-Entrepreneurship.

6. Adam Grant, *Originals: How Non-conformists Move the World* (New York: Viking,
2016), 94.

7. Stuart A. Kauffman, *Investigations* (New York: Oxford University Press, 2000).

8. Steven Johnson, *Where Good Ideas Come From: The Natural History of Innovation*
(New York: Riverhead Books, 2010).

9. Harry McCracken, "How Japan's Line App Became a Culture-Changing,
Revenue-Generating Phenomenon," *Fast Company*, February 19, 2015,
https://www.fastcompany.com/3041578/most-innovative-companies-2015/
how-japans-line-app-became-a-culture-changing-revenue-generat.

10. Michael E. Porter, *Competitive Advantage: Creating and Sustaining Superior
Performance* (New York: FreePress, 1985).

11. Michael E. Porter, "What Is Strategy?," *Harvard Business Review*, November/
December 1996, https://hbr.org/1996/11/what-is-strategy.

CHAPTER 3: NEUROSCIENCE OF LEADERSHIP, OR THE LAWS OF HOW ALL LIVING THINGS WORK

1. Matthew J. Parry-Hill and Michael W. Davidson, "Thomas Young's Double Slit
Experiment" (interactive tutorial, Optical Microscopy Primer, Physics of Light

and Color, Molecular Expressions, Florida State University, Tallahassee, January 2017) http://micro.magnet.fsu.edu/primer/java/interference/doubleslit.

2 . Francis Heylighen and Erik Rosseel, eds., *Self-Steering and Cognition in Complex Systems: Toward a New Cybernetics*, Studies in Cybernetics, bk. 22 (New York: Gordon and Breach Science Publishers, 1990).

3 . Eugene P. Wigner, "Remarks on the Mind-Body Problem," *Symmetries and Reflections* (1961), 171.

4 . Irving Wladawsky-Berger, "Big Data, Complex Systems and Quantum Mechanics," *Irving Wladawsky-Berger* (blog), December 10, 2012, http://blog. irvingwb.com/blog/2012/12/big-data-complex-systems-and-quantum-mechanics. html.

5 . Jean-Louis Rivail, Manuel Ruiz-Lopez, and Xavier Assfeld, eds., *Quantum Modeling of Complex Molecular Systems*, Challenges and Advances in Computational Chemistry and Physics, bk. 21 (New York: Springer, 2015).

6 . Daniel J. Siegel, *Mindsight: The New Science of Personal Transformation* (New York: Bantam, 2010).

7 . Eleanor A. Maguire et al., "Navigation-Related Structural Change in the Hippocampi of Taxi Drivers," *Proceedings of the National Academy of Sciences* 97, no. 8 (2000): 4398–403.

8 . James Watson, *The Double Helix: A Personal Account of the Discovery of the Structure of DNA* (London: Hachette UK, 2012).

9 . Francis H. C. Crick, "On Protein Synthesis," *Symposia of the Society for Experimental Biology* 12 (1958): 138–63.

1 0 . Daniel J. Siegel, *The Developing Mind, Second Edition: How Relationships and the Brain Interact to Shape Who We Are* (New York: Guilford Publications, 2015).

1 1 . Siegel, *Developing Mind*.

1 2 . Daniel J. Siegel and Mary Hartzell, *Parenting from the Inside Out: How a Deeper Self-Understanding Can Help You Raise Children Who Thrive* (New York: TarcherPerigee, 2013).

1 3 . Joseph LeDoux, "The Emotional Brain, Fear, and the Amygdala," *Cellular and Molecular Neurobiology* 23.4 (2003): 727–738.

1 4 . LeDoux, "Emotional Brain."

1 5 . Antonio R. Damasio et al., "Subcortical and Cortical Brain Activity During the Feeling of Self-Generated Emotions," *Nature Neuroscience* 3, no. 10 (2000): 1049–56.

1 6 . Horacio Fabrega Jr., "The Feeling of What Happens: Body and Emotion in the Making of Consciousness," *Psychiatric Services* 51, no. 12 (2000): 1579.

1 7 . J. Douglas Bremner, "Traumatic Stress: Effects on the Brain," *Dialogues in Clinical Neuroscience* 8, no. 4 (2006): 445.

1 8 . D. M. Curlik and T. J. Shors, "Training Your Brain: Do Mental and Physical (MAP) Training Enhance Cognition Through the Process of Neurogenesis in the Hippocampus?," *Neuropharmacology* 64 (2013): 506–514.

19. Neil Burgess, Eleanor A. Maguire, and John O'Keefe, "The Human Hippocampus and Spatial and Episodic Memory," *Neuron* 35, no. 44 (2002): 625–41.

20. Daniel J. Siegel, *The Mindful Brain: Reflection and Attunement in the Cultivation of Well-Being* (New York: W. W. Norton, 2007).

21. Charles J. Limb and Allen R. Braun, "Neural Substrates of Spontaneous Musical Performance: An Fmri Study of Jazz Improvisation," *PLoS One* 3, no. 2 (2008): e1679.

CHAPTER 4: EFFECTIVE SELF-MANAGEMENT: THE FOUNDATION OF QUANTUM LEADERSHIP

1. Rachel Feintzeig, "'Nice' Is a Four-Letter Word at Companies Practicing Radical Candor," *Wall Street Journal*, December 30, 2015, http://www.wsj.com/articles/nice-is-a-four-letter-word-at-companies-practicing-radical-candor-1451498192; Jodi Kantor and David Streitfeld, "Inside Amazon: Wrestling Big Ideas in a Bruising Workplace," *New York Times*, August 15, 2015, http://www.nytimes.com/2015/08/16/technology/inside-amazon-wrestling-big-ideas-in-a-bruising-workplace.html.

2. Daniel Kahneman and Angus Deaton, "High Income Improves Evaluation of Life but Not Emotional Well-Being," *Proceedings of the National Academy of Sciences* 107, no. 38 (2010): 16489–93.

3. Sunnie Giles, Twitter post, July 20, 2016, 11:42 AM, https://twitter.com/sunnie_giles/status/755835336815546368.

4. Lilianne R. Mujica-Parodi et al., "Chemosensory Cues to Conspecific Emotional Stress Activate Amygdala in Humans," *PLoS One* 4.7 (2009): e6415.

5. Smiljana Mutic et al., "You Smell Dangerous: Communicating Fight Responses Through Human Chemosignals Of Aggression," *Chemical Senses* (2015): bjv058.

6. Richard Boyatzis and Annie McKee, *Resonant Leadership: Renewing Yourself and Connecting with Others Through Mindfulness, Hope and Compassion* (Boston: Harvard Business Press, 2013).

7. Lauri Nummenmaa et al., "Bodily Maps of Emotions," *Proceedings of the National Academy of Sciences* 111, no. 2 (2014): 646–51.

8. Jerry Useem, "Power Causes Brain Damage," *Atlantic*, July/August 2007, https://www.theatlantic.com/magazine/archive/2017/07/power-causes-brain-damage/528711.

9. Dacher Keltner, "Don't Let Power Corrupt You," *Harvard Business Review*, October 2006, https://hbr.org/2016/10/dont-let-power-corrupt-you.

10. Dacher Keltner, *The Power Paradox: How We Gain and Lose Influence* (New York: Penguin, 2017).

11. Daniel Goleman, "Emotional Intelligence: Why It Can Matter More than IQ," *Learning* 24, no. 6 (1996): 49–50.

1 2. Julie A. Ruth, Frederic F. Brunel, and Cele C. Otnes, "Linking Thoughts to Feelings: Investigating Cognitive Appraisals and Consumption Emotions in a Mixed-Emotions Context," *Journal of the Academy of Marketing Science* 30, no. 1 (2002): 44–58.

1 3. Leon Festinger, *A Theory of Cognitive Dissonance* (Stanford, CA: Stanford University Press, 1962).

1 4. Timothy A. Judge and Joyce E. Bono, "Relationship of Core Self-Evaluations Traits—Self-Esteem, Generalized Self-Efficacy, Locus of Control, and Emotional Stability—with Job Satisfaction and Job Performance: A Meta-Analysis," *Journal of Applied Psychology* 86, no. 1 (2001): 80.

1 5. Robin Martin et al., "The Role of Leader-Member Exchanges in Mediating the Relationship Between Locus of Control and Work Reactions," *Journal of Occupational and Organizational Psychology* 78, no. 1 (2005): 141–47.

1 6. Angela Roddenberry and Kimberly Renk, "Locus of Control and Self-Efficacy: Potential Mediators of Stress, Illness, and Utilization of Health Services in College Students," *Child Psychiatry & Human Development* 41, no. 4 (2010): 353–70.

1 7. Maureen J. Findley and Harris M. Cooper, "Locus of Control and Academic Achievement: A Literature Review," *Journal of Personality and Social Psychology* 44, no. 2 (1983): 419.

1 8. Herbert M. Lefcourt, *Locus of Control: Current Trends in Theory & Research* (New York: Psychology Press, 2014).

1 9. Carol Dweck, *Mindset: The New Psychology of Success* (New York: Random House, 2006).

2 0. Danny Miller and Jean-Marie Toulouse, "Chief Executive Personality and Corporate Strategy and Structure in Small Firms," *Management Science* 32, no. 11 (1986): 1389–409; Mohammad Saud Khan, Robert J. Breitenecker, and Erich J. Schwarz, "Entrepreneurial Team Locus of Control: Diversity and Trust," *Management Decision* 52, no. 6 (2014): 1057–81.

2 1. Stephen L. Mueller and Anisya S. Thomas, "Culture and Entrepreneurial Potential: A Nine Country Study of Locus of Control and Innovativeness," *Journal of Business Venturing* 16, no. 1 (2001): 51–75.

CHAPTER 5: PROVIDING SAFETY

1. David V. Day, ed., *The Oxford Handbook of Leadership and Organizations* (New York: Oxford University Press, 2014).

2. Arne Öhman, "Automaticity and the Amygdala: Nonconscious Responses to Emotional Faces," *Current Directions in Psychological Science* 11, no. 2 (2002): 62–66.

3. Stephen W. Porges, "The Polyvagal Theory: Phylogenetic Substrates of a Social Nervous System," *International Journal of Psychophysiology* 42, no. 2 (2001): 123–46.

4. Richard Boyatzis and Annie McKee, *Resonant Leadership: Renewing Yourself and Connecting with Others Through Mindfulness, Hope and Compassion* (Boston: Harvard Business Press, 2013).

5. Boyatzis and McKee, *Resonant Leadership*.

6. J. Douglas Bremner, "Traumatic Stress: Effects on the Brain," *Dialogues in Clinical Neuroscience* 8, no. 4 (2006): 445.

7. David R. Euston, Aaron J. Gruber, and Bruce L. McNaughton, "The Role of Medial Prefrontal Cortex in Memory and Decision Making," *Neuron* 76, no. 6 (2012): 1057–70.

8. Boyatzis and McKee, *Resonant Leadership*.

9. Tracie J. Rogers, Brandon L. Alderman, and Daniel M. Landers, "Effects of Life-Event Stress and Hardiness on Peripheral Vision in a Real-Life Stress Situation," *Behavioral Medicine* 29, no. 1 (2003): 21–26.

10. Thomas W. Kamarck et al., "Exaggerated Blood Pressure Responses During Mental Stress Are Associated with Enhanced Carotid Atherosclerosis in Middle-Aged Finnish Men," *Circulation* 96, no. 11 (1997): 3842–48.

11. Roland von Känel et al., "Effects of Psychological Stress and Psychiatric Disorders on Blood Coagulation and Fibrinolysis: A Biobehavioral Pathway to Coronary Artery Disease?," *Psychosomatic Medicine* 63, no. 4 (2001): 531–44.

12. Boyatzis and McKee, *Resonant Leadership*.

13. Pinar Yilmaz et al., "Brain Correlates of Stress-Induced Analgesia," *Pain* 151, no. 2 (2010): 522–29.

14. Kelly A. Butts et al., "Glucocorticoid Receptors in the Prefrontal Cortex Regulate Stress-Evoked Dopamine Efflux and Aspects of Executive Function," *Proceedings of the National Academy of Sciences* 108, no. 45 (2011): 18459–64.

15. Benno Roozendaal, Bruce S. McEwen, and Sumantra Chattarji, "Stress, Memory and the Amygdala," *Nature Reviews Neuroscience* 10, no. 6 (2009): 423–33.

16. Simon Sinek, *Leaders Eat Last: Why Some Teams Pull Together and Others Don't* (New York: Penguin, 2014).

17. Susan Rose-Ackerman and Bonnie J. Palifka, *Corruption and Government: Causes, Consequences, and Reform* (New York: Cambridge University Press, 2016).

18. Rose-Ackerman and Palifka, *Corruption and Government*.

19. Coral Garnick, "Costco Increases Entry-Level Wage for First Time in 9 Years," *Pacific Business News*, March 4, 2016, https://www.bizjournals.com/pacific/blog/morning_call/2016/03/costco-increases-entry-level-wage-for-first-time.html

20. Liz Torres, "Walmart raises Starting Wage for Department Managers, $13/Hr," *Monster*, https://www.monster.com/career-advice/article/walmart-raises-starting-wage-for-department-managers-to-13-hour.

21. Krystal Steinmetz, "Costco Boosts Hourly Pay for Entry-Level Workers," *MoneyTalksNews*, March 6, 2016, https://www.moneytalksnews.com/costco-boosts-hourly-pay-for-entry-level-workers/

22. Phil Wahba, "How Walmart Is Helping New Employees Get Raises Faster," *Fortune*, January 27, 2017, http://fortune.com/2017/01/27/walmart-raises-salaries-wages.

23. Alex Bennet and David Bennet, *Organizational Survival in the New World* (New York: Routledge, 2004).

CHAPTER 6: CREATING DIFFERENTIATION

1. Zhengjun Xi, Yongming Li, and Heng Fan, "Quantum Coherence and Correlations in Quantum System," *Scientific Reports* 5, no. 10922 (2015): doi:10.1038/srep10922.

2. "Coherence," *Encyclopaedia Britannica*, November 23, 2011, https://www.britannica.com/science/coherence.

3. Michael P. H. Stumpf et al., "Estimating the Size of the Human Interactome," *Proceedings of the National Academy of Sciences* 105.19 (2008): 6959–64, doi:10.1073/pnas.0708078105.

4. Daniel J. Siegel, *Brainstorm: The Power and Purpose of the Teenage Brain* (New York: Penguin, 2015).

5. Göran B. W. Söderlund et al., "The Effects of Background White Noise on Memory Performance in Inattentive School Children," *Behavioral and Brain Functions* 6, no. 1 (2010): 55.

6. Peter K. Joshi et al., "Directional dominance on stature and cognition in diverse human populations," *Nature* 523 (2015): 459–62.

7. Stuart A. Kauffman, *Investigations* (New York: Oxford University Press, 2000).

8. Matt Bromley, "Improving Teaching and Learning with the Bayesian Method," *SecEd*, September 12, 2013, http://www.sec-ed.co.uk/best-practice/improving-teaching-and-learning-with-the-bayesian-method.

9. Jim Giles, "Internet Encyclopaedias Go Head to Head," *Nature* 438 (2005): 900–901, doi:10.1038/438900a.

10. Scott E. Page, *The Difference: How the Power of Diversity Creates Better Groups, Firms, Schools, and Societies* (Princeton, NJ: Princeton University Press, 2008).

11. Scott E. Page, "Making the Difference: Applying a Logic of Diversity," *Academy of Management Perspectives* 2, no. 4 (2007): 6–20.

12. Deborah H. Gruenfeld et al., "Group Composition and Decision Making: How Member Familiarity and Information Distribution Affect Process and Performance," *Organizational Behavior and Human Decision Processes* 67, no. 1 (1996): 1–15.

13. Sunnie Giles, "The Most Important Leadership Competencies, According to Leaders Around the World," *Harvard Business Review*, March 15, 2016, https://

hbr.org/2016/03/the-most-important-leadership-competencies-according-to-leaders-around-the-world.

1 4. Per Bak and Kim Sneppen, "Punctuated Equilibrium and Criticality in a Simple Model of Evolution," *Physical Review Letters* 71, no. 24 (1993): 4083; Christopher H. Loch and Bernardo A. Huberman, "A Punctuated-Equilibrium Model of Technology Diffusion," *Management Science* 45.2 (1999): 160–77.

1 5. Ethan Bernstein et al., "Beyond the Holacracy Hype," *Harvard Business Review*, July/August 2016, https://hbr.org/2016/07/beyond-the-holacracy-hype.

1 6. Bernstein et al., "Beyond the Holacracy."

CHAPTER 7: STRENGTHENING CONNECTION

1. James P. Neelankavil and Anoop Rai, *Basics of International Business* (New York: Routledge, 2014), 204.

2. Siddhartan Ramamoorthy, *Lean Six-Sigma Applications in Aircraft Assembly* (master's thesis, University of Madras, India, 2007), https://soar.wichita.edu/bitstream/handle/10057/1167/t07043.pdf.

3. John Hagel, "The Power of Power Laws," *Edge Perspectives with John Hagel* (blog), May 2, 2007, http://edgeperspectives.typepad.com/edge_perspectives/2007/05/the_power_of_po.html.

4. Steven Johnson, *Where Good Ideas Come From: The Seven Patterns of Innovation* (London: Penguin UK, 2011).

5. Johnson, *Where Good Ideas Come From.*

6. Luis M. A. Bettencourt, Jose Lobo, and Deborah Strumsky, "Invention in the City: Increasing Returns to Patenting as a Scaling Function of Metropolitan Size," *Research Policy* 36.1 (2007): 107–120.

7. "2015 GRI Report" (Global Reporting Initiative Report 2015, PepsiCo, Bureau Veritas North America, Cleveland, OH, June 2016), http://www.pepsico.com/docs/album/sustainability-reporting/final_pep_2015_gri.pdf.

8. Jim Whitehurst, *The Open Organization: Igniting Passion and Performance* (Boston: Harvard Business Review Press, 2015).

9. Whitehurst, *Open Organization.*

1 0. Tom Spahn, "Law Firms Competing on the Edge of Chaos: Pro Bono's Role in a Winning Competitive Strategy," *University of Hawai'i Law Review* 35 (2013): 345.

1 1. Michael Kosfeld et al., "Oxytocin Increases Trust in Humans," *Nature* 435 (2005): 673–76.

1 2. Paul J. Zak, Angela A. Stanton, and Sheila Ahmadi, "Oxytocin Increases Generosity in Humans," *PloS One* 2, no. 11 (2007): e1128.

13. Simone G. Shamay-Tsoory et al., "Giving Peace A Chance: Oxytocin Increases Empathy to Pain in the Context of the Israeli–Palestinian Conflict," *Psychoneuroendocrinology* 38, no. 12 (2013): 3139–44.

14. Kosfeld, "Oxytocin Increases Trust."

15. Franziska Plessow et al., "Intranasal Oxytocin Reduces the Expression of Impulsive Behavior in Overweight and Obese Men," *Regulation of Energy Balance*, Endocrine Society, April 2, 2016, OR19-3.

16. Michael W. Kraus, Cassey Huang, and Dacher Keltner, "Tactile communication, Cooperation, and Performance: An Ethological Study of the NBA," *Emotion* 10, no. 5 (2010): 745.

17. Vittorio Gallese et al., "Action Recognition in the Premotor Cortex," *Brain* 119, no. 2 (1996): 593–609.

18. Peter Totterdell et al., "Can Employees Be Emotionally Drained by Witnessing Unpleasant Interactions Between Coworkers? A Diary Study of Induced Emotion Regulation," *Work & Stress* 26, no. 2 (2012): 112–29.

19. Nicholas A. Christakis and James H. Fowler, "Social Networks and Happiness," *Edge*, December 4, 2008, https://www.edge.org/conversation/ nicholas_a_christakis-james_fowler-social-networks-and-happiness.

20. General Stanley McChrystal et al., *Team of Teams: New Rules of Engagement for a Complex World* (New York: Penguin, 2015), 94.

21. Katherine O. Burleson and Gary E. Schwartz, "Cardiac Torsion and Electromagnetic Fields: The Cardiac Bioinformation Hypothesis," *Medical Hypotheses* 64, no. 6 (2005): 1109–16.

22. Rollin McCraty et al., "The Electricity of Touch: Detection and Measurement of Cardiac Energy Exchange Between People," in *Brain and Values: Is a Biological Science of Values Possible?*, ed. Karl H. Pribram (Mahwah, NJ: Lawrence Erlbaum, 1998): 359–79.

23. Martha K. McClintock, "Menstrual Synchrony and Suppression," *Nature* 229 (1971): 244–45.

24. Maharishi Mahesh Yogi, *Creating an Ideal Society: A Global Undertaking* (Bremen, Germany: MERU Verlag, 1976), 123.

25. John L. Davies and Charles N. Alexander, "Alleviating Political Violence Through Reducing Collective Tension: Impact Assessment Analyses of the Lebanon War," *Journal of Social Behavior and Personality* 17, no. 1 (2005): 285.

26. Mary D. Salter Ainsworth et al, *Patterns of Attachment: A Psychological Study of the Strange Situation* (New York: Psychology Press, 2015).

27. Malcolm L. West, *Patterns of Relating: An Adult Attachment Perspective* (New York: Guilford Press, 1994).

28. "Strange Situation," Wikipedia, last modified October 19, 2017, https:// en.wikipedia.org/wiki/Strange_situation.

29. "Strange Situation," Wikipedia.

30. James A. Coan, Hillary S. Schaefer, and Richard J. Davidson, "Lending a Hand: Social Regulation of the Neural Response to Threat," *Psychological Science* 17, no. 12 (2006): 1032–39.

31. Naomi I. Eisenberger and Matthew D. Lieberman, "Why Rejection Hurts: A Common Neural Alarm System for Physical and Social Pain," *Trends in Cognitive Sciences* 8, no. 7 (2004): 294–300.

CHAPTER 8: FACILITATING LEARNING: THE PINNACLE OF LEADERSHIP COMPETENCIES

1. Roberto Benzi, Alfonso Sutera, and Angelo Vulpiani, "The Mechanism of Stochastic Resonance," *Journal of Physics A: Mathematical and General* 14, no. 11 (1981): L453.

2. Steven Johnson, *Where Good Ideas Come From: The Seven Patterns of Innovation* (London: Penguin UK, 2011).

3. Mike Hockney, *The Holographic Soul* (Morrisville, NC: Lulu Press, 2016).

4. Niles Eldredge and Stephen Jay Gould, "Punctuated Equilibria: An Alternative to Phyletic Gradualism," in *Models in Paleobiology*, ed. Thomas J. M. Schopf (San Francisco: Freeman Cooper, 1972): 83.

5. Robert Rosenthal and Lenore Jacobson, "Pygmalion in the Classroom," *Urban Review* 3, no. 1 (1968): 16–20.

6. Pete Collins, ed., *Air Crash Investigations: Miracle on the Hudson River—The Ditching of US Airways Flight 1549* (Morrisville, NC: Lulu Press, 2014), 145.

7. Arthur Conan Doyle, *Sherlock Holmes: The Complete Novels and Stories*, vol. 1 (New York: Bantam Classics, 2013), 379.

8. Malcolm Gladwell, *Blink: The Power of Thinking Without Thinking* (New York: Back Bay Books, 2007).

9. Kathleen M. Eisenhardt and Donald Sull, "Strategy as Simple Rules," *Harvard Business Review*, January 2001, https://hbr.org/2001/01/strategy-as-simple-rules.

10. Sunnie Giles, "Turning Performance Reviews into a Vehicle for Radical Innovation," *Forbes*, March 28, 2017, https://www.forbes.com/sites/forbescoachescouncil/2017/03/28/turning-performance-reviews-into-a-vehicle-for-radical-innovation.

11. Marcus Buckingham and Ashley Goodall, "Reinventing Performance Management," *Harvard Business Review*, April 2015, https://hbr.org/2015/04/reinventing-performance-management.

12. Claire Zillman, "IBM Is Blowing Up Its Annual Performance Review," *Fortune*, February 1, 2016, http://fortune.com/2016/02/01/ibm-employee-performance-reviews; Lillian Cunningham, "In a big move, Accenture Will Get Rid of Annual Performance Reviews and Rankings," *Washington Post*, July 21, 2015, https://www.washingtonpost.com/news/on-leadership/wp/2015/07/21/

in-big-move-accenture-will-get-rid-of-annual-performance-reviews-and-rankings.

1 3. Buckingham and Goodall, "Reinventing Performance Management."

1 4. Zillman, "IBM Is Blowing Up."

1 5. Su Hyun Lee, "Companies Turn to South Korea for Product Testing," *New York Times,* November 10, 2010, http://www.nytimes.com/2010/11/11/business/global/11iht-sk-consume.html.

1 6. Wendell Cox, "World Urban Areas Population and Density: A 2012 Update," *New Geography*, May 3, 2012, http://www.newgeography.com/content/002808-world-urban-areas-population-and-density-a-2012-update.

1 7. Cox, "World Urban Areas."

1 8. Yun Hee Lee, "[2016 Household Finance] Seoul House Furniture, Average Debt . . . 1.5 times the national average" [in Korean], *Joins*, December 20, 2016, http://news.joins.com/article/21022610.

1 9. Mark McDonald, "Home Internet May Get Even Faster in South Korea," *New York Times*, February 21, 2011, http://www.nytimes.com/2011/02/22/technology/22iht-broadband22.html.

20. "Smart Seoul 2015" (Basic Strategic Plan for Informatization of Seoul Metropolitan City, Hi Seoul, Soul of Asia, February 19, 2014), http://english.seoul.go.kr/wp-content/uploads/2014/02/SMART_SEOUL_2015_41.pdf.

2 1. Gretchen R. Vogelgesang, Hannes Leroy, and Bruce J. Avolio, "The Mediating Effects of Leader Integrity with Transparency in Communication and Work Engagement/Performance," *Leadership Quarterly* 24, no. 3 (2013): 405–13.

CHAPTER 9: HIGHER COMPLEXITY AND RADICAL INNOVATION

1. John Cleveland, "Complexity Theory: Basic Concepts and Application to Systems Thinking," *Innovation Network for Communities,* March 27, 1994, https://www.slideshare.net/johncleveland/complexity-theory-basic-concepts.

2. Mitchell M. Waldrop, *Complexity: The Emerging Science at the Edge of Order and Chaos* (New York: Simon & Schuster, 1993).

3. Richard P. Feynman, Robert B. Leighton, and Matthew Sands, *The Feynman Lectures on Physics,* vol. 1 (Boston: Addison-Wesley, 1963), ch. 46–5.

4. Niles Eldredge and Stephen Jay Gould, "Punctuated Equilibria: An Alternative to Phyletic Gradualism," in *Models in Paleobiology*, ed. Thomas J. M. Schopf (San Francisco: Freeman Cooper, 1972): 83.

5. Per Bak and Kan Chen, "Self-Organized Criticality," *Scientific American* 264, no. 1 (1991).

6. Robert E. Krider, "Empirical Evidence of Long-Run Order in Retail Industry Dynamics," *Academy of Marketing Science Review* (January 2004).

7. Per Bak and Kim Sneppen, "Punctuated Equilibrium and Criticality in a Simple Model of Evolution," *Physical Review Letters* 71, no. 24 (1993): 4083.

8. Stuart A. Kauffman, *Investigations* (New York: Oxford University Press, 2000).

9. Bela H. Banathy, *Guided Evolution of Society: A Systems View* (New York: Springer Science+Business Media, 2013).

10. Jeffrey L. Fannin and Robert M. Williams, "Neuroscience Reveals the Whole-Brain State and Its Applications for International Business and Sustainable Success," *International Journal of Management and Business* 3, no. 1 (2012).

11. J. Nina Lieberman, *Playfulness: Its Relationship to Imagination and Creativity* (New York: Academic Press, 2014), xi.

12. Daniel J. Siegel, *Brainstorm: The Power and Purpose of the Teenage Brain* (New York: Penguin, 2015).

13. Britta K. Hölzel et al., "Mindfulness Practice Leads to Increases in Regional Brain Gray Matter Density," *Psychiatry Research: Neuroimaging* 191, no. 1 (2011): 36–43.

14. Siegel, *Brainstorm*.

15. Daniel J. Siegel, *The Mindful Brain: Reflection and Attunement in the Cultivation of Well-Being* (New York: W. W. Norton, 2007).

16. Daniel J. Siegel, *Mindsight: The New Science of Personal Transformation* (New York: Bantam, 2010).

17. Elissa Epel et al., "Can Meditation Slow Rate of Cellular Aging? Cognitive Stress, Mindfulness, and Telomeres," *Annals of the New York Academy of Sciences* 1172, no. 1 (2009): 34–53.

CHAPTER 10: QUANTUM LEADERSHIP IMPLEMENTATION

1. Alia J. Crum and Ellen J. Langer, "Mind-Set Matters: Exercise and the Placebo Effect," *Psychological Science* 18, no. 2 (2007): 165–71.

2. Rachel Emma Silverman, "So Much Training, So Little to Show for It," *Wall Street Journal,* October 26, 2012, https://www.wsj.com/articles/SB1000142405297 02044259045780729505185583 28.

3. Jim Whitehurst, *The Open Organization: Igniting Passion and Performance* (Boston: Harvard Business Review Press, 2015).

4. Robert Kabacoff, "Develop Strategic Thinkers Throughout Your Organization," *Harvard Business Review,* February 7, 2014, https://hbr.org/2014/02/develop-strategic-thinkers-throughout-your-organization.

5. "Performance with Purpose: 2025 Agenda" (Sustainability Report 2015, PepsiCo, 2016), https://www.pepsico.com/docs/album/sustainability-reporting/pepsico_sustainability_report_2015_and_-2025_agenda.pdf

6. Paul Sparrow, Hugh Scullion, and Ibraiz Tarique, eds., *Strategic Talent Management: Contemporary Issues in International Context* (Cambridge: Cambridge University Press, 2014).

7. Clayton Christensen, *The Innovator's Dilemma: When New Technologies Cause Great Firms to Fail* (Boston: Harvard Business Review Press, 2013).

8. Reed Hastings, "Netflix Vacation Policy and Tracking," SlideShare, August 1, 2009, https://www.slideshare.net/reed2001/culture-1798664/71-Netflix_Vacation _Policyand_Trackingthere_is.

9. Chelsey Dulaney, "Best Performers in the S&P 500 in 2015," *Wall Street Journal*, December 31, 2015, https://blogs.wsj.com/briefly/2015/12/31/5-best-performers-in-the-sp-500-in-2015; Kathy Kristof, "Best S&P 500 Stocks of 2013," *Kiplinger*, January 6, 2013, http://www.kiplinger.com/article/investing/T052-C008-S003-best-s-p-500-stocks-of-2013.html

10. "What Makes GE The Worlds Most Admired Company," *Business Standard*, January 27, 2013, http://www.business-standard.com/article/specials/what-makes-ge-the-worlds-most-admired-company-198031101012_1.html.

11. Cari Tuna and Joann S. Lublin, "Welch: 'No Such Thing as Work-Life Balance,'" *Wall Street Journal*, July 14, 2009, https://www.wsj.com/articles/SB124726415198325373.

12. Dylan Law, "Flexibility Helps This Dad Have the Best of Both Worlds," MyGE Story, June 16, 2016, http://www.mygestory.com/flexibility-helps-this-dad-have -the-best-of-both-worlds.

13. Katie Jacobs, "GE Leadership Development 'Going Back to Basics'," *HR*, June 26, 2014, http://www.hrmagazine.co.uk/article-details/ ge-leadership-development-going-back-to-basics.

14. Nelson D. Schwartz, "In an age of Privilege, Not Everyone Is in the Same Boat," *Business BVI*, June 15, 2016, http://www.businessbvi.com/business/ item/1119-in-an-age-of-privilege-not-everyone-is-in-the-same-boat.

15. "GE Global Learning Leader Paul Fama," YouTube video, 8:52, posted by Entelo, December 22, 2016, https://www.youtube.com/watch?v=38TEF6fJSNo&t=298s.

16. Jeff Immelt, "Why GE is Giving Up Employee Ratings, Abandoning Annual Reviews and Rethinking the Role of HQ," *LinkedIn Pulse*, August 4, 2016, https://www.linkedin.com/pulse/why-ge-giving-up-employee-ratings-abandoning -annual-reviews-immelt.

17. "GE Career Benefits," Working at GE, GE Careers, https://www.ge.com/careers/ working-at-ge.

18. Susan Peters, "How Will You Lead in the Emergent Era?," *LinkedIn Pulse*, May 8, 2017, https://www.linkedin.com/pulse/how-you-lead-emergent-era-susan-peters ?trk=mp-reader-card.

19. Whitehurst, *The Open Organization*.

ACKNOWLEDGMENTS

I am grateful for the radical innovators in many disciplines who provided their pioneering thought leadership in the adjacent possible and helped me see the common thread of evidence that cuts across all of them.

Huge thanks go to Dr. Joseph Choi at Raytheon, who edited the quantum mechanics content, and Dr. Jason Shepherd at the University of Utah, who edited the neuroscience content, for their generous gift of time.

I am truly grateful to Amy Bernstein at *Harvard Business Review* for challenging me to quantify the impact of my theory through research. That opened many doors for me. and became a genesis of this book. Thank you for taking a chance on me, a first-time writer.

I am grateful to my editor, Vy Tran, at BenBella for challenging me to clarify my thoughts through many iterations in the editing process, and also to my agent, Giles Anderson, and my publisher, Glenn Yeffeth, at BenBella for seeing the potential of this book.

I am indebted to Greg Butterfield and Colleen Edwards for believing in me and for their generous gift of time, support, encouragement, and friendship as I got started as a first-time author, and to all of my clients who have provided me with real-life insights on how to actually implement the principles covered in the book. All of the case examples in this book come from real life client stories, of course disguising names and situations to protect their confidentiality.

And I am grateful to God, who has carefully directed my life so I could find him and my place in eternity.

INDEX

Note: *Italic* page numbers indicate illustrations

A

Aalto University (Helsinki), 65
AC Nielsen, 200
academic achievement, 70, 147
Accenture, 17, 154, 169
accountability, 110, 210–211
accuracy
  communication and, 182
  connection and, 128
  efficiency and, 114
  perfect, 13
  sacrificing, 83
  simple rules and, 152
  speed over, 61–62, 65, 78, 156
  Wikipedia and, 101
actions, 70–71, 85, 134, 171, 179, 197
adaptability, 8, 12, 31, 63–64, 114, 167
  boundaries and, 72
  feedback and, 153–159
ADHD, 96
adjacent possible, 32, 37, 167–169
Adobe, 154
adrenaline, 80, 82
AdSense, xiv
advocacy, 88–89
Africa, 4–6
agility, 12, 65
Aillis app, 35
Ainsworth, Mary, 130–132
AirBnB, 200
al-Assad, Bashar, 2
Alexander, Charles, 129–130
AlphaGo, xi–xiii, *xiv,* xv–xvi, xvi–xviii, 10, 13, 29, 150
Amazon, 37, 59, 109, 199–200, 201, 203
ambiguity, 3, 12, 64, 153, 156, 211
American Museum of Natural History, 168
Android, 199
Antioco, John, 203

anxiety, 52, 63
Arab Spring, 2
ARM, *201*
artificial intelligence, xi–xviii, 9, 204. *See also* AlphaGo
AT&T, 201, 204
attachment
  brain and, 51
  communication and, 131
  connection and, 126–136, 129, 133
  differentiation and, 131
  infants and, 130–132
  insecure, 131
  positive, 174
  secure, 130–134, 173
  survival and, 174
attention, focused, 10, 64, 66
attitude, 52, 70
authenticity, 63, 84–86, 171–172
autocatalysis, *107*–108, 117, 136, 151–152
Avex Group, 34

B

B612 app, 35
balance, 72–74, 157, 164–165, 170–171, 174–175, 183, 205
Ball and Buck, 105
Bánáthy, Béla, 170
Bayes, Thomas, 143–144
Bayesian discipline, 100, 142–145, 159, 161
belief system, 69, 149–150, 153, 180–182, 181–182
belonging
  compensation and, 59
  connection and, 134
  environment and, 12, 135–136
  Maslow's hierarchy of needs and, 58
Ben Ali, Zine El Abidine, 2
Benzi, Roberto, 140–141
biodiversity, 29, 96

ABOUT THE
AUTHOR

Dr. Sunnie Giles is president of Quantum Leadership Group. She catalyzes leaders to produce radical innovation and redefine the rules of the game as individuals and organizations. She is a TEDx speaker on radical innovation.

She is an adviser at Stanford Business School's Institute for Innovation in Developing Economies. Her research on global leadership for innovation has been published by the *Harvard Business Review*. Her thoughts have been published in *Forbes, Inc., World Financial Review*, the *Korea Times*, the *Korea Economic Daily*, and Management Matters Network.

Sunnie received her MBA from the University of Chicago Booth School of Business and her PhD in systemic psychology (Marriage and Family Therapy) from Brigham Young University.

Readers can connect with her the following ways:

- Homepage: www.sunniegiles.com
- Twitter: https://twitter.com/sunnie_giles
- LinkedIn: www.linkedin.com/in/sunniegiles
- Facebook: www.facebook.com/DrSunnie